Third World — Second Sex

Women's Struggles and National Liberation

Third World Women Speak Out

Compiled by Miranda Davies

Zed Books Ltd., 57 Caledonian Road, London N1 9BU

Third World, Second Sex was first published by
Zed Books Ltd., 57 Caledonian Road,
London N1 9BU, UK, and 171 First Avenue,
Atlantic Highlands, New Jersey 07716, USA,
in 1983.

Book designed by Jan Brown Designs.
Cover designed by Andrew Corbett, based on
design by Jan Brown Designs.
Spanish translation by Maria Mercedes Uribe.
Printed and bound in the United Kingdom
at The Bath Press, Avon.

4th impression, 1987.

British Library Cataloguing in Publication Data

Third world, second sex.
  1. Women and socialism   2. Underdeveloped
areas socialism
I. Davies, Miranda
305.4'2'091724   HQ1870.9

ISBN 0-86232-017-8
ISBN 0-86232-029-1 Pbk

Contents

FORTHCOMING – Autumn 1987

Third World, Second Sex 2

Following the continuing success of *Third World, Second Sex*, now in its fourth impression, in Autumn 1987 Zed Books is publishing *Third World, Second Sex 2*, also compiled by Miranda Davies, with a Preface by Kumari Jayawardena, author of *Feminism and Nationalism in the Third World*. *Third World, Second Sex 2* embraces new women's movements and new issues from more countries, reflecting the growing vitality of women's struggles in Africa, Asia, Latin America and the Middle East.

Acknowledgements

This book came together with the help of women from all over the world. My special thanks to ISIS who gave me access to all their documentation and without whom I would probably never have tackled the book.

For help in finding sources, thanks also to Tany Alexander, Margaret Ling, Jane MacIntosh, Ann Murray-Hudson, Bobby Ortiz, Vibhuti Patel, Majida Salman, Sylvia Stevens, Marilyn Thomson, Jenny Vaughan and Candice Wright.

Finally I want to thank all the women whose words fill the following pages and whose support and co-operation made this book possible.

Preface

This book is a compilation of interviews and articles by women from the Third World. The voices speaking here are very diverse. They belong to women from countries as different as Oman, Bolivia, India, Mauritius and Zimbabwe. These women share no one single approach to women's liberation, but together they all show the revolutionary emergence of a new feminist consciousness amongst women in the Third World.

In some ways the specific situations that give rise to this consciousness will be unfamiliar to feminists in the West. For example, few Western feminists, with the exception of women in Northern Ireland, know what it's like to be directly involved in armed struggle. At the same time, many aspects of the experiences described in these pages will be only too familiar. Whether at home, in the street, in the workplace or fighting in a guerrilla army, we all experience sexism in our daily lives. By revealing the deep-rooted similarities, as well as some of the many differences between women's struggles in the West and in the Third World, the following collection aims to help build some of the links needed for the development of women's liberation on a truly international scale.

The subject of women and liberation in the Third World covers a huge spectrum and putting together this collection could have been approached in many different ways. It is becoming an increasingly respectable area for academic research and so has generated a lot of theoretical studies, some of which might well have been included in this book. However, I didn't set out to compile a book of academic essays. The achievements of any liberation movement clearly depend on the ways in which theory is developed through practice and, from the beginning, my aim was to publish little-known material based entirely on the direct experiences of women activists from the Third World.

Taking this starting point, the book concentrates on one main issue, the issue of women and organization. What is it that leads women in Africa, Asia, Latin America and the Middle East to challenge their situations, to abandon their traditional roles and become subversive? How do these women get together and organize themselves and which particular issues most concern them? These are the kind of questions which lay behind my search for original material from the Third World.

The accounts published here come, directly or indirectly, from women from at least 20 Third World countries. They show that women's struggles in the Third World have given rise to organization on a number of levels, both in the private and the public sphere. In Bolivia, for instance, women are organizing themselves directly around their family role in support of their men. This is described in Domitila Barrios de la Chungara's pamphlet *Women and Organization*, translated here for the first time, where she outlines the work of Housewives Committees in the mining community of Siglo XX. Elsewhere they have organized more as an extension of their defined roles in society. This happened very much in the early stages of national liberation struggles in Chile, Oman and Eritrea when, often hiding their men underground, women acted as nurses, cooks and couriers. And now although, as Miriam Galdemez from El Salvador puts it, 'There's a long way to go before women pick up a gun as easily as a casserole!', more and more women in these movements are taking up the gun.

Other forms of organization discussed by women in this collection are less obviously bound-up with the question of national liberation. They include campaigns against rape and against the dowry system (very much focal points in the Indian women's movement), organization for better health-care and safe legal abortion, and the growing participation of women in trade unions.

Looking at these different forms of organization, it is possible to make a broad distinction between women's struggles for liberation inside and outside the context of national liberation movements. The distinction has been convenient for the structure of this book, but its use should never obscure the fact that these struggles are 'inevitably linked', a point emphasized again and again by the women speaking here. To quote a statement from the Association of African Women for Research and Development (AAWORD): 'Moreover, fighting against genital mutilation without placing it in the context of ignorance, obscurantism, exploitation and poverty etc., without questioning the structures and social relations which perpetuate this situation, is like "refusing to see the sun in the middle of the day".'

Much of the material in this compilation comes from women actively fighting for the liberation of their countries and most of them belong to some form of political party. Therefore, their concern is to free not only women, but an entire oppressed people. At the same time, in countries such as India, Sri Lanka, Peru and Namibia, despite vast social, economic, political and cultural differences, there is a growing awareness of the additional need to fight against the double oppression of women, as women and as half the oppressed population of the Third World.* This is explained very well in an editorial from the Indian feminist magazine *Manushi*. Entitled 'Drought: "God-Sent" or "Man-Made" Disaster?' the article uses the tragic effects of drought in India to illustrate how women bear the major brunt of poverty and exploitation: 'Are not women 50% of the poor, the *Harijans*, the *Adivasis* and of every other oppressed group in this country? Are not women in rural India affected even more disastrously by drought — the first to be hit by malnutrition and disease, the first to die, the first driven into destitution and prostitution? In the cities is it not women who suffer the worst consequences of scarcity and price rises. . . ?'

As they begin to recognize and identify the specific nature of their double oppression, many women in the Third World realize that, when needed, they may join guerrilla movements, participate in the economy, enter politics and organize trade unions, but at the end of the day they are still seen as women, second-class citizens, inferiors to men, bearers of children, and domestic servants.

This new consciousness has led to increasingly outspoken criticism of the way in which the subordination of women has consistently been ignored by political parties. Here again, as Gladys Diaz says from her experience as an activist, first in Chile and later as a militant exile, 'Women have had to fight to earn their place in political and mass organizations with an effort double that of men.' Just as women in the West have learned to fight back against a history of male prejudice in revolutionary organizations, so are women in Third World countries refusing to tolerate this attitude in silence. They now see glaring contradictions between the revolutionary principles of national and social liberation and a passive, unchallenged acceptance of female subordination.

Some, like the Peruvian women fighting for workers' control in the factories of Lucy/Cornell, reach this understanding through trade union organization. Others discover it in the process of armed struggle where a woman soon learns that whatever her role — and she is usually given so-called lesser tasks — she is still seen first in terms of her gender. As one guerrilla puts it, 'even with a gun in my hand I am seen as a woman by my comrades'.

Along with lessons learned from the continuing need to struggle

* According to the International Labour Organization (1980) women are 50% of the world's population. However the ratio obviously varies according to individual countries. In India, for example, women make up only 46% of the population, largely as a result of female infanticide, malnutrition etc.

for women's liberation in such post-revolutionary societies, as Cuba and Mozambique, this emergence of a new feminist consciousness amongst women in national liberation movements has largely been responsible for the birth of organizations such as the Asociacion de Mujeres Nicaraguenses Luisa Amanda Espinoza (AMNLAE) in Nicaragua, SWAPO Women's Council in Namibia and the Omani Women's Organization. In the words of Anabella Rodriguez from Mozambique: 'It was easier to eliminate colonial, bourgeois influences that were imposed on us and identified with the enemy, than to eliminate generations of tradition within our society', a fact clearly understood by the Omani women who write that, 'The liberation of women cannot be achieved through men making concessions to women, but through constant organized struggle by women on the economic, social and political levels'. Giving an indication of the problems that Third World women are faced with, Anabella Rodriguez cites polygamy, the dowry system and initiation rites, as just three traditions which Mozambican women are still trying to abolish.

Another theme that emerged more than once in the material I collected concerns Third World attitudes towards Western feminism. Not only has the question of women's liberation traditionally been bypassed by revolutionary organizations in the Third World (as it has in the West), but (again this applies to groups in the West) it has also become a target for hostility from the Left — especially in Latin America. This hostility stems partly from a strong economistic bias which has tended to neglect social, let alone sexual, relations in the revolutionary process. But it also arises from an over-simplified view of women's liberation struggles in the West, often referred to as one single movement emanating from the United States and, therefore, another manifestation of US imperialism.

This distorted view of feminism and the women's movement comes out in the writings of Domitila Barrios de la Chungara. Although she strongly defends women's rights and the importance of women taking an active, leading role in politics, Domitila is quick to denounce what she sees as the decadent influence of Western feminism. Referring to the 1975 United Nations International Women's Conference in Mexico, she says: 'I could see two types of liberation. One type involves those who think women will only be free when they have equalled men in all their vices. This is called feminism. It means that they must fight against men for the right to smoke and drink as they do . . . . the other type of liberation consists of women being respected as intelligent human beings, capable of solving problems and of participating in everything in the field of culture, art, literature, politics and trade-unionism.' Domitila thus rejects feminism as typifying the demands of wealthy

American women, but then, speaking directly from her own experience, goes on to point out the undervalued nature of housework and describes many of the fundamental problems that unite women in struggle throughout the world.

The most significant aspect of the kind of anti-feminism found in the Third World has been the dismissal of such issues as sexuality, abortion and rape, as the unique concern of women in the West. Anyone who believes that sexual issues are the prerogative of Western feminists, however, has only to look at the campaign against rape in India where, for poor low-caste women, rape is a consequence of poverty itself. As the *Manushi* article explains, 'In UP it has been reported that tribal women who collect firewood and go to sell it in towns, are sexually exploited by ticket checkers because they have no money to pay for the short train-ride from the village to the town'. Here we have yet another illustration of women's double oppression. Indian women are fighting poverty and tradition, but they also know from experience that a poor male is unlikely to suffer the added dimension of sexual harassment and often downright violence.

Amongst all the Third World countries represented here India, with its incredibly complex pattern of sex, class and caste oppression, appears to have produced the one women's movement which is truly anti-patriarchal and anti-capitalist in character. But it is clear, especially from the recent material coming out of Asia and Latin America, that more and more, sexuality is becoming a leading issue amongst Third World women, and with it a new debate about sexism, racism, imperialism and their relationship to patriarchy is opening up. Inevitably, this debate will feature increasingly in future collections of women's voices from the Third World.

Finally, a few words about how this book was compiled: I wrote to groups and individuals in more than 40 countries, the areas approached being largely determined by initial contacts and the ways in which they built up. However, the final selection attempts to give a fairly balanced representation of women and organization in Africa, Asia, the Middle East and Latin America. There are still geographical gaps. For instance there are no accounts from Vietnam, the Philippines or South Africa, all of which have their own progressive women's organizations. There are also gaps and limitations in terms of specific issues; not only is sexuality neglected, but the fundamental question of autonomy by women is frequently overlooked, especially in national liberation movements. It would have been impossible to cover every aspect of women's struggles in the Third World, but these gaps are in themselves significant.

In addition, the selection of material was obviously restricted by

language — the only translations are from French, Spanish and
Portuguese — which was a pity. I would have liked to include
extracts from a booklet in Creole, published by Muvman Liberasyon
Fam of Mauritius as part of their campaign against rape. There were
also the inevitable hazards of international communication and an
often erratic postal service. At times this was very frustrating as
letters crossed, some never arrived and addresses were frequently
out of date.

As material for the book began to pile up, I was very soon faced
with the problem of structure. The initial idea was to divide it
according to country, but gradually it seemed to make more sense
to classify material by theme. Although divisions were by no means
always clear, articles and interviews soon began to fall into broad
categories which, by focusing on certain key issues or themes,
appeared more useful than regional headings, for two main reasons.
First, I was presented with a lot of documentation from some
countries and very little from others. This was partly a result of the
limitations mentioned above and doesn't automatically reflect the
uneven development of women's movements in different parts of
the world. The use of purely geographical headings might well have
been confusing in this respect. Secondly, and more important for
the purposes of this book, dividing material by country wouldn't
help to identify the actual issues which, linked together, are the
main foundation for the international women's movement.

Classification of the material may sometimes seem a bit arbitrary,
for instance, the division of sexuality between 'health' and 'violence'.
This overlapping of various themes obviously follows in part from
material limitations: the fact of relying entirely on existing material,
researched over a period of ten months. It does, however, also
point to the interconnections and different possible interpretations
of questions being raised by women's movements all over the world.
In addition, the accounts which follow have undergone little, if any,
editing. This was not only because of the difficulties of contacting
the original authors, but because of the danger of forcing the
freshness and urgency of these women's voices into an alien and
stilted style.

Finally, I must point out that a number of valuable contributions
came from sources in Britain, as well as further afield. Some of
these interviews and articles first appeared in British publications
such as *Spare Rib* and *Feminist Review*. Others were received
directly from Third World women living in Britain, many of them
political exiles. Amongst them are groups such as SWAPO Women's
Campaign, the Anti-Apartheid Women's Committee and the London Latin American Women's Group (Carila), as well as a number
of individuals. I am particularly indebted to Maria Mercedes
Uribe who became involved in the project in its very early stages.

As well as helping to find and translate material from Latin America, Maria read and commented on articles from other parts of the world, and our notes and discussions together formed the basis for this Preface. I am also very grateful to Shaila Shah who spent hours obtaining and editing material from India and whose encouragement helped to dispel some of my uneasiness about being a Western feminist, commissioned to select documents from women in the Third World. The experience has taught me a lot.

There is no single road to women's liberation. Women in the Third World are constantly searching for new answers and creating new strategies for change. As the following testimonies show, these don't develop through theory alone. They depend on organization and practice, determined by specific conditions in each country, but also guided by an understanding of the universal and not simply the specific nature of women's oppression. Only in this way, through making connections, can we hope to construct a new life and a new purpose for women throughout the world.

Miranda Davies
August 1982

Part I: Women, Politics and Organization

Awake

The mountain-moving day is coming
I say so, yet others doubt.
Only awhile the mountains sleeps.
In the past
All mountains moved in fire,
Yet you may not believe it.
Oh man, this alone believe,
All sleeping women now will awake
and move.

Akiko Yosano
Japan

1. Drought: 'God-Sent' or 'Man-Made' Disaster?
Manushi Collective

The following article is an editorial from the Indian feminist magazine *Manushi* (No.6, July-August 1980). Drought, famine and
floods, resulting in food scarcity, are annual occurrences in India
and many other Third World countries. Their frequency has
numbed the severity of their impact, strongly assisted by news
coverage which commonly upholds the belief that such calamities
are 'natural' or 'god-given' and therefore quite beyond the control
of the mass of people who die as a result. Though not primarily
concerned with women and organization, by giving an excellent
introductory insight into what drought and poverty mean for the
rural poor of India — and especially women — this article affirms
how crucial it is for women to analyse their position and organize
together against different aspects of poverty and exploitation. The
women of *Manushi* specifically requested that their original editorial should not be shortened or altered in any way.

'Why are you writing about drought? What has it got to do with
Manushi, with women?' We were repeatedly confronted with these
questions while working in libraries and talking to activists from
different regions, trying to collect information on drought.

Such questions spring as much from ignorance as from arrogance,
both of which lead men to assume that not only running the
affairs of the country, but also messing around with the problems
they have created, are their prerogatives; that women, if they are
to speak at all, should confine themselves to women's issues such
as dowry and birth-control.

The attitudes and assumptions behind these questions push
women into invisibility. Are not women 50% of the poor, the
Harijans, the *Adivasis* and of every other oppressed group in this
country? [*Harijan*, meaning 'child of God', is the name which
Gandhi gave to people of low caste, formerly referred to as un-
touchables. *Adivasis* are tribal people.] Are not women in rural
India affected even more disastrously by drought — the first to be

John Ogle

hit by malnutrition and disease, the first to die, the first driven into
destitution and prostitution? In the cities, is it not women who
suffer the worst consequences of scarcity and price rises; struggling
harder and harder to feed their families and themselves on an ever-
shrinking budget; standing in long queues to buy essential commodities, having to work harder in order to substitute their own labour
and time for services they can no longer afford? For the middle-
class woman this means every kind of drudgery, from unravelling
old woollen sweaters to reknit them, to cutting down on her own
consumption and needs so that the children's [school] fees can be
paid and their shoes bought, or not being able to afford the occasional, short scooter-ride and having to crush herself into over-
crowded buses, regardless of her age, her health and of what she
may be carrying. Or else she has to put off visiting the doctor,
consider her own health unimportant so that she can save a few
rupees and prevent the family's standard of living from sinking too
rapidly. For the poor woman, the privations are even more pro-
nounced and the labour input more backbreaking. It means standing
in endless queues to buy kerosene, fetching water from distant and
erratic taps, being forced to turn from kerosene stove to cowdung

chulha [stove], getting up earlier to grind the wheat herself, in order to save a few *paisas* [100 *paisas*: 1 rupee], walking miles just to buy at a slightly cheaper market, cutting down on her own food so that there is enough to go around, being forced to supplement the family income by doing poorly paid, menial jobs.

The 'Unprecedented' Drought

While in the cities, soaring prices and artificial scarcities are taking a heavy toll of women's lives and labour, in the rural areas, want takes a much more brutal form. Two hundred million people, that is, one-third of the total population have been in the grip of famine for the last ten months or more. In the seriously affected areas, villagers have no food stocks left, no employment and no money with which to buy anything. They are just starving, stilling the pangs of hunger by chewing leaves and digging up roots. Even these have got exhausted over the months. It is during such times that poor peasants and landless labourers are pushed even more deeply into debt, and forced to mortgage their land to landlords and money-lenders.

Women Are Always The Worst Hit

As food and water resources have grown scarce, thousands have been driven to migrate to cities in search of work, the consequence being that women are often left behind in the villages to fend for the children and the old.

As people are forced to live in sub-human conditions, as human lives are systematically devalued, degraded, it is women who suffer most, are the first to be sold or exchanged for food, the first to die. It is not surprising then that an overwhelming number of the starvation deaths so far reported have been those of women (*Hindustan Times*, 31.3.80). Even in normal times, women in this country as elsewhere in the world, have always borne the brunt of poverty and malnutrition. In every family, women eat the last and the least. This, and many other forms of neglect and devaluation of women within the family seem to be on the increase. No wonder then that the mortality rate among women even in 'normal' times is much higher than that among men. (Between 1951 and 1971, the number of females per 1,000 males decreased from 946 to 930).

Here is a living example of how this comes to be. This is how Ratna Chamar described the death of his wife at Hanna relief work project in Uttar Pradesh to Inder Malhotra of *Times of India*

(September 1979): Ratna claimed and others confirmed that on the day of her death the poor woman had worked on the canal relief project all day and then had collapsed on reaching home. 'If you have survived all this time, why do you say that she starved to death?' he was asked. His reply was: 'We get very little grain and we get it very late. . . . It was her habit to feed me first, then the children, and not eat enough herself.'

Thus the traditions built into male-dominated society, which force women to see their own lives as less valuable and to think that virtue lies in self-sacrifice, mean the slow starvation of the woman when the family is living at bare subsistence level.

The Double Burden

It is because of this devaluation that women accept as inevitable their double burden of work — paid and unpaid. Their daily toil begins hours before the men's 'working day'. The burden of fetching water for the family has, for instance, always been a woman's burden. So when all nearby water sources dry up, it is the woman who walks anything from one to three kilometres in search of water, scrapes it out of a river bed or spends hours scooping it out of a nearly dry well. (*Statesman*, 22.5.80). Added to this strain is that of gathering some kind of edible or procuring it by longer hours of backbreaking labour. A woman political worker from Chattisgarh district reported how one landless labourer with three children and a father-in-law to support, took to gathering firewood to eke out a living. She had to daily walk miles to a distant jungle, collect firewood and carry the heavy load to the city. This strained her so much that one day she started bleeding profusely and just collapsed.

When the erratic Food for Work projects appear, women from surrounding villages have been flooding them. At certain sites the percentage of women far exceeds that of men. They have to walk miles carrying the children, work on the project, again walk miles to the Block Development Officer's (BDO) office and wait hours for the grain to be distributed, and then somehow convert the virtually non-edible grain into food for the family.

Women put all their energy into food gathering activity *Adivasi* women and girls rise before daybreak and rush to sweep up mahua flowers to feed the family. Even these resources have been slowly snatched by the local rich to feed their animals since even fodder has been scarce. (*Patriot*, 17.4.80). In parts of Orissa, tribal girls who go out to collect basic *Adivasi* foods such as bamboo shoots, have been arrested and clapped into jail for the crime of trespassing into bamboo groves which have always belonged to the tribals, but have now been taken over and 'protected' by the government without as much as informing the tribals. Since all edible roots, leaves and fruits have been slowly exhausted, people have been driven to eat poisonous churuhla grass, wild kesari dal which causes terrible skin diseases, body swellings, blindness and paralysis. (*Indian Express*, 10.3.80) Here too, women have been usually the worst hit, the first to die of starvation — which the government conveniently chooses to label as deaths due to malnutrition or poison — since in some cases deaths occur after rather than before consuming poison.

As all sources of food went more and more out of reach of the rural poor, families have had to sell their last possessions from domestic animals to utensils to even doors and windows. (*Patriot*, 16.5.80) In parts of East Uttar Pradesh, one ragged sari has to be shared by all the women in a family so that if one goes out wearing it, all the rest must hide in the hut. And finally, when there is nothing left to sell, the least valued human beings, that is the girls and women, are sold. Year after year, newspapers report how the sale of women into prostitution shoots up during times of drought.

In Nawapara, Orissa, girls in the age group 10 to 14 are reported to have been sold for anything from Rs 15 to Rs 55. (*Patriot*, 7.5.80) Businessmen from Madhya Pradesh purchase these girls and sell them to vice dens in the cities at very high prices. One Raja Nayak of Komma village, sold his eight-year-old daughter Premlata to a businessman for Rs 40: 'I could not give her food for days together and my entire family starved so I preferred to sell her. She can now survive on the food given by her master and my family can survive for a few days on the money I got by selling her.'

Another report sums up very succinctly how women are being used, and then accused and punished by administrators who are supposed to be administering so-called relief: 'Recently, police apprehended a woman in the vicinity of Food for Work food grain stores at Kadar village . . . She was in possession of a bag of rice. . . Working on the suspicion that she might have stolen it from the stores, the police took her to the Block Development Officer's residence. . . . It took the BDO quite some time to open the door. . . . a young girl in a dishevelled state was also in the room . . . BDO introduced her as a close relation. . . But when the woman with the bag of rice entered the room, the girl rushed towards her, crying "Ma!" Finding himself thoroughly exposed, the BDO immediately raised an alarm and asked the police to arrest both mother and daughter on a charge of pilfering grain from the stores. He said that he had called the woman to his room for interrogation. The matter is still under investigation and no action has been taken against the BDO so far.' (*Blitz*, 26.4.80)

In UP it has been reported that tribal women who collect firewood
and go to sell it in towns, are sexually exploited by ticket checkers
because they have no money to pay for the short train ride from
the village to the town. The Tripura government recently uncov-
ered a major interstate racket wherein about 2,000 tribal men and
women, mostly unmarried girls, are exported from Bihar every
week, and many more from Orissa and Madhya Pradesh, to work in
privately owned brick fields in Tripura. The women were sexually
exploited as well. (*Organiser*, 22.6.80) In another typical case:
'. . . migration of landless labourers and small farmers in Singhbhum
is not unusual. What is unusual is that while male members are
finding it difficult to get employment outside the state, the women
are being trapped by unscrupulous contractors . . . who lure them
by promising them a daily wage of Rs 10 . . . this year's drought
has made the task of the contractors even easier . . . the girls are
sent to brothels or dumped in private homes to do domestic work.
In most cases they are not paid anything except two meals a day.
Failure to obey orders of the master invites torture and beating . . .
there are also instances where girls have been sent back to their
homes after their "utility" in brothels is over. . . .' (*Statesman*,
27.11.79) These cases go to show how poverty acquires doubly
brutal dimensions for women. While for a man, poverty means
starvation, for a woman, it invariably also involves rape and a
myriad forms of sexual exploitation.

Women are made so much more vulnerable in poverty that the
distinction between voluntary and forced action seems to completely lose its meaning: 50 destitute girls aged between 20 and 30
years, went to a magistrate's court in the famine stricken district
of Rangpur and registered themselves as prostitutes . . . the girls
filed affidavits before the magistrate, declaring they were voluntarily accepting prostitution as their profession because of
"extreme economic hardship." Prostitution, they felt, was better
than begging. (*Times of India*, 28.9.79) These cases are the mere
tip of the iceberg because big newspapers either systematically
under-report or never report what is really happening to the poor,
especially women, in this country. Such facts are given occasional
coverage simply to provide titillation by sensationalizing atrocities
on women. A cursory glance at the newspapers makes it clear that
most of the space is occupied with tracing the political games and
manoeuverings of those in power.

Relief — The Myth and The Reality

The government has been piously promising relief on a 'warfooting'.
But how have the much-vaunted Food for Work programmes been

functioning? On the one hand, government officially admits that there is no absolute scarcity of food in the country, that tons of food are lying in state godowns. It is also know that tons of food-grains lie hoarded by private traders. On the other hand, the government bureaucrats, in their airconditioned offices, pretend to be as helpless before the calamity as the starving landless themselves.

All the political parties, including those in power at the centre and in the states, are only making political capital out of people's misery. Those in power blame the previous regimes while those in opposition blame those in power.

Between the exploitative landlords and the hypocritical relief schemes, the landless poor are trapped. Often, these two connive to rob the workers of their rightful earnings. The landlords, because of their political connections, can ensure that the Food for Work project be shortlived so that the poor become more dependent and are forced to accept any wage they may decide to fix, or even work in some form of bonded labour. In Madhya Pradesh, the landlords are reported to have sent their bonded labourers (known as *Kamia Mazdoors*, since the *term* 'bonded' though not the *fact* has been banned) to worksites; they then pocketed the wages of the labourers and gave them the usual meagre ration of food. Furthermore, there have also been reports of poor labourers preferring work on the relief project to work in the landlord's fields, only to find that the whole project is in control of the landlord who then takes his revenge on them.

Reports from all over the country show that those who work on the relief projects are being cruelly cheated of their rights. Almost everywhere, large scale bungling has been reported, involving every power holder from village heads to relief officers and some social workers who are supposed to be running voluntary organizations. The wages which actually reach the labourer's hands are far lower than what is allocated on paper. In Palamau, for example, only three kilos of wheat were given to the workers instead of the promised four kilos. Worse still, in Bundelkhand region, all the food was reported to have been diverted to the open market where it was sold at high prices, the profits being pocketed by contractors and government staff. Workers were given 50 *paisas* for a whole day's toil. (*Patriot*, 28.4.80) Another form of government relief is to flood 'fair price' shops with food — where it lies unbought because the people in these areas have no money at all.

In many places, the workers are not paid. Who are they to complain to, when the authorities are themselves the exploiters? In Kundra, for instance, the only relief work undertaken was the construction of a dirt road five kilometres long. This was completed within three weeks last September and the wages had not yet been paid as of March. This delay in distributing the meagre wages is a common feature at most relief works. The villagers have no means of knowing when food distribution will begin. In Banda district after 26 days of work the people were given certificates and had to walk miles to the block headquarters to collect their food. In other places, they had to wait hours in the sun before distribution started. Women at most of these sites were being paid much less than men — by the same government which boasts of having passed the Equal Remuneration Act!

A study conducted by the Planning Commission shows how well-organized this robbery is. In one state, foodgrains meant for the labourers were sold, and crockery and furniture was bought for government inspection bungalows. In another, the money was used to beautify the collectorate building. Some contractors selling food in the market said that labourers were not used to eating wheat anyway! In other cases, good quality foodgrains were sold off by contractors and ration shop owners, and inferior grain distributed. (*Patriot*, 14.2.80)

Often, the wheat distributed is not fit for human consumption. Also, as Shyama, a woman in Durgapur, pointed out, is plain wheat food? For a whole day's hard labour, 'Would it be too much if they gave us a pinch of salt or a handful of chillies to go with it?' she said. (*Times of India*, 22.5.80) The women trying to make do with the meagre quantities of sub-standard grain, are often forced to adulterate it still further so that they can feed the whole family. They mix sawdust with the flour to make *chapatis* [bread] of it. (*National Herald*, 20.3.80)

And then of course, there is the usual phenomenon of the sexual abuse of women by contractors and petty officials at the work-sites. For example, in a rich contractor's camp near a road building site in Palamau district, the *Sunday* magazine reporters saw eight young tribal girls taking care of him — one pressed his limbs while another held his head and so on. (*Sunday*, Special Drought Issue)

Who Suffers Most And Who Benefits?

When we are told by the government and the mass media that Madhya Pradesh, Orissa, Rajasthan, UP, Bihar and parts of West Bengal, Jammu and Kashmir, Assam, Punjab, are affected by drought what does this actually mean? Who are the people made to bear the burden of this calamity?

A new dimension of barbarity to famines and starvation in the present day world is added by the fact that millions are being con-demned to starvation in the midst of plenty and opulence, and worse, that such occurrences have become good occasions to speculate, hoard and make super profits. What is scarcity for the poor becomes a blessing for the rich. Government policy is doubt-less giving an impetus to this trend.

Even during this so-called unprecedented drought, the victims are largely landless agricultural labourers and poor peasants. The rich farmers and landlords have remained immune from its destructive effects. For instance, the Kharif crop was supposed to have been badly hit, but the arrivals in the market have far exceeded the government targets and stand close to the level of the bumper harvest of 1978. (*Indian Express*, 7.12.79) Clearly, those who have a marketable surplus to sell are invariably rich farmers and landlords.

'Natural' Or 'Created' Disaster?

Is it any longer true that famines and droughts are unavoidable 'natural' calamities? Or is this just another myth, like that of the natural inequality between men and women?

That the drought is not a mere natural calamity is evident from the fact that even though Punjab and Haryana had no rainfall last year, they have, on the whole, maintained their level of production. This is because rich farmers in these states are relatively better off and have irrigation facilities. Even in the worst hit and traditionally 'backward' areas such as Madhya Pradesh, the rich farmers, able to afford private irrigation facilities, managed to harvest 60 to 70% of the crop. (*Indian Express*, 17.12.79)

Drought, like price rises and inflation, has its own politics and there are powerful vested interests which seek to perpetuate such misery because they gain by it. The government has computed the loss in farm incomes due to the current drought at Rs 10m *crores*. But it is the poor peasant and landless labourer who seem to have almost exclusively borne this loss because it is they alone who produce for consumption and not for market. The rich farmers who can hoard the surplus and later sell it at higher prices have actually benefited from scarcity.

The drought has further accentuated pauperization in the countryside. The rural poor have been driven further into debt and newer forms of servitude, forced to mortgage or sell what little land they had left. Thus, the stranglehold of the landlord-money-lender combine has been further strengthened and the process of concentration of assets and land — which has been going on steadily even while there has been so much talk of land ceilings and agrarian reforms — has been accelerated.

The government, by increasing the procurement support price of foodgrain, makes matters worse. This helps only the rich who have surplus foodgrain to sell and prevents even a little relief to the urban poor, by keeping prices artificially inflated even during times of plenty.

The so-called national calamity is therefore not a calamity for the whole nation. To the frequenters of five star hotels, it makes no difference whether sugar sells at Rs 7 or Rs 5 a kilo. Thus even while there is so much talk of shortages, the consumption of the rich has in fact become even more luxurious. Witness the sudden spurt in big cities over the recent year, of exotic eating places such as fancy ice cream parlours, pizza joints, French, Arabic and Mughlai restaurants.

Meanwhile the rural poor are flocking to the cities in the hope of a few crumbs. They are seen eating garbage, begging, and are reduced to committing petty thefts and robberies. For the government, they merely represent a law and order problem left to be dealt with by the police and anti-begging squads.

Droughts, floods and other such calamities have become good occasions for the Indian government to pour out hypocritical concern for the poor and to seek in them excuses for the politics of perpetuating poverty that it has pursued since independence.
'. . . It was at Kithana in UP that a tribal woman told me something that nearly made me cry. The drought, she said, had done her family some good. Because of a relief work project close to the village, she and her children were eating *rotis* made of wheat. What the Kols eat normally — thick chapatis made of extremely coarse grain mixed with jowar stalks — I tried to eat at Manha Kolan but could not. And I do not think I will ever live down my shame and sorrow for the pain I inflicted on a boy of 14 at Simawar by asking when he had eaten *dal* [lentils] and cooked vegetables with his *rotis*. He tried to answer my question, stammered for a while and then began to sob. His mother told me in a matter-of-fact way that she had never been able to feed her son *dal* or cooked vegetables.' (Inder Malhotra in *Times of India*, September 1979)

This is the context in which the 'unprecedented' drought occurred. The achievements of this 'great democracy' in the 33 years since independence are indeed spectacular. More than 150,000 villages, according to the government's own figures, are without potable drinking water throughout the year. And when the government says 'potable drinking water' it does not mean clean drinking water because that is not available even in cities like Delhi with their elaborate waterworks!

And it is in so-called normal times that more than 70% of people in this country live below the poverty line — the government's idea of the poverty line being an income of Rs 30 per month for urban areas and Rs 20 for rural areas — an income even at this level unequally distributed. It is in this context of increasing pauperization of the mass of the people that the phenomenal price rise and inflation acquire the aspect of life and death issues.

When rice sells at Rs 2.80 to Rs 7 a kilo, sugar at Rs 7 a kilo, milk at Rs 3 a kilo, any attempt at 'holding the price line' or selling in 'fair price' shops acquires a farcical character, aimed only at fooling the urban middle class. It has absolutely no relevance to the lives of millions living below the subsistence level. And it is in 'normal times' that sale of human beings goes on despite government's pious platitudes about having abolished bonded labour. Take for instance the case of Prasen Korwa from Bandna village near Garwa. It was during 'normal times' that he borrowed 12 kilos of rice from the *sarpanch* (a government official) Shivdutt Mahato in 1971. At that time, the value of the rice was Rs 20. But the interest on his debt started multiplying. He has already given the landlord two goats worth Rs 150, a bullock worth Rs 170, and around 12 kilos of pulses costing Rs 16. In addition he worked without pay for 15 days and returned Rs 150 in cash. But the *sarpanch* is still not satisfied. Since that fateful day, Prasen Korwa works on Mahato's fields with only a meal a day. . . . (*Sunday* magazine, Special Drought Issue)

Is it true then, as the government would have us believe,that the state is trying to help people, that it is only inefficiency and corruption which prevent schemes from working? Or is there some method in this madness? Is this corruption not part of a larger pattern wherein the owners of resources are able to devise newer and newer ways to keep the poor in such a state of sub-human subsistence that it becomes easier to crush whatever little possibility of revolt can exist under such circumstances?

The government is very efficient when it comes to unleashing violence and crushing struggles of the oppressed and the poor. It is very efficient in ordering police firings on unarmed workers demanding their rights, as in Kanpur, Faridabad, Pantnagar. Why is it then, that the government cannot ensure a supply of clean drinking water in villages where Campa Cola can manage to be supplied regularly? Why is it that the government cannot ensure that the food under the Food for Work project reaches those who work for it, instead of ending up in the pockets of the corrupt bureaucracy?

For years now, we have been fed with lies about the problem of poverty that our government is trying to cope with. But if one looks at the policies and programmes of the whole governmental set-up, it becomes clear that all its efforts are directed towards perpetuating inequality and strengthening the position of the economically powerful. How else would one explain the government's attempt to go in for colour television — a project that might cost anything up to Rs 300,000,000 crores (1 million rupees) — at a time when more than 150,000 villages are without drinking water, when water is at places selling for Rs 3 a bucket (*Patriot*, 19.4.80) when millions are dying of starvation? The politicians in power boast of allocating Rs 141 crores to relief work (of which only a fraction manages to reach the affected) but how is it that the budget for 1980 to 1981, presented to Parliament in March has sanctioned over Rs 37 million to defence? Why is it that the government can afford to go on buying more and more sophisticated arms from abroad, but cannot show the same keenness in procuring deep digging bores to provide much-needed water? Similarly, 32% of the total budget is being spent on maintaining a corrupt, inefficient bureaucracy whereas the budget spent on providing irrigation facilities is substantially less than this, even though droughts in India are acquiring the regularity of the seasons.

In spite of the utter destitution and powerlessness to which the mass of people in this country have been reduced, there have been attempts – some spontaneous, some organized – to express their anger and demand their rights.

One silent but no less significant way in which people expressed their anger, was by keeping away from the recent state assembly elections. Many villages boycotted the elections en masse. Here is one of the many examples: 'Residents of drought-hit Khandekama village of Barmer district refused to vote unless drinking water was provided to them immediately. Not a single voter turned up at the Sundara polling station until 1 p.m.' (*Statesman*, 29.5.80)

In Chattisgarh region (Madhya Pradesh) too, attempts were made by the people to march to the local Food Corporation godowns [basement stores] where food was lying rotting in the open because of inadequate storage space with the demand that food be distributed to the hungry. But the protesters could not reach the food godowns because of the heavy police guard. These godowns are as heavily guarded by police and security men as are the government's defence establishments! (Reported by a local activist)

Dahanu district in Maharashtra is one of the worst affected in the state. But no relief work was provided because the government, for its own reasons, did not declare it as a famine-stricken area. To put pressure on the government, the Kasthakari Sangathana organ-ized the tribals to demand Employment Guarantee Schemes in the village. On April 23, they went in a demonstration to the Tehsildar's office and got an assurance that work would be started, but while they were returning to the village they were brutally attacked by local goondas, shopkeepers and landlords. Many women, children and men received serious injuries. As usual, the police refused to take notice. No arrests were made till May 31. In fact, the activists of the Kasthakari Sangathana are being threatened with arrests and are being intimidated by both police and goondas. (Report sent to us by an activist)

An even more revealing case: 'In Karwi sub-division where a population of 392,000 has been affected, only 35,000 were employed in relief projects. A mob of starving Harijans allegedly raided the shop of a grain dealer Baijnath Shivhari, looted four quintals of grain at Bira village, Banda district, and distributed it equally among themselves. The said: "We were starving and this greedy profiteer was selling his foodgrains across the district border in Madhya Pradesh." ' And what was the state's response? 'A case of dacoity [banditry] was registered against the Harijans at Shivrampur police station'! (*Times of India*, 12.11.79)

Who Are The Thieves?

Does this not clearly show that the laws of our country are weighted in favour of the propertied? What could be called the highest form of social justice is labelled *dacoity* by the guardians of the law. After all, it is these landless *Dalits* [tribal peasants] who work on the fields and produce the foodgrain. Through this act, they had tried appropriating the fruits of their own labour and distributing it justly. Do we not need to ask who decides what is to be called theft in law? For whose benefit do these laws operate?

How is it that 12% of the richest rural farmers owning more than half of total rural assets including land, is not called theft? Is it not theft that 80% of the country's resources are controlled by 20% of the people? And if one dares call this theft, one is accused of creating a law and order problem! Surely no supernatural powers conferred such property rights on a few chosen ones! Why is it that starvation deaths, when there is plenty of food rotting in godowns, both private and state-owned, are not treated as murder? Why is it that all the laws of the country protect this unfair ownership of resources by a few?

Solutions From Above?

Since this is the record of the government, how have opposition parties reacted to the situation? There have been sporadic attempts by some parties to highlight these issues, but most of the agitations ended in slogan shouting before the blank walls of a government office and the handing over of a memorandum to some official or the other. The following are instances of action under the aegis of some political party or the other:

'Recently, thousands of men and women with empty pitchers and buckets paraded through the streets of Giridih and demonstrated before the Deputy Commissioner's office handed over a charter of demands.' (*Patriot*, 14.4.80)

'In Etawah 2,000 *kisans* [farmers] demonstrated on March 18 at the district centre. A charter of demands was submitted to the District Magistrate.'

'Forty women belonging to the Anti Price-Rise Committee, for 15 minutes gheraoed V.P. Sathe and demanded proper distribution of kerosene and other essential items and steps to bring down sugar prices.' (*Times of India*, 29.2.80) 'In Faizabad district, Kisan Sabhas and the Khet Mazdoor Sabha jointly led a demonstration of 2,000 peasants and agricultural workers in Akhbarpurtehsil, demanding a proper running of the state tubewells in view of the drought conditions, ending blackmarketing and strong steps to check price rise.'

This tendency of sporadic political agitations to end in deputations and memorandum-giving has, over a period of time, bred in people a sense of despair and futility, the feeling that nothing ever changes. And political parties through such agitations, help foster the myth that solutions will come from above, that government can be pressurised into becoming more considerate.

We have come across a few other such instances of different kinds of collective action being reported in the press but by and large, such instances seem to be systematically censored or under-reported. It seems as though the press is only too happy to be part of this conspiracy of silence. Here is one instance that we ourselves witnessed. On 30 June 1980, all the traffic at India Gate was stopped for an hour by thousands and thousand of poor *Adivasis* who had come to the capital and braved the pouring rain to protest against their deteriorating economic, social, cultural conditions, and demand a separate Jharkhand state. This got only a few lines on the third page of national newspapers. And the *Adivasis* were treated with equal callousness by the government. They were heavily fined and clapped into prison for travelling back home without tickets! Since the press under-reports events in the capital, what chance do small local protests have of getting to the people through the mass media?

The mass media helps isolate people's struggles so that they do not get forged into a widespread movement. It is this isolation of small, local struggles which demoralizes them on the one hand, and on the other, breeds the feeling of helplessness and despair among all of us — the feeling that nothing is being done to bring about change and that nothing can change.

To give an example from our experience. Many women from small towns and cities which have no active women's organizations,

have told us that for the first time, as they read in *Manushi*
reports of women's collective struggles in some parts of the
country, they begin to develop a new feeling of power, of strength:
'If women in Patna or Bombay or Bangalore can organize, we can
do it too.' And it is this feeling which is helping many of us overcome our diffidence and initiate new women's groups.

Even more revealing was what the mother of one of the dowry
victims had to say the other day, at one of the anti-dowry demonstrations in Delhi. Satyarani Chadha's daughter was burnt to death
by her in-laws a year ago. And the culprits have gone scot-free.
Today, Satyarani is a leading participant in all anti-dowry demonstrations. She wanted us to help her organize a demonstration
outside the house of her daughter's in-laws. We asked her why she
didn't do this immediately after her daughter died. Her answer:
'I didn't know then about these *morchas* [demonstrations]. Otherwise, I would never have let the hundreds of women of my community who came to mourn the death of my daughter, sit around
crying with me. We would have gone together and demonstrated
outside their house, put pressure on the neighbourhood to socially
ostracize the family, and got justice for ourselves.' [For more
about Indian women's organization against the dowry, see section
on women and violence.]

It is this sense of power to effectively intervene in our own lives
and to fight for justice that the mass media in conspiracy with the
powers-that-be, wants to deny us. The only time it chooses to
highlight such atrocities and militant action by people is when some
political lobby takes an interest in it. For instance, in the Baghpat
rape murder case, the fact that Charan Singh and Company have
jumped into the fray to settle scores with Indira Gandhi is in no
small measure responsible for the publicity the case is receiving.
Similarly, when the Belchhi atrocities took place, Indira Gandhi's
elephant ride, what she said, seemed more important to the press
than the fact of atrocities on Harijans. Why does the mass media
give more coverage to the Prime Minister's various appointments or
the many vague, empty pronouncements by the horde of Ministers
than to the starvation of 200 million people? Surely, not a case of
mistaken priorities, but a systematic attempt to make some people
into larger than life figures, to build cults around them, and make
the power games of a handful of such people seem the only events
of importance in the national life. All this contributes in no small
way to making the mass of people feel small and helpless. It is made
to seem as if a single stroke from Indira Gandhi's pen, a wave of her
hand or a frown on her face is more potent than the anger of
thousands against unhuman living conditions. This feeling of small-
ness, helplessness, of struggling in isolation against the ever-increasing
might of those we are made to put in power, are important factors

in making people 'accept' their predicament.

Our Battle Begins Here

We feel that a lot more is happening by way of people's resistance protest, and efforts to create change, than ever gets known through the established mass media. So we have to collect and disseminate this information on our own. We must do this vigorously, systematically. This is an important way in which we can win back for ourselves the belief in our own power to change things. Only thus can small local struggles get linked and grow into a widespread movement.

Women in large numbers have participated in consumer movements against inflation like that which swept Maharashtra and Gujarat in the early 1970s. But these movements have been led by the urban middle class. The worst sufferers – working-class women – remained largely uninvolved. That is why these movements had a short term minimal impact. The issue of price rises in this country must be linked to the issue of a living wage. As long as landlessness, indebtedness, bondedness, unemployment continue to be life conditions for the mass of people their total destitution will keep prices out of reach for them in any case.

During the recent drought too, there were local agitations against food scarcity in villages, and against price rise in cities. Why is it that these struggles remained fragmented? What is it that prevented the anger and discontent from exploding into a widespread movement? What are the factors that act as a hurdle or as safety valves? It is in this context that we hope that *Manushi* readers will help us gather information on this drought (and no floods that are already beginning their havoc) — particularly, the details of how such calamities affect people's lives, accelerate the process of indebtedness, bondedness, pauperization, traffic in women, prostitution. Even more important, what role did women play in agitations and struggles during this period?

Since all these problems — poverty, bondedness, lack of living wage, unemployment, landlessness — affect women much more, since women bear the major brunt of poverty and exploitation, must not these issues also become women's issues? Can women not organize around these issues? What role can women's organizations play in taking up these issues? We invite our women readers to send their views, especially those based on experience of struggle and women's participation in struggle. Also, women's reactions, responses, to the problems of drought or inflation as they feel them in daily life.

What form should the struggles take? We have seen over the years, the inadequacy of protest demonstrations, submitting demand charters which are aimed at reforming the government and pressurising it into becoming more 'considerate', and since political parties have so far organized in this direction only, there has been a growing cynicism about the effectiveness of mass action itself. But in places the poor and landless did try other means, as for instance the Harijans in Karwi sub-division, who raided the local merchant's shop and distributed the grain equally among themselves. Or the poor villagers in Jhakni and Jaurhari, who physically restrained rich farmers from taking their wheat stocks to sell in neighbouring markets.(*Patriot*, 18.10.70) Perhaps these instances point the direction in which the solution lies: in people realizing and asserting the need to exercise collective control over privately owned resources.

2. Women and Politics in Lebanon
Yolla Polity Sharara

The following article has been reproduced from *Khamsin* (No. 6, 1978), a journal of revolutionary socialists of the Middle East, and formed part of a special issue on Arab women. Very little is known about the author, Yolla Polity Sharara, who apparently wrote the article for a French, local Middle Eastern newspaper whilst she was studying librarianship some time ago in Grenoble. It was later translated for *Khamsin* with her sister's permission.

Mothers build homes and sons build countries

The mother who rocks her newborn son with her right hand does not shake the world with her left hand

(Arab sayings)

I think I experienced my relationship with politics as the transgression of a taboo. Of course, in the 1960s we were no longer living in the era of the veil. Lebanese society, despite its reputation for Westernization and modernism, was none the less still carefully partitioned: boys' schools and girls' schools, girls' games and boys'

games, motherhood and homemaking for women, professional work
for men. . . . This division of roles and behaviour, seldom trans-
gressed in practice, was instilled very early on within the family.
Boys were openly preferred to girls, and girls were intensively prepared for their role as wives and mothers. Housekeeping skills and
docility were the qualities most appreciated in a young girl ready
for marriage. Women and politics were two opposite poles, or two
spheres which never intersected. Politics was 'public', 'outside
activity', 'history'. A woman was everything that was most private,
most eternal and 'ahistoric', the 'within', the 'at-home' that everyone, boy or girl, found in the home, the mother.

Politics was the preserve of men. We had obtained equal civic
and political rights in 1953, we could vote and we could be elected.
But it was good form not to make too much use of these rights.
We would go and vote with our fathers or husbands, and we would
vote the same way they did. Was it worth stirring up trouble in the
family to vote for or against people we did not know from Adam
or Eve, men foreign to our family? Was it worth the ridicule to
stand as a candidate, as two women had done just after we had
obtained the right to vote? Political questions were settled for us
at the level of what is 'done' and what is 'not done', of what was
or was not suitable for a woman. Although legally citizens, we continued to be ruled by our families and we had few, if any official
relations with the state.

To engage in politics, or to 'enter politics' as we put it, was not
the done thing for young women. We entered despite the opposition of our frightened parents. We joined as though we were joining
a religion, eager to learn, to catch up on secular backwardness,
serious and hardworking, obeying all the bizarre rules which gover-
ned meetings and demonstrations. The world of politics had the
taste of forbidden fruit. We were proud to have been admitted,
proud to meet celebrated leaders in the corridors, and especially
proud finally to be taken seriously. Men, our comrades, listened
carefully and with respect, and we were at ease discussing economic,
historic or international problems with them. We were flying
high, far from the kitchens of our mothers, and far from the
embroidery work destined for our trousseaus.

It is necessary to have lived in these closed societies, where roles
are rigidly defined from infancy, to understand our euphoria and
also our blindness. We thought we had escaped the usual fate of
women. We had slipped through a breach into the world of men.
We tried to acclimatize ourselves to that world, always thinking our
setbacks were due to our own ignorance. We were not yet ready
to bring men and their values into question, and still less to question
'politics'.

Our elders who, like us, could not bear their situation, did not have the same opportunities as we did. In their time, political parties did not admit women, and no woman dared to meet men publicly who were not known to her family. So they founded women's charitable and social associations. For a long time they denied that they were involved in politics. When they took a position on a political or national problem, they took great care to show why, as mothers, they could not accept this and why, as wives, they demanded that. They led a campaign for political rights, and from 1953, they tried vainly to bring women into political life.

These women's organizations saw the problem as solely at the level of national power. Politics was the world of deputies and ministers. Women were excluded, and that was unfair. Several unsuccessful attempts to get themselves elected to the legislature were occasions for diatribes by these organizations against backward voters, and against women who did not understand their own interests, were traitors to their own sex and lacked confidence in the ability of women to represent them. There were diatribes also, and especially, against the power of money, electoral fraud and the manoeuvres of politicians whose victims were women candidates. Pure and innocent women mounting an assault on a corrupt electoral system were defeated by the forces of Evil (Men) and corruption. [There is an untranslatable pun in the last sentence — *Mal* — evil, *Male* — Men]. All of which said to the most indulgent 'they can't make the grade' and to others 'Its a good thing; they shouldn't mix in matters which don't concern them.'

Although disgusted by these defeats, the women did not give up their project. During a meeting before the last legislative elections one woman speaker made an apologia for the Syrian and Egyptian regimes, which had allowed women into the body of deputies. Conceding that these women had not been elected but designated on the lists of single parties or simply nominated by the executive, this speaker, warmly applauded by the audience, demanded that in Lebanon as well, a certain number of seats be reserved *ex officio* for women nominated by the *Conseil General des Femmes* and the President of the Republic. This support for a system of nomination was astonishing on the part of women who otherwise swore by democracy in Lebanon, and criticized the absence of freedoms in neighbouring Arab countries. But the advantages they saw in this system led them to gloss over everything which accompanied it.

Thus, they said 'the woman would remain dignified, would not be obliged to have her photo on the walls of the town, nor be confronted with the base material considerations of an election campaign. She would not lose her femininity, nor run the risk of a humiliating defeat and would gain power.' Alas, all this required an amendment of the Constitution and the electoral law, a difficult process in Lebanon.

Perhaps the dream of gaining power could be achieved more easily and more quickly at the level of ministerial posts? Every time there was a change of Cabinet (which was frequent during these troubled years) we saw these same women's organizations rushing to the newly-nominated head of the government during his consultations: 'women are under-represented, you must give us a portfolio . . .' The same thing happened every time: the Prime Minister received them courteously while they were served titbits to eat, and the press, in ironic mood, noted the visit; meanwhile everyone waited for the women to finish their activities so that serious matters could be dealt with.

It was pathetic. These women took their sex literally as the reason for their exclusion from power, and presented themselves as women, without any consideration of political tendencies, religions, parties, programmes, international or Arab affiliations — the essence of the political game. It was also pathetic because it took the authorities, who presented themselves as democratic, at their word: representatives of all citizens, without distinction of sex, class or religion, a just and egalitarian power. It was as though the right to something was sufficient to obtain it; as though the exclusion of women resulted from an oversight, which would be rectified on the spot once it was realized.

The women who joined political parties were less naive. They regarded politics as something requiring time and work. They had transferred their ambitions for power to the party. The majority thought that the conditions of women would change if they joined political parties. They expected that political and social transformations would make reforms possible. According to which party they belonged to, they struggled for Arab unity, the Lebanese nation, or socialism, but very little for the cause of women. It was very important for them to be recognized as full members of the party. They disliked being assigned to the women's section and wanted to prove that they were as capable as men at dealing with any problem. Thus they avoided talking about women, a minor subject, in order not to be put down. Within the many parties which, while admitting women, kept them in separate groups, the women met among themselves, waited for instructions from a party leader and were mobilized particularly when the party had to show its strength in demonstrations and especially in electoral campaigns. In these situations, women were suddenly necessary and even indispensable.

In 1975, as part of the activities of International Women's Year, the Democratic Party invited representatives of Lebanese political parties to a meeting to draw up a balance sheet of the participation of women in political parties and to consider the possibility of agreeing on a platform of demands and common action. Women from the Phalangist Party, the National Bloc, the Progressive Socialist Party, the Ba'ath Party, the Communist Party, as well as other women belonging to small groups, all met together; distrustful, rivals, convinced in advance that no agreement was possible.

However, agreement was possible. It was sufficient to point to the one or more paragraphs in each party's programme devoted to women, to realise that all the parties — at least in principle — were for equality between men and women, for optional civil marriage, for the application of the law on equal pay, for the generalization of education for girls, for better professional training for girls, for an extension of creches etc . . . That this preparatory meeting was not followed by others, was officially because of the war: the leftist parties ordered a boycott of the Phalangist Party, so women from the left-wing parties could not sit down at the same table with Phalangists. In fact, it was because of the anguish provoked by the agenda.

The first question was strictly political: 'What is the position of your party on women's questions?' Everybody, both on the left and on the right, was doubtful whether they would agree. How would a Communist look if she found nothing either to criticize or to add to what was proposed by a Phalangist? How was it possible to end up with only differences of detail in demands over women, starting from so many different and antagonistic ideologies representing the whole organized Lebanese political spectrum? Was it sufficient to attribute the agreement to the demagogy of the right, which in its programmes made promises to women which it had no intention of keeping? This was not a serious approach, and one felt that it revealed a grave problem, that of an inadequate analysis of the exploitation and oppression experienced by women in Lebanese society.

The second question, although also political, was of a more existential nature: 'In your party, what is the number of women members, and the number of women who are in leading positions? What problems do they have because they are women?' Of all those present, only the Democratic Party could point to women in its politburo. No woman representative would agree to give figures or even a rough estimate of the proportion of women members in relation to the total membership of the party. There was great reticence in admitting there were problems at all. Thus, if there were few women in the party, this was because women lacked consciousness; if they did not hold responsible positions, this was because they were not sufficiently competent — the party itself did not discriminate. Women found themselves using standard male modes of thought in regard to other women: they talked like men. The same mechanism that makes women loth to complain of their lot in front of women they do not know, especially if they are

Liberation! Victory! The message is an armed struggle for peace in the women's poster.

rivals, was at work there. These women militants, when they were conscious of the discrimination of which they and their comrades were victim, when they were not themselves token women in the party, preferred to wash their dirty linen at home. They refused to question publicly the men from their own party, to recognize that their party, their men, were not the most advanced, the most egalitarian, or the most revolutionary. Alienated, and preferring their hard-won identity as members of the party to the less prestigious identity of committed women, they left without having really met, without having talked, or listened.

The possibility of politicizing the women's question, i.e. applying the same criteria as that applied to any other question, analysing it in terms of relations of power, of positions through which one group of people (in this case men) control another group (women) seems to be a long way off, for at least the majority of Lebanese women. But some women began to do this. They had been militants

for several years in the left parties. They had lived with and undergone subtle or brutal discrimination from society, from militants
of other parties — but especially from their own comrades. They
had been confronted with the disastrous consequences of the
etiquette of principal and secondary contradictions, the contradiction between the sexes being, of course, always secondary. They
had realized the futility of any revolution which kept intact the
basic unity of exploitation and oppression, that of one sex over the
other, of masculine over feminine. They had also lived through the
laceration of the war, in which, although perhaps in different
forms according to the side, the male order had been the sole
victor.

It is this reflection, still embryonic, which I want to account
for. To try to see in the present political situation in Lebanon an
antagonism of class and of religious communities, but also an
antagonism between the sexes, to try to see the war through, and
starting from, the feminine universe (cf. Mao and also M.-A.
Macciocchi 'les Femmes et la traversee du fascisme' in *Elements
pour une analyse du fascisme*, Paris, 1976, p.128.)

It is hardly astonishing that in Lebanon more than in other
places women experience politics as something foreign in their
daily lives, since their lives are ruled by community, and not national laws. The principal moments of their lives are punctuated by the
intervention of men from their communities and religious authorities, rarely from the state. It is essential to understand, that in
Lebanon, all matters relating to personal status depend on confessional laws and tribunals. There is no civil marriage. There are as
many different laws for women as there are religions. Marriage,
divorce or separation, relationships, guardianship of minors, inheritance, all these problems have different solutions according to
whether one is a Maronite Christian, a Greek Orthodox, Greek
Catholic, or a Sunnite or Shi'ah Muslim. Of course the state also
intervenes: education policy, employment policy, wages, prices. . .
But these problems are secondary, or rather experienced as
secondary by most women, with the exception of politicized
women who are interested in them.

In 1975 the women's organizations held a congress to discuss
the laws relating to personal status, and demanded optional and
non-compulsory civil marriage. A law forbidding discrimination
against women in the family was presented by women from the
Democratic Party and adopted by the congress. All the parties
which declare themselves opposed to confessionalism talk about
the necessity of having unified and secular laws in all spheres of
life, especially that of personal status. The left parties add that this
reform is all the more necessary because the present laws are dis-
advantageous to women, but their declarations remain at the level

of principles, and everyone carefully avoids entering into details.

However, at the moment of civil war, the question of women became the central point of negotiations between the right and the left, and it is not irrelevant that it also became the point of rupture.

The 'Committee for National Dialogue', laboriously created during one of the many cease-fires that marked the war, attempted to list points of disagreement and bring together different points of view. It broke down over the question of secularization. The left demanded total secularization, as did the Christian right. The Muslims wanted political and administrative secularization, but refused secularization of personal status, considering it a matter of private and non-political problems. Since the beginning of the war the left had been a prisoner of its Muslim allies. Its leader, Kamal Jumblatt, known for his misogyny and political opportunism declared that since the 'Muslim and national side' was not ready for such a reform, they could put the question of civil marriage to one side. One could not open a breach in alliance over such secondary problems! The important thing was to remain united in the face of the enemy and to deal with 'political' and military problems. It should be noted that this abandonment by the left of the women's cause went almost totally unnoticed.

The Christian right affirmed that for its part it wanted civil marriage. Assured of a Muslim rejection, it could allow itself all sorts of proposals to give itself a modern and Western image. In a recent interview with *Le Monde*, Beshir Gemayel stated: 'Alone, we achieved secularization a long time ago.' Describing the federal structure he supported, he said: 'Each community should rule itself according to its own laws, and no one should impose their views on others.' But isn't this precisely what happened before the war? As for secularization, that is a trap-word for women. For the Napoleonic Code was a secular code, as was the Rocco Code, drawn up by Mussolini in fascist Italy. What sort of code then, are the Phalangists and the Guardians of the Cedar, allied to the Lebanese monks, preparing for us?

Here we touch on a very important aspect of intercommunal relations. We are dealing with two communities struggling for power, for leadership. Within each community, masculine domination over women takes place under different conditions and according to different laws, but it is none the less implacable. It is a matter of keeping the women for the men of the community. However, Muslim men have legal access to Christian women; the reverse is not true. A Muslim woman cannot marry a non-Muslim without at least converting and in that case losing her inheritance. Marriages are very common between Lebanese Christians and foreign Christians. Mixed marriages are very rare between Christian men and Muslim women, and often in these cases the man converts to Islam.

When civil marriage is discussed, traditional Muslim men immediately imagine a cohort of young women, their daughters and sisters, rushing into the arms of Christian men the minute the law is passed. This threat is absolutely untenable. One exasperated Muslim said to me: 'When we discuss secularization with Christians they ask me: will you give us your daughter in marriage? Would that they would leave our women alone!'

For centuries, these communities have lived side by side with myths concerning the women of the other community. In the Muslims, the Christians see the East with all its seduction, its sensuality, and its docility, in short — the harem. The Muslims imagine Christian women as being more advanced, more educated, and more modern than their women. To join them is a promotion, But as intercommunal relations remained relatively rare, because of the fear of reprisals from jealous fathers and brothers (sometimes leading to crimes, qualified as 'crimes of honour') negative myths grew up, helping to make frustration tolerable: 'bunch of whores' said Muslims of Christians who rejected them; 'stupid and ignorant women' said the Christians of Muslim women they lusted after, but who were inaccessible.

A kind of rule operated in peace time, an implicit understanding between the males of the two communities, recognizing the mutual right of each over the women of their respective communities. This *entente*, based mainly on fear of reprisals, protected women of the two camps in the first stages of the war. Few women were kidnapped, and if they were arrested they were quickly released. They could move around more easily than men; militiamen on barricades did not ask them for identity papers. One got the impression that if one side broke this agreement and started to seize women, it would be terrible. If the walls, which held back repressed and aggressive desires, suddenly broke, the consequences would be uncontrollable.

These walls were effectively broken at times, when the war reached extremes of violence: Quarantina, Damour, Clemenceau, Tel El Za'atar. These were points of no return, where through the association of sexuality with power, by the rape of women and young girls, the aggressors signified their absolute (but momentary) domination over the other camp. In all the random shelling, houses in flames, banks looted, hotels destroyed, factories sacked, some elements of the patriarchal order — religious, political and military leaders and women's property — were spared. This 'gentlemen's agreement', based on a cult of authority and hierarchy, and on an extraordinary respect for force and violence, as much in their own camp as within the enemy camp, led to some aberrations: Hawi, military leader of the Phalangist militias, was captured by the

Palestinian resistance and released several hours later. When people wanted to hit Chamoun, they executed his nephew; and as a reprisal, it was Jumblatt's sister that was assassinated.

If certain of the leaderships were hit during this war, those who survived emerged even more ingrained with authoritarianism and violence. Both sides attributed their previous 'defeats' to the softness of their leaders; they wanted the strongest leaders, the best armed militias, the most organized — that is the most easily controllable — population. Any questioning of authority had to be fought, any criticism or reservations were put down to laxity, politics was no longer a citizen's right, only guns talked. These were phallic values *par excellence*.

The people had to be mobilized to accept the infernal life that gripped the combat areas, Beirut in particular, scarcity and sometimes total lack of water, electricity, bread, vegetables and meat, children without schools, workers without jobs, stealing and looting, destruction and death. Those responsible for the war were aware that it was the women who bore most of the burden of everyday life. They attempted to gain their support. Radio programmes were specifically directed at women from both sides. Despite references to the 'Cedar of Lebanon' — or the Arab destiny of the same Lebanon — these programmes were very similar. They talked about 'the necessary contribution of women to the national cause', and of 'the price to be paid'. They exalted the spirit of sacrifice of the mothers who had borne the heroes. Heroes, yes, but how to acknowledge their deaths, and the death of so many victims of random shelling and the bullets of snipers? *'Ommash-shahid'*, the mother of the martyr, became the object of endless glorification. The violence of the apparatus and rituals of funerals was useful as a means of making death unreal, and silencing the women's grievances: the profusion of guns, shots in the air, the bodies removed to the wailing of the women, and the men accompanying the hero-martyr to his final resting place.

Pathetic as always, women from the women's organizations, corroded like everybody by the confessional evil, completely bypassed by events and not knowing what to do, took up a position against the war. One day they tried to remove the barricades of the militias and this led to kidnappings. Going from east Beirut to west Beirut, from Phalangist barricade to progressive barricade, they spoke in the name of wives, mothers and sisters. They wanted an end to the killing. They had built homes and now, contrary to the saying, the sons were destroying the country. Of course, their campaigns had no success, although it reflected the feelings of many people.

Women belonging to parties, and many others who joined in during the war, organized assistance and food for both camps. Not having been able to leave the area controlled by the progressive forces and the Palestinian resistance during the whole of the war, I don't know in detail what happened in the Christian camp. However, everything leads me to believe that women from both sides ran into the same problems.

On the progressive side the disorganization would have reached unmanageable proportions without the participation of the women. They formed aid teams, provided help for the injured, welcomed refugee families, gave food for the fighters, sewed sheets and linen for the hospitals. An incredible amount of energy was and continues to be expended. Very few men militants took part in this work unless they were overseeing it. This was considered to be women's work, and regarded with contempt; men who participated in it felt themselves diminished, and were mocked by their comrades. Everything was just the same as in the family. For women, the servile jobs, for men, the noble jobs; in war the noble jobs are carrying arms and fighting.

Women did take part in the fighting — and their presence was considered to be neither natural nor obvious. On the surface, men were proud to have women fighting in their ranks. This conformed to the scheme of 'people's war'. In actual fact, the presence of women was felt to be an intolerable blow to their virility. They defended themselves by attacking: sexual and verbal aggression or attempts to put the women down. The attitude of military instructors was full of condescension, as though they were saying: 'I'm too important to waste my time with women.' The military commanders were no better. Women fighters were always given the least prestigious arms with the excuse that they had not had enough training, and the worst places on the pretext of 'protecting' them. To be treated as equals, the women had to be more courageous and more competent than the men, and at that point they became the token women, heroines. Each party and each militia had a few of them.

In addition, the women fighters had to defend themselves against the ever-present accusation of being whores. 'In the trenches, it's an orgy', was a fantasy often expressed by men fighters talking about the enemy camp or rival militias. Women had no right to be there, they were a nuisance. Every pretext was good.

And why were we there?

Why, even by taking up arms, did we fill precisely that role given to us for all (patriarchal) eternity: that of the beautiful woman fighter, or the avenging mother defending her little ones? Why were we involved in a struggle from which we would gain nothing?

Why did we let ourselves into this sinister adventure?

3. Roles and Contradictions of Chilean Women in the Resistance and in Exile Gladys Diaz

This paper, subtitled 'Collective Reflections of a Group of Militant Prisoners', was first presented by Gladys Diaz in Venezuela in 1979. She is an exiled member of the Central Committee of MIR (Movement of the Revolutionary Left) and the occasion was the plenary session of an International Conference on Exile and Solidarity in Latin America. The paper was translated by the Women's International Resource Exchange Service (WIRE Service) who also distribute it and many other interesting articles by women all over the world.

We see the women's struggle, our struggle, in the context of the class struggle and, therefore, we consider the struggle of our people to be a priority; that is why we conceive of exploited men and women as a group, as one single class. We women are an important sector of that class, 50% of it, a sector which has been doubly exploited, oppressed since time immemorial, relegated, misunderstood, and for the most part ignored when it comes to important discussions. In the struggle for the liberation of our people, we face all the many contradictions implied in being workers, mothers, housewives, and, at the same time, committed and thinking women. That is why we carry on a double struggle, the struggle for freedom alongside our people and the often tiring and wearing struggle for our own emancipation. Experience has shown us that our struggle is only part of the battle to regain dignity, to once again become protagonists in, instead of mere observers of, history.
  We understand that our liberation will not occur within capitalist society. The struggle for liberation will only really begin seriously when the working class has conquered power. We are convinced, and history and experience show us, that our liberation as women is not a gift which will automatically be given with socialism. Our struggle is a long one, as long as the history of the enemy's ideological presence within us, within our *companeros*, and within all of society; and that is why the struggle is necessarily long and difficult — that ideological battle to erase distortions,

prejudices, obstacles which the present situation of women in society has created and which women suffer even in the relationship with their mates.

During the last two decades, Latin American capitalism has exacerbated the exploitation and misery of the masses. The dominant pattern of economic development in Latin America must of necessity rest on authoritarian governments, which may take the form of military dictatorships or of controlled democracies which, in turn, rest on super-exploitation and repression.

It is in this framework, therefore, that women have been brutally confronted with the gradual loss of gains made over the years with so much sacrifice. Under Pinochet's dictatorship, Chilean women have come to understand that they have nothing to gain from the military, and that alone, as individuals, they cannot stop the steady encroachment onto those small areas that had been won. The military regime has destroyed the family, arresting, executing, or 'disappearing' women's brothers, husbands, fathers, sometimes all of these. Entire families have been forced into unemployment. During these six years, in addition to depriving women of the right to assembly, free speech, and organization, by virtual sleight-of-hand they have taken away nurseries, free kindergartens, family medical services, and both the half litre of milk for children and school breakfasts have also been suspended.

The backward hands of the clock of time have thrust women into darkness, back into a period where they are no longer even second or third class citizens, but rather society's pariahs. In 1972 a large number of Chilean women, including women from sectors of the middle class, were used by the ruling class as a support base and as one of the springboards for the *coup d'etat*. Once the dictatorship was installed, however, women were plunged into a paradoxical situation. On the one hand, the dictatorship has annihilated women socially, deprived them of material and cultural means for survival, of their development as human beings, as workers; and on the other hand, by burying women under decrees and decisions which have progressively isolated them, thrusting them with even greater force back into their traditional roles, they are filled with hatred — hatred which bit by bit will become power decision. The dictatorship forces women to leave their homes in search of food, to fulfil a more important role in the economy of the home. Women once again become the centre of the home, as they were a thousand years ago, because their mates have been imprisoned, disappeared, assassinated, or are unemployed or earning the minimum wage, which is inadequate for subsistence.

And on going out to look for work, to wash clothes in the houses of the rich, to beg for charitable aid in the parish or neighbourhood, Chilean working women leave the ghetto, enrich their vision of what is happening, and achieve primary, and at times diffuse forms of consciousness. They become restless, they ask questions, they find answers, or they seek them from other women. They exchange points of view with the wives of the other prisoners standing on the interminable lines in front of the gates to the concentration camps. That is how the first organizations arose: committees of relatives of those who had 'disappeared', of relatives of prisoners, soup kitchens for the unemployed, workers' associations that meet in private homes, mothers' centres, shanty-town women's centres, etc. These groupings represent the search for a collective answer to the women's problems, to their most deeply felt demands.

A persecuted *companero* might appear, and one of these women might offer him her home, doing so with a fear which is overcome because she thinks of her own *companero* who is in prison or also a fugitive. Another woman might pick up an underground leaflet, read it on the sly and tear it up; on another occasion this woman might risk showing it to a sister, to her relatives, to a woman neighbour. Later on, perhaps, this woman might speak of it in the grocery store, as she shops. Women like these slowly incorporate themselves into the Resistance, in either its semi-legal or clandestine forms. There are women who once belonged to a party and had dropped out, who now seek to reconnect with their old contacts; if they do not find them, they will continue working on their own, in the parish or in a Resistance Committee.

There are also women who had never been involved politically, but who now begin to be interested, to participate, to feel useful. These women take on increasingly complex tasks; daily they dare to do more and more. And one day, one of them might, for example, become part of the underground network organized by the Resistance. She will remember that day as an important one in her life, and she will feel stronger and more confident. Women like Domitila Barrios de Chungara are not created from one day to the next; they are produced by their history and by an awakening to their doubly exploited status and by their patient and constructive commitment to their people's cause. [Domitila Barrios de Chungara is a militant Bolivian woman from the country's mining region. She has long been a motive force in the network of Housewives' Committees, in miners' strikes, in prison hunger strikes. A recent pamphlet she wrote on women and organization follows on in this volume.]

In Chile today, the dictatorship (and its concomitant repression) is a giant forge where hundreds of Domitilas, hundreds of heroic and anonymous women, are being tempered, women who, alongside the men, build and create the growing network of the Resistance. This is the only explanation for the huge 8 March demonstration which took place this year (1979), this is the only explanation for the heroic hunger strikes of the wives of the 'disappeared'.

Today, thinking Chilean women, committed to their class, are present on the three battle fronts which the Resistance has set: underground, prison, and exile. On all these fronts women are writing an important page, seeking to win a protagonist's role, to be a part of the fighting army which will one day free our people. With the firmness of a conscientious artisan, with a deep sense of responsibility, of discipline, of creativity, the women in this struggle have been learning and teaching their *companeros* and organizations that they are capable of doing all types of jobs, that they ask for an opportunity to demonstrate this, that they hope for understanding so as not to be denied the right to be party members or active members of the Resistance, without abandoning their integral development as women, in relation to their mates, their families, their children.

This is a subject we used to speak about in the dark, late into the night, evading the guards' vigilance, in the Tres Alamos concentration camp. Women have had to earn their place in political and mass organizations with an effort double that of the men. Women have constantly had to prove themselves if they were to be trusted. Before the military coup, it was common for women members in the left parties to be assigned tasks that accorded with those that society permitted them in their social roles. During the first years of the Resistance, party women began functioning as couriers or who had hidden *companeros*. Women who had held men were the principal targets of the repression and, for a short time, the enemy was less rigorous in its vigilance and searching of women.

The absolute sexism of the military favoured women's mobility. In 1975, a majority of the women prisoners had functioned in these capacities and as a result had been victims of the repression. Today, there are dozens of disappeared women, women who were couriers or who had hidden companeros. Women who had held positions of responsibility in the intermediate or higher leadership were in a minority.

That was in 1975. Today no one would dream of saying that the tasks of liaison should be done only by women. The fact is that the *companeras* did the liaison job well, under the inclement sun or in the rain, leaving their children alone at home or carrying them along, thus claiming the right to participate without giving up motherhood, love, joy. And from this, from these small and routine tasks of liaison, women moved on to organize Resistance Committees, to participate alongside the working class in the elaboration of tasks for the front or a small programme for a factory. They began working on the underground newspaper which was so harassed by the enemy.

The *companeras* in Chile are growing accustomed to more responsible tasks and are learning how hard it is to be leaders of the Resistance. In the same way, armed propaganda has become one of their tasks as party members. The bourgeois press pointed to this with contempt in reporting that a woman had led the armed action, in which a Madeco bus full of workers was intercepted, leaflets distributed, and speeches made. In another report, they attempted to show that the morale of the Resistance must be low, for them to resort to using women to lead the armed entry into the canteen of the Quimantu publishing house, full of workers during their lunch hour, in order to carry out a lightning political demonstration.

Yes, our *companeras* are winning space; but it has not been easy and it is not enough. There is still a very, very long road to be travelled. Now we have women in the front lines of the working class, there are now women among those who, tomorrow will be the vanguard and who will lead decisive battles. And this role has been won fundamentally during these six years of struggle against the dictatorship. Thus we are witnessing the enormous revolutionary potential of the 50% of us who are women. Nor has it been a linear process. Like the struggle of the masses, it is a process which advances irregularly. In 1975, only 8% of the first women prisoners in Tres Alamos had really done sustained mass work as party members, and only 5% had been in high or intermediate leadership positions. The majority of the women had only had experience in rank-and-file conspiratorial activities, or in the reproduction of materials and ideas which others had elaborated. We know that today the situation has improved considerably, but we also know that it could be even better.

The party women have now proved themselves in many battles, like their male comrades, they have had their ordeal by fire. This was at the moment of torture.

In the case of the women, this was a difficult moment, but also one of a brutal encounter with the role to which the capitalist system has assigned us, and one of an equally brutal and cruel encounter with all the contradictions yet to be overcome; all this we women had to carry with us in the interrogation by the enemy.

Like us, the military have a deep class hatred, but they doubly despise those of us who have committed ourselves to the people's cause. They despise us because we are their class enemies, they despise us because we have dared to break out of the roles to which we had been assigned. Because we have dared to think, because we have dared to rebel against the system. And the ferocity of the military is redoubled in angry and active response to the women's emancipation from that traditional role.

They would threaten to bring a woman's children and kill them in her presence, if she did not speak. Or they would already have them there and would make them cry in a neighbouring room in order to remind the woman of her basic maternal function. They undressed the women, they ran their hands over their bodies, they raped them, they gave them electric shocks on their naked bodies which had developed in a context of modesty and virginity. They beat women on the face and on the body in order to mutilate them, because within the conception of femininity, society has given great importance to symmetry, to bourgeois models of beauty. Some women were forced to confront their bleeding, dying *companeros;* the torturers hoped that this would demoralize the men, that the women would beg their men to confess. Thus they were forced to weigh their love for their *companeros* against their love for the people and the cause of freedom.

This is why we women prisoners in Tres Alamos were proud that 95% of us had heroically resisted torture. This sense of proletarian pride was not because we thought ourselves braver, stronger, or as strong as our male *companeros*. The sense of pride came from having been able to reject our traditional role at a critical moment. Of having been able to see the priorities clearly, as committed and fearless fighters, transcending the tears which we all held back in order not to show weakness.

The women prisoners, despite the fact that most had not had leadership positions, despite the fact that most were very young and inexperienced politically, mastered their limitations, their weaknesses, and took a qualitative leap in their emancipation as women as well as in their revolutionary commitment. Once they had lived through the first stage on this second battle front which prison represents, the women went on to live another enriching experience, out of solitary confinement and into the prison community.

There, there were no male *companeros*, always so good at organization and organizing us; in spite of this, the task of organizing was carried out rigorously and carefully. Discipline, a spirit of sacrifice, solidarity, dignity in the face of the enemy, the creation of activities and workshops to fill the lives of the women and avoid stagnation. Each woman had to contribute what she knew, each one had to be generous with her knowledge, with her experience, and with the maturity she had already achieved. If there was anything of importance learned there, it was how to share — to share food, joys, tasks, knowledge, and pain. And there we did exactly what political prisoners all over the world, have done: we converted the prison into a school for well-trained

cadres. for combatants, for human beings who were free, even
behind bars, to love more than ever in those conditions the freedom
which had been so cruelly torn from them.

Just like our *companeros*, we women prisoners built our freedom
every day. In the absence of freedom of the press, we created wall-
newspapers which would be put up and taken down, depending
on the degree of vigilance. In the absence of freedom of expression,
we responded by creating poems, songs, theatrical works, dances
which reflected our lives and our hopes. We learned that children
are not individual property but rather the children of the collectivity. Miguelito was arrested in Rosa's womb, at seven months.
Miguelito was born in the prison and was freed when he was 16
months old, when he was already dancing to the song about *'el
negro Jose'* [a traditional Chilean song which came to be
extremely significant, in a symbolic manner, in the prisons, where
it would be sung each time a prisoner or a group of prisoners was
released] and would clap his hands to announce the arrival of the
daily meals. Miguelito, along with Amanda, Alejandrito, and so
many others, lived a new conception of the family. They were the
children of one mother and of a hundred aunts. Their feeding,
education, entertainment, clothing, bathing, etc. were tasks and
responsibilities of the collectivity. The mother's responsibilities
toward her child were the same as those of each one of us.

The majority of women reached exile with this accumulated
experience. With the mutilation inherent in the loss of loved ones,
with the traumas remaining from the moments of horror lived
while in the hands of the brutal enemy; but also with their
hearts overflowing with solidarity received and shared. Extern-
ally we were older, but inside we felt renewed by having been able
to meet our responsibilities. We arrived at an obligatory but
temporary exile, another battle front, less comforting, less gratif-
ying, but as useful as the previous front – as useful and as
necessary. This is the temporal space in which the rearguard is
constructed and developed, a rearguard which nourishes, which
denounces, which propagandizes, which accumulates international
forces while basing itself on the actions carried out on the front
lines of the battle. An exile in which we must also prepare the
conditions for returning to Chile improved, renewed, strengthened,
better than before.

But what we have just defined as our task is being accomplished
with difficulty, with advances and retreats. Once again, in exile,
party women face the daily contradictions implicit in being a
woman, a worker, a mother, a housewife, and a party militant.

In prison, after having thrown off our traditional role in the
torture chamber, we reflected at length on our lives, became aware
of many things, wrote to our *companeros* who were also in prison

or on the outside, in order to communicate our thoughts. We questioned the unproletarian relationship which existed between men and women, we wanted to develop an ideological discussion on that theme. And the debate, which often became collective, began. In the light of the growth achieved, the whole concept of the couple was reformulated. In exile, the topic has been brought up more energetically, sometimes advancing the discussion, at other times hampering it, and at still others leading to the break-up of the couple, because women and men emerged from a rich but difficult experience and because both had grown, but not always in parallel ways. Exile has tended to create an inhospitable framework for discussion.

Women were forced to confront the reality of the period recently lived through. The forced separation from our children was follo-wed by reunion with them; in addition to joy, this meant the resumption of an interrupted relationship which had been dramatic for the children and which brought together mother and child as virtual strangers. We women had to learn to walk in the streeets and watch the sunsets with the knowledge that never again would we feel the warm hands of those whom we loved who had fallen in battle. We had to swallow our pain in an alien setting, hearing a language which was not ours, and absorbing a culture which others had created. The deprivation of freedom was a thing of the past, but with that situation we women also left behind the collective experience, the hundreds of voices, discussing each day in order to dig deep into the truth of each moment. Children were once again individual property, so much so that we could not even depend on our *companeros* to share this with us, because they were too busy.

Now we have to summon up the strength to understand that we cannot live in the past, not in the good nor in the bad which has remained of it; that from the marvellous human group in which we had lived we must take the strength and the lessons in order to project them into the future; that the suffering of yesterday must be relegated to a small corner of our memory and acknow-ledged only when weakness appears, as a way to remind ourselves of how much is yet to be done.

Women party members, because of our experience, had more self-confidence on reaching exile. We expected more of ourselves, but also more of our *companeros*, of our families, of the collect-ivity. And there was no coherent response to our expectations, not from the *companeros*, not from the families, not from the organizations comprising the collectivity. It was taken for granted that the *companeros* had advanced: they washed the dishes, set the table, went out with us to shop. The *companeros* helped, but did not commit themselves wholeheartedly. Tasks were not equally

divided, they were merely lightened a bit. The women continued
to bear the major responsibility. Responsibility for what? For
accepting everything twice over: double exploitation, doubly
difficult exile, because while we face the same difficulties as the
exiled men, we also have had to face the job of integrating *all* our
roles, of coordinating them. Once again women have had to make
a double effort in order to meet their responsibilities, so as not to
be obliged by others to opt for one role at the expense of another.
We aspire to be integral women, to have children while fighting
on the front lines or in the rearguard, to bring them up, to be part
of a revolutionary relationship, to be workers, to have homes. We
women have had to work much harder than men to fulfil all our
responsibilities, but when we do so we blame ourselves because
we are always giving our time to one role to the detriment of the
other.

So, where is the solution? We do not have the answer. The
collectivity should give the answer, we women and you men,
companeros. Clearly the situation is not to find a woman who will
do the housework in exchange for an hourly wage. Nor is it to send
the children off to those relatives with more time because they
are not involved in the struggle. Nor is it to choose one or the
other role, giving up our integral quality. Neither do we believe
that the solution would be for women to take on all those roles in
a voluntarist manner, like superwoman, making tremendous
physical, psychic, and intellectual efforts, and in the long run
disintegrating.

In order to find the solution, men must make our struggle for
autonomy theirs. The solution necessarily requires a great debate
which, clearly we women must push for but which must involve
us all, all those who by questioning capitalist society aspire to build
a better world, a just, united, and socialist world. If we set ourselves up as the forgers of freedom, if we want to be consistently
revolutionary, we cannot separate the theme of exile, of solidarity,
of the struggle of our people, from the present condition of women.

We represent 50% of humanity, and we have revolutionary
potential. Only a privileged sector of women has had the chance to
prove this. There are two great battles to be won: the incorporation
of more and more women into vanguard positions and, in addition,
the assurance that the existing vanguard of women continues to
develop without interference. We must support this sector so that
it does not falter midway.

The people will never be free if women do not join the struggle
en masse. There will be no revolution if women are kept on the
side-lines, as inferior, third class beings.

In the early dawn of history, women played important roles in
the social group, and when the rules of the game were changed, the

relegation of women was implacable, cruel, pitiless. That was the beginning of a history of suffering and humiliation. The regaining of our lost identity, the advancing along the road of our liberation as women, the winning of our emancipation, and the assurance of support and comprehension, will be part of a process, a process which we acknowledge to be slow and fraught with difficulties. The job of initiating it is ours, but it is obvious that millions of women all over the world have already begun to move. History begins anew each day, when in some corner of the Resistance a woman ceases to be a simple courier because, by working twice as hard, she has won the right to organize, to create, to lead. The history of our emancipation begins each day that a woman in Chile, in Latin America, in any part of the world, joins the struggle of the exploited and learns to expect that if she falls, the generous hands of the people will raise her children, learns to walk beside her *companero*, at the same pace as he, toward the definitive victory.

It is certain that this 50% wants the right to be heard regularly, and to be present and participate in all levels of decision-making. It is our aspiration to be not only a quantitatively important sector, but also a qualitatively vital one.

4. Women and Organization
Domitila Barrios de la Chungara

This is the entire text of a pamphlet by Domitila Barrios de Chungara which was first published in Bolivia in March 1980. As far as we know it has never been translated into English before.

Domitila's pamphlet is based on a series of talks that she gave to peasant women; the original contains many more cartoons than we were able to reproduce here. Her analysis stems from almost 20 years experience working in the Housewives Committees of Siglo XX, one of Bolivia's largest mining complexes situated high up in the Bolivian Andes. Siglo XX is well known for its long history of violent struggle against the succession of ruthless military regimes which have oppressed the country's people for so many years.

Domitila was born in the mining encampment at Siglo XX in

1937. Like the children around her, she grew up in great poverty.
Most mineworkers' children receive little, if any, formal education,
but thanks to her determination and a strong desire to learn she
finished primary school. Domitila is married to a miner and has seven
children. She set up the first Housewives Committees in 1963 and
they have taken up a large part of her time ever since. In 1975,
the United Nations invited her to speak at their International
Women's Conference, held in Mexico, and in 1977 she published a
book about her life, *Let Me Speak.* During the elections in 1978,
Domitila stood as candidate for Vice-President of the Republic,
representing the Party of the Revolutionary Left. She has been
exiled since the latest of Bolivia's military regimes came to power
in a coup on 17 July 1980. Unfortunately, we have been unable
to contact her for permission to reproduce this pamphlet, but we
are grateful for permission from her publishers, Unitas Cidob, La
Paz.

Introduction: The Woman's Problem

First we shall talk about the woman's problem in general. Woman,
not only in Bolivia, but all over the world, is being subjugated,
relegated to a fourth place in society. She is subjugated in such a
way that she is not allowed to participate — as we can see in
everyday life — even at the level of trade union organization.

We are looked down upon right from birth. Let us begin by
looking at what happens to the woman in the home. When a boy
is born, *companeras*, what does the father do? He goes off and
celebrates because a man has been born. There has to be celebration because the child is male. Isn't this true? But what do they say
when it's a girl? 'Ah this good-for-nothing, what use is she, let her
die!' And even the women sometimes say: 'What a shame it's a
little girl, what use is she? It would be better if she died.' They
have taught us to look down on ourselves, isn't this true?

Where would the world be without women? It wouldn't get
very far. But we are used to looking down on ourselves and under-
mining our own abilities. There are women who criticize us for
being in trade unions or political parties. They say: 'Those idle
women have nothing to do. Why do they interfere?' Thus, even
women criticize us because, since birth, we have been brought up
in this way, with this mentality, not only in Bolivia but in the
whole world. Throughout history, however, women have shown
themselves just as capable of taking part in cultural, political and
union activities as men. They have also shown that they can fight
on battle-fields, fight beside the men. We have many examples of
this in our country, the women who fought alone in La Coronilla,

other women who fought alongside the men in the War of Independence. Men and women have also fought together in other countries, such as Nicaragua.

What I want to tell you, *companeras*, is that we women were born with all our rights. In Bolivia there is a law that guarantees women's participation in everything. In 1948, all the countries of the world came together in the United Nations. There, laws were created about human rights, and amongst these was one that gave women the right to participate in everything, as human beings. Thus, we women have the right to participate in clubs, in unions, in political parties, We have the same rights to education as a man does, and the right to receive equal wages with men. We are all covered by these laws. Even Bolivia has said 'We agree that Bolivian women should participate in everything', and the government has signed this document. But, since 1948 up to the present day, what government has really bothered about educating, training and encouraging women to participate? None. If they have created laws for women, it has only been so that they can use them to serve a certain political party, a certain social class. Later the women are forgotten. A woman is like a piece of cloth, used to clean a dirty table and then hidden away in a corner until next time. This is how they use us, and it is we ourselves who are to blame. We allow ourselves to be used and manipulated. We criticize ourselves. How many times have we been called lazy and idle when we participated in unions? They also say that we join the union looking for an affair with one of the leaders and the leaders themselves sometimes think that we go to the meetings to flirt with them. What we must do is decide exactly what we are looking for, because women all over the world are fighting for their liberation in different ways and for different reasons.

At the International Women's Conference in Mexico in 1975, I could see two types of liberation. One type involves those who think women will only be free when they equal men in all their vices. This is called feminism. It means that women must fight against men for the right to smoke and drink as they do. For example, they said in this conference: 'If the man goes out to enjoy himself tonight, tomorrow I must go out and do the same.'

But *companeras*, do we really want to smoke cigarettes? Do we really want to go out drinking and living it up like our husbands? I don't think so. If the man has ten mistresses, does this mean I have to do the same? What would we be doing? We would be degrading people, nothing more. But we should not fight against our *companeros* or imitate their vices, but we should try to imitate our husbands' good points.

This fight is typical of the wealthy, women who have everything and only want to imitate men's bad habits. But for us, from our class position, what type of liberation do we want? The liberation that rich women and American women want? Or the other type, which consists of women being respected as human beings, who can solve problems and participate in everything — culture, art, literature, politics, trade-unionism — a liberation that means our opinion is respected at home and outside the home! Because sometimes even as mothers are we not allowed to give our opinion or correct our children, because the father comes along and beats us and takes away our authority. In the end, the children lose all respect for us, and when their father dies they tell us to shut up and treat us like idiots. Isn't that true? And why does all this happen? Because it has been proved in practice, women are more thoughtful, more firm in their positions, more honest. When a woman reaches a position of leadership, she doesn't sell out like a man because she has fewer vices, and is more conscious in her struggle. That is why our exploiters don't want us women to get involved in anything.

Jenny Matthews

Many comrades say that women should organize themselves in unions, but sometimes, what happens is that they are very enthusiastic at first, then later they get demoralized. There are times when our husbands are conscious, helping in the struggle. Then, when the repression comes, what does the woman do? She starts saying to her husband, 'Well, now you must choose between me and your children, or the union and your party.' Or she says 'You're not going to the union, or I will leave.' This is why they sometimes blame us women, saying that instead of being a help, and encouraging them to go on with the fight, we are a hindrance. Some women have actually denounced their own husbands.

It is good if we women are interested in why our husbands organize themselves. We must encourage them and work together with them. Because, what also happens is that when women begin to emerge, the men become jealous, and think their wives are going to take over. By working together, this problem could be solved.

I was saying that there were international agreements saying that women can participate, but that in practice this does not happen. For example, in Bolivia, broad guarantees have been given out to many of those women's organizations who serve whichever government happens to be in power at the time. There's CONIF (National Confederation of Feminine institutions), the Rotary Club, the Lions ladies, the civic action groups and I don't know what else. Last year they remembered that thousands of children get no breakfast, so they gave them all cups of chocolate, and with this they thought that they had wiped away the misery those children had suffered for all the year. These organizations are supported by the government. They know no repression, these women get all types of support. But what happens when the wives of workers begin to organize in a conscious way? They are repressed. It follows us just as it follows the men. They want to shut us up, they want to scare us, and sometimes we are scared and we say, 'Well, I'm not going to get involved any longer'. And who benefits when we do this? The capitalists who exploit us.

We know, from our own experience, that women are not used to being activists. We never dared to be; since we were little we were told that the man's place was in the street, and the woman's was in the home, that the woman must look after the kids, and cook and sew while the man could go into the street, get involved in politics and go to the cinema or to meetings. Isn't that right? They even use religion to keep women down because religion says that 'the head of the family is the man'. So, even if the man is unjust, we must obey him in everything because he is the boss. He made him in His own image and likeness; then He made a woman. But did He make her from man's head, so that she could be above him? Or perhaps from the soles of his feet, so that he could walk all over her? No, It says that to make woman, God took one of man's ribs, this means that she is his companion. She is neither superior, nor inferior, to be walked over by man. Man and woman should go together and be trained in the same way.

Happily, there is an awakening all over the place — not just in Bolivia — of women who want to start to participate and to be trained. In our country there are already groups of women who are well oriented and who are doing something.

The Housewives Committee of Siglo XX

I am now going to tell you how the Housewives Committee of
Siglo XX arose, formed by the wives of the mine workers.

1) How the Housewives Committee was created

In the mining centres, as in the countryside, women are not
allowed to take part in the struggle. But repression began to grow
and leaders were taken prisoner, so, one by one, women went to La
Paz to complain and to get their husbands back. One of the wives
often went with her children, and they [the authorities] wanted
to take her prisoner too — to pressure her husband. So the women
went back to Siglo XX, and went to the Union and saw that about
60 leaders had been taken prisoner; they cried for them. But one of
them had an idea and said 'If, instead of going on our own to
complain, we all went, as a group of 60 and refused to move until
they freed our husbands, perhaps we might get somewhere.' So the
60 women went to La Paz where they were on hunger strike for
nine days until their husbands were set free.

That was in June 1961. During that nine days they were
together, they had agreed that aferwards they must organize themselves into some sort of union. The result was that, when they got
back to Siglo XX, they called a meeting of all the housewives and
organized the first Housewives' Committee of Siglo XX.

But the women did not lose heart. Instead, they went on working,
using the radio, writing letters complaining about different things,
about organization! They're bound to fight, it won't last 48 hours!'
Luckily, this committee had a good leader, Norbeta de Aguilar. I
was not in the committee then, I was just watching and listening.

The *companeras* of the committee identified each other by
little flags, that they wore. They would be in the butchers, checking
that they were given good meat, so that we weren't tricked about
its weight or price. If we had a problem, we looked for the women
with the little flags, we complained to them, and they sorted it
out. Some time later these *companeras* went to their first Miners'
Union meeting, but how were they received? The *companeros* just
whistled at them. They wouldn't let them say one word and, finally
threw them out of the meeting with a shower of banana skins and
orange peel. The women left almost in tears. And what were the
men shouting at them? 'These women should be looking after our
kids, mending socks, and cooking.'

But the women did not lose heart. Instead, they went on working
using the radios, writing letters complaining about different things,
and asking for solidarity from their *companeros*. The Union didn't
take much notice of them, even though they had managed to free
their leaders. Instead, they tried to damage the women's reputations,

saying that they were going to the meetings to find lovers, and other such things. What problems these women were made to suffer, even in the home: The *companeras* continued in this way more or less until 1963.

2) How I Joined the Housewives Committee

In 1963, I joined the Committee, because a *companera* invited me, when some of the Union members had been imprisoned. My husband thought it was just a one-time thing, and that afterwards I would go on hiding myself away in the house. But I began to attend meetings every Thursday, from five till six. We'd spend half an hour talking about the Union and so on, and the other half hour we made embroideries and other things we liked. Then we went home. My husband just sat back and watched me go to these meetings, until pay-day came — then he didn't give me one penny! The next pay-day came and still he gave me nothing. Instead he got drunk and wanted to beat me. I didn't know why he was like this, and he didn't tell me not to go to the meetings.

At the end of the third month he still didn't give me any money. I'd had enough, and asked him for an explanation. Do you know what he said? 'You're going to the Union. You're going to meetings. What good is all that to me, go and ask for your wage from the Union.' I said it was only for an hour; and besides, I said, I have learnt to sew — but he wouldn't listen. I couldn't convince him. According to him, I had to rely on the Union now as I spent all my time there! So who was doing the cooking, the washing, and looking after the kids at home then?

I felt very bitter, I didn't know what to do. Then one day, I met one of the leaders in the street, Don Federico Escobar; he is dead now. He asked me why I hadn't been going to the House-wives' meetings and I decided to tell him what had happened. Then he said, 'And haven't you told your husband who does the washing and cooking, and who is looking after the children? You must complain, or would you like me to go to the house and talk to him?' 'No, no, I said. If you do that he will be even worse.'

Another week passed. I was no longer his wife, my husband would come and go, talking to the kids but not saying a word to me. This was hard to bear, because until then we'd shared everything. His going on like this hurt me a lot.

One day I thought: 'He says I don't do anything, so from now on I won't', and I began to cry. My father came round and saw that I had not swept the house and wasn't cooking, and he said why. So I told him what had happened. Then he said, 'Daughter, women should never be angry with their pots and pans. You must go on cooking. So I started cooking again, but very grudgingly and I didn't sweep the house or do the washing. I didn't even wash the

nappies of the two youngest children, so there were lots of dirty nappies all over the place. . . .

When my husband got back he saw that everything was still dirty. I was afraid he would hit me. I was ready to run away. He said to me, 'I see that nothing has been done', so I said 'Well, since you say I do nothing, you can bring somebody in to do the things: the washing and cooking, and to clean the nappies.' He didn't reply. 'I have cooked your food' I said, 'but I shouldn't even have done that.'

A week went by like this and I still didn't wash the nappies. I didn't have any to put on my children, so I cut up some curtains and used them! I even cut up some of my husband's trousers to use as nappies. I didn't like doing this and I was scared! I thought that my husband would kill me. But I also thought he had to be made to understand. Every day I asked him to bring somebody to do the washing, saying I would only cook for him for one more day.

I had a terrible week. I couldn't sleep. I was scared of what my husband would do, until one day he just threw me out. He told me to get out of the house. That day, I had an idea: I went to buy a notebook — you know why? — to write down everything I did every day and see what it would cost. It was the first day of the month and I began to make a note of everything; the washing, cleaning, cooking, ironing, everything. I made a note, every day, of how many dozens of things I washed, how many I ironed, and so on, for the whole month.

The end of the month came, my husband and I were on better terms, he was happier because everything was clean and tidy once more. So, on the 30th, I said to him, 'Well, Don Rene, now we must sort out the money. I have washed and ironed so many clothes, and cooked for so many days, and I've been working it out, and the total is such and such.' It worked out at 240 *pesos* and my husband at the time earned about 80 *pesos*, so what I had done was worth three times his salary. Then I said to my husband, 'You say I do nothing, that I don't support you. Well, I have shown that I do. But you don't want to understand me'. And in that way I showed him that I did help him, but that I also wanted to learn other things about other problems. Finally, we came to an agreement: he wouldn't go out enjoying himself, or go to the cinema, and I wouldn't go to the Union.

My husband went a month without going out, even to the cinema. He was very bored, moaning all the time he was in the house, until one day, a Saturday, he went out on the town and came in late at night, asking me to forgive him. 'It's all right Rene,' I said, and left it at that. The next day, Sunday, he went off to cure his hangover and got drunk again. He came in on Monday, but

I didn't say anything. I always used to tell him off when he came in drunk, but this time I didn't say anything. He must have been very puzzled because he asked to forgive him again. I was very understanding and said it didn't matter. But when Thursday came I got the children ready and said, 'Rene, its four o'clock, I'm going to the Union meeting. You said you weren't going to go out any more and I was going to forget about my meetings. We had an agreement. So, you've been out twice — I can go to the Union twice.' He didn't like it and we fought, but I still went.

As it happened, that day it poured with rain. When the time came to go, we couldn't, it was raining so much. As I was with the children, my husband felt sorry for us and came to meet us with an umbrella. When he got there the President asked him in and told him what we did in the meetings. She showed him the things we had made and said to him, 'You men are better trained. We would like to invite you to our next meeting to talk to us about the trade union movement.' My husband didn't know what to say — and so he accepted.

The following Thursday, he was ready first and hurrying me. This is how my husband came to understand me and, since then, he has worked in everything with me. This is the battle I have had to win at home.

However, *companeras*, I'd like to say that our struggle must not degenerate into a struggle against our husbands. They act like this because of the system that teaches them to think that way and to criticize women.

Since then, my husband has had to suffer a great deal because of me, because of my activism. He has been beaten up, imprisoned and even his bosses at work have victimized him. I will tell you one thing they did. None of the workers in the mine can have food brought to them from home — only the clerical staff can do this. But to make problems for him, the company, told my husband he must have his food brought in from home. 'Your food must be here at 9.30 in the morning,' they told him. Then, at 9.25, the boss was standing there and said to my husband, 'Well, where is your food? Of course, since your wife has been in the Union, who is there to cook? Why don't you make her do her woman's work first?' Happily, we are now left in peace because even the bosses have begun to understand that women must participate. Only the other day one of the bosses said to my husband 'Will you forgive us, Chungara, I didn't know how important everything is that your wife is doing . . .' And why was this? Because this very man had been sacked, and thanks to a strike which we women held, he was reinstated.

So, *companeras*, there have been many problems. They always try to stop women participating. And why? Because when we women get involved in anything we are more persistent and give more help to our *companeros*. This is because even when we are not being active in the Union, or in politics, we know that our husbands must be in the Union, and work in the political party, and we must support them. This helps the *companero* and, as well, helps our struggle for liberation from the capitalists who exploit us. But, if we are fighting men against women, we are playing right into the hands of the capitalists who have made *machismo* (meaning that men don't want help from women) and use it to divide us, so that we cannot fight together. And capitalists have made feminism, to make women fight against men.

I remember once, in a Union meeting — my *companeras* were very young and I wasn't all that old either — one of the leaders came up to me and said 'Hello Fatty, how are you? Let's go for a drink somewhere', and he wanted to put his arm round me in front of everyone. I got up and asked to speak, and said 'Mr Secretary, please make this man understand that the Union is, for us, like a temple which must be respected. We have come here to share ideas, to fight for the people, not to look for lovers. I ask you to punish this man for treating us in such a way. . .' From then on they began to respect us — we ourselves have made them respect us.

There are some women, above all young immature women, who think that when they are leaders they can forget all their other responsibilities, that a woman leader need no longer worry herself about being a wife, a mother or a housewife. But we leaders must do things even better, as an example to the other woman. To be a leader doesn't mean that I am now equal to my husband, I can go out and that's that. I work for my organization and my family. I must do the washing, prepare the food at night to cook next day if I'm going to be busy with my duty as a leader.

3) The Committee's Experience in the Struggle

I would also like to say that, even with all the problems we've had in the mines over the last 15 years, we have had experience, that have taught us a lot. I would like to fell you a bit about them so that you can see which way to go.

The most important thing is organization. If the people are organized, they respond, there is unity and everything is possible. This has been my experience. But, if the people are not organized, they are not well-oriented, and they cannot achieve anything. Sometimes enthusiasm can make things go wrong, as I will now tell you.

a) The Defeats:

We had no medicine in the hospital. The Housewives Committee had sent a letter to the COMIBOL company giving them 48 hours to bring the medicine. If not, we would take measures.

The company took no notice of us, we wasted no time and
went to block roads that lead to Siglo XX. After a week of this
we were out of bread and meat. We had nothing. The workers
complained to the company, and the boss said to them, 'And what
are we supposed to do if the Housewives have blocked all the
roads, the meat is rotting only a kilometre from here, in three
lorries.' Flour and sugar were also stuck in lorries; it rained and
everything became one big mess. Everything had to be thrown out,
and the company paid the suppliers, though we had eaten nothing.
The measures we had taken, which we thought right, had worked
against us. The whole thing was a disaster.

And what did the workers say? They almost beat us up for what
we had done. We had been mistaken, but also, afterwards, we were
misunderstood by our *companeros*. I went home, crying, 'I'll
never get involved again, we sacrificed ourselves, making our children cry day and night, making sure nobody got in, and still the
miners talk to us like that, and want to hit us. Let them go to hell.
I'm going home'. And so, very bitter, I went. We didn't realize that
the measure we had taken would go against our own companeros.
Wanting to do good, we had made things worse.

So, the first thing we must do is organize ourselves. In every
town people fight against the bourgeoisie, against the capitalists,
against the government. But we must look at and think what
measures to use because of their consequences. You never know
what might happen, suddenly they start harassing us a lot and
then the army comes in.

This is why you must know if all the people are ready to respond, to give support. This is why organization is the most
important thing.

Not everything we did was a failure. I would like to tell you
about something else that took place after the 1978 elections in
Siglo XX.

They stopped delivering us meat, rice, soap and paraffin — for
a whole month we didn't have any of these things. So the
Housewives Committee got together and decided that I should
go and speak to the director [of COMIBOL], and if he took no
notice, we would take action. They didn't take any notice, so the
members decided that the leaders of the Committee (there were
15 of us) should do what we thought necessary. So the 15 of us
got together and began to think about what we could do. Some
women had the same idea — blocking the road again, and closing
down the shops. But we now knew that this went against our own
people. The director could no longer buy us off with food. If our
husbands were to go on strike this would also go against us as we
wouldn't have their salaries.

What could we do? It happened that that day, 300 tons of

minerals were leaving in 20 lorries. 'We must stop these lorries
leaving,' we said. This was directly against the company because
COMIBOL had a deadline to meet with the delivery of the minerals,
and if they broke their contracts they would be blacklisted.

The next day, at nine in the morning, we went with a group of
women to where the lorries were. Some had started to leave and
some of the drivers pretended to take no notice of us. They just
wanted to go. But we've always been a bit wild – so they say –
so we'd taken some sticks of dynamite with us. We got into one
of the lorries and said to the driver: 'If you drive off, we'll light
this stick of dynamite and everything will go up. . .' 'No, no, I'm
getting out,' he said, and got out quickly. We managed to stop them
leaving, and organized ourselves in shifts. Three *companeras*
would look after the lorries from seven in the morning till three
in the afternoon, while other women cooked for them and looked
after their children. Then, at three, they would go to the lorries
until eleven at night, and the other *companeras* would cook and
look after the children. Another shift began at eleven at night till
seven o'clock in the morning, while others looked after their
families.

When we want to achieve something we have to be organized
and everyone must take part. If not, everything will fail. We spent
a week like this. At first the director laughed at us, but when he
saw that we didn't even leave the lorries at night – we'd even
taken our beds there – he began to get desperate. So, to try and
persuade us to give up he brought food for us. There were two
shops in Siglo XX, one large, one small. He filled up the small one
and told us, 'There's the food you wanted', so we Housewives went
to see – and it was true, the shop was full. But a leader, *companeras*, must know for sure how much is eaten in a day. I sat down
to work out how many days' supplies there were. I counted the
sacks of sugar and found that they had only brought enough for
one day.

Since they had tried to trick us, we went on with the blockade.
The director was desperate. He told us he would sign a document.
We said we would have to consult the others first. Finally at
eleven o'clock at night, after a week's blockade, he came to us
with a document he had signed. Then we said to him, 'We're sorry
sir, but we only deal with shop problems during office hours. Just
now we are resting,' and we went to sleep. That is just what the
director always tells us – he will never see us at his house, even if
we're dying. He always says, 'I'll see you during office hours'. We
also said that the others would have to study the document first
before any decision was made.

At six o'clock in the morning, the director went to the radio
station to call the Housewives to a meeting. The Union leaders also

went and, well, it was decided to come to an agreement. But before this, in a press conference, the *companeras* said, 'What the director has signed is worthless, for he is just a pawn for COMIBOL. We want a guarantee from La Paz that he will comply with this document'. So, it was confirmed in La Paz and at three in the afternoon we called off the blockade.

This time we were triumphant, *companeras*, because we didn't act against the people but against the government, and because we were better organized. When all the underdogs are united we can strike a very heavy blow against our enemy. But if we don't unite, if we do things on our own, we could well harm our *companeras*.

I must say, *companeras*, that getting organized isn't easy. Even in Siglo XX, though you wouldn't believe it, there are still people who are against the organization, and will only be mobilized when there is a lot of pressure. When Banzer was in power he put up the price of bread which, before was one *peso* for five loaves. Then he put it up 50 *centavos* a loaf. We held a demonstration and, to punish us, they closed the store, the shops and everything. We had nothing to give our children to eat. I called the Housewives together, and we decided to send a letter to the company, and if they didn't respond we would have a demonstration and go on strike. We gave them 24 hours. After that time we called the *companeras* together for the demonstration, but not even ten people turned up. How was I to hold a demonstration, after threatening the director with a strike, with so few people?

So, do you know what we did, *companeras?* We — those of us who were there — we locked the store. I called a press conference and said on the radio, 'My *companeras* don't need food — that is why they haven't come to the demonstration — so those of us who have come, as a protest against our *companeras*, will shut the store until they need food. We are going to stay here, inside the store, with our children, cooking what there is. This way we'll be able to last, even if it's for a whole year.' At about one o'clock in the afternoon, all the women with their children were ready. A large group of us went to Catavi to state our claim to the director. He would not listen, but the people were so furious that we stayed there until midnight so as to solve the problem. Our children, in the meantime, were wandering around all over the place, with nothing to eat. But we didn't move from the director's door and we didn't let the director leave his office, not even to have his lunch. Did he think our husbands were having *their* lunch? The director wanted coffee, well there was no coffee, he had to stay, sitting with us, until he agreed to increase the value of our food coupons.

When at one o'clock in the morning we finally went home, many *companeros* beat their wives for having gone. 'You're a

53

housewife not a politician, what do you think you're doing abandoning our children like that. . . ?' That is how they treated us. The next day, when they came to tell me this, I made a broadcast over the radio, saying, 'Unfortunately, *companeros*, our action has not been well accepted by the Nationalists, by the Banzerists, who have beaten their wives for having got a small rise in the coupons'. And I told them that next time we would give out all the names of the Banzerists. They say that then the *companeros* begged their wives not to go out, so that no one would see they had been beaten and they asked to be forgiven. But the people did notice, and workers said to them, 'Ah, you have beaten your wife, you are a Banzerist'. These *companeros* complained to my husband saying, 'Listen Chungara, tell your wife not to molest us so much, she is going too far.'

I have told you this in great detail, *companeras*, so that you can see that not everything is nice and rosy, Sometimes our own people are against us, they don't understand us, or they have been enthusiastic, but when the time came, they have not acted. This is why I repeat to you that the main thing is organization. When every woman can set up blockades, work shifts, go on strike with others, do what she likes without her husband stopping her; when we have women like this, then we will be able to do anything, but, meantime, it's difficult. We must be sure of ourselves so that we don't get demoralized.

How We Must Fight as Working Class Women

1) We must be Firm in the Struggle

We have a very serious commitment, *companeras*, which is the future of our children. This is why we must fight, why we must be conscious and strong. There are people who say to me, 'Dona Domitila, you have suffered so much, why don't you give up, after all, what have you got out of it?' Forgive me talking about my personal problems, but perhaps you know that some of the very people I have fought for have slandered me, and even accused me of being a thief. In these moments, you can become very disillusioned and want to give up everything but, if you know you are fighting for your people, for your own children, so that they have a better future, so that they don't suffer what we have suffered, you don't get demoralized that easily. All the same, it's not easy.

Our struggle is not just for paraffin or for palliatives that don't solve the main issue. For example, we fought for meat and got it, but we are also short of rice and when we get the rice, we will still be short of medicines. Go to the store in Siglo XX and you'll see

full shelves — everything is there — because there isn't the money
to buy it. People from outside come in, see the store and say, 'Ah,
the miners have everything!' I call this store 'the tinned food
museum' because the tins of food have been there for years; drying
up. So, *companeras*, we must be aware that the problems are not
solved just like that.

2) We Must Fight Alongside the Men

We, *companeras*, are man's other half. If this half does nothing it
could mean there's no fight, because man has so many problems.
How can he fight on his own? At times he is unaware of things
isn't he? A lot depends on us and there are many ways in which we
can make our husbands understand, but the main thing is not to
separate from them. I think that the best thing *companera* Norberta
de Aguilar did was when she invited my husband to the meeting
that time. Since then, he and I have always been together. He knows
where I go, what I am doing, everything. My husband always
trusts me, so much that at times I go to meetings where I'm the
only woman, but he trusts me and the *companeros* respect me too.

So, these barriers, these taboos and the criticism are disappearing.
All these things have been imposed on us by the capitalists to keep
us from rising up, for the more ignorant we women are, the longer
it will be before we liberate ourselves.

3) We Must Learn New Skills

If we women are ignorant, our children will be ignorant. For
example, our sons; we don't make them share the housework —
we bring them up to go out on the street and no more. But we say
to the little girls, 'You, you are a girl, you must do this and that;
little girls belong in the home'. This is how we bring them up
isn't it? And in this way we help the capitalists. That is why I think
that we women must learn skills, we need to, much more than
men, because who do the kids question? The mother. I haven't been
to school, so I don't know what to do when the children don't
understand something — they ask me and I don't know. They're
hardly going to ask their father. When the man comes in, usually
he is tired and fed-up with his own problems, isn't he? He'd
probably shout at them and make them afraid of him. This is why our
responsibility is so great. We must educate ourselves for our children's
sake, so that they're not easy to fool [easy prey for imperialism].
'Ignorant people are deceived with half a loaf of bread' is what they
say, isn't it? We must talk to our children about all our problems.
We mustn't say, 'Ah, he's only little, he doesn't understand'.
Instead we must think 'This child must learn all I have learnt and
more', because when we die, what will happen? Who will take over?
Our struggle must be passed on to our children.

I know two families in Siglo XX, the fathers were killed in the San Juan Massacre of 1966. One of the widows was left with eight children, and when they cried with hunger, or when they asked for shoes or anything from their mother, she would say to them, 'Yes, cry, and curse those who assassinated your father. Go and ask the police for these things. Thanks to the army, thanks to Barrientos, you have no father, go and complain to them.'

This woman, she didn't know much, because her husband never made her participate, but she knew who was behind the death of her husband and she brought up her children with this idea in them. And now they are good leaders.

But the other woman, she was also left widowed, was never interested and has never spoken to her children about who killed their father, and now they are police agents, working with the people who tortured and killed their father — the people who should be their sworn enemies for ever. This is what can happen when a woman doesn't know how to guide her children.

Now there are also great fighters, great revolutionaries who think that women should not participate in the struggle. 'One revolutionary in the house is enough,' they say. And when the revolutionary falls, the wife doesn't know how to behave, and many times, instead of defending her husband's position, she seems to betray it. We have often seen this in times of repression.

I have a relative who was a militant in a political party which agreed that women should take part. He was one of those who said, 'One revolutionary is enough in my house'. One day, the police took him, and he told them that he had been a militant of such and such a party at one time, but he hadn't been involved again since he got married, and that he knew nothing. The agents wanted to know who his *companeros* were. The result was that the woman innocently went to the police to complain about her husband's detention. 'My husband isn't involved in anything,' she said. 'But so-and-so was his friend, and he has denounced him,' the agents told her. 'He said that on such-and-such a date your husband went out distributing leaflets. . .' They went on like this, and the woman began to talk. 'What liars, what bloody men, it's a lie, sir, my husband was no longer involved, so-and-so probably came to the house and gave the propaganda to my husband, someone else did this, and so-and-so did something else. . .' and she told them everything. The agents, who had taped everything she had said, then went to her husband and said, 'After denying everything, listen now to what your wife has been saying. She has denounced you. On such-and-such a date you gave out leaflets, on this date you had a meeting at your home.'

Without meaning to, this woman betrayed her husband. This wouldn't have happened if she had taken part with her husband —

if she had been better educated. Maybe she would have helped her husband to deny everything and then everything would have worked out all right. Later, when this man (my cousin) was released, he wanted to beat his wife. I said to him, 'She is not to blame; she knows nothing. You would never let her take part'. Finally he understood. Now, she participates in everything.

Men should not feel jealous, or think that we are going to start ruling the place. We women can mobilize not only other women but also the men. If our sons are well brought up and shown the way by us, they too will become mobilized. There are young children who have suffered tortures and misery and have never denounced their *companeros* because they have taken part in the struggle along with their fathers.

Men on their own or women on their own can never carry out the fight. We must be united, first in the home, as a family, and then in the whole community and the entire country.

Final Words to Women in the Countryside

1) First of All, Organization

The first thing you must do in your communities, *companeras*, is to get yourselves organized. Because if there isn't organization, no matter how beautiful the plans may be, and even if *companeras* give up their lives in the struggle, we shall achieve nothing. We shall be making useless sacrifices; nothing will come of them. You may be prepared to die, but our lives must help us move forward.

2) Secondly, We Must Teach Our Companeras

Believe me *companeras*, I am not happy when I'm cooking bread to sell because I think of all the people who need to learn, who need to be taught. You, *companeras*, must teach and guide other women. For us in the mines it's easier, you see, when we're in the queue at the store, we are talking, we are always commenting on these things. You must find ways, places where you can talk. In the Mothers' Centres, which are for sewing and knitting . . . you must talk about your problems there and in other places like these. Of course, in these organizations that are run by the government, they say 'No politics'. But *companeras*, we are political from the day we are born, When a human being starts to cry he or she is already making politics, in wanting you to give it milk, or wanting you to change its nappy.

When you complain about lack of paraffin, you are all being political, this is Left-wing politics. Our exploiters are also political, but they are Right-wing. That is why we cannot say that we are apolitical. We are political, we are revolutionaries because we want changes, we want to see an end to this exploitation, we want better living conditions, so that we, in this country, can enjoy the riches in our soil. I beg you, *companeras,* that all we women educate ourselves and join in our people's struggle and, wherever we go, wherever we may be, that we preach what we have talked about here.

Part II:
The Role of Women in National Liberation Movements

The Mother

has changed her clothes.
Her skirt has turned into pants,
her shoes into boots,
her pocketbook into a knapsack.
She no longer sings lullabyes,
she sings songs of protest.
She goes unkempt and crying
a love that envelopes and frightens her.
She no longer loves only her children,
nor does she give only to her children.
She clasps to her breast
thousands of hungry mouths.
She is the mother of ragged children
of little children who spin tops on dusty sidewalks.
She has given birth to herself
feeling — at times —
unable to support so much love on her shoulders,
thinking of the fruit of her flesh
— far off and alone —
calling her in the night without answer,
while she responds to other shouts,
to many shouts,
but always thinking of the one and only shout of her flesh
one more shout in that clamour of the people who calls her
and pulls from her arms
even her own children.

Gioconda Belli

Translated by Electa Arenal and Marsha Gabriela Dreyer.

5. Fighting on Two Fronts: Conversations with Palestinian Women
Soraya Antonius

The following conversations have been selected from transcripts first published in the *Journal of Palestine Studies*. They were gathered together by Soraya Antonius who was formerly editor of the *Middle East Forum* and who has also served on committees of the General Union of Palestinian Women (GUPW). The conversations are preceded by a slightly shortened version of the introduction she wrote to accompany them.

The salient characteristic of the women's movement in Palestine and in exile has been its identification, since the early part of this century, with the national movement against Zionism. It is this that distinguishes it from the women's movement in Egypt or in Western countries: among Palestinians there has never been a broadly-based grassroots movement for women's rights; the major efforts have been devoted to political, national ends, and the emancipation of women has come as an accidental consequence of their determination to carry out some political action, such as a demonstration, which entailed a flouting of conventional mores.

The Palestinian women who first demonstrated against Zionist immigration in 1921 were heavily veiled and rode in closed cars. Then, in 1929, two hundred delegates from all over the country attended the first Arab Women's Congress of Palestine. 'It was a bold step to take in view of the traditional restrictions which, until then, prevented the Arab woman in Palestine from taking part in any movement which might expose her to the public eye.'[1]

After this Congress, delegates asked to present a petition to the British High Commissioner's wife, since prevalent conventions made it improper for them to appear before a man; when the British refused this request, they decided that they 'had no other alternative but . . . to ignore all traditional restrictions.'[2] In 1933, 'for the first time in history a Christian lady delivered a political speech from the pulpit of a mosque'[3] (the mosque of Omar facing the Church of the Holy Sepulchre), in which she recalled the

Muslim and Christian conquerors of Jerusalem and compared Omar's honoured pledge to Sophronius with Allenby's broken word, and then a Muslim lady made a speech standing before Christ's tomb in the Holy Sepulchre.

Between these pioneering ladies and Leila Khaled, Dalal Mughrabi, and their contemporaries, lie four wars, a dozen major 'incidents', the destruction of a society and the exile of a nation, yet they are recognizably the inspirers and progenitors of the women activists of today. Women still demonstrate, present petitions, make bandages and cook for the wounded, still die from bullet and bomb, as they did 50 years ago.

But in spite of these affinities there are two major differences in the world surrounding Palestinian women today. From 1919, when the first women's association was founded in Jerusalem, until 1969 when the Resistance organizations gained power in the Palestine Liberation Organization, Palestinian women had never had the backing of a national or governmental authority, nor had they faced the responsibilities that this backing inevitably entails. The earlier groups were almost entirely apolitical, except for one small Marxist group, and they dealt with alien governments imposing a policy inimical to men and women alike. Since 1969, however, Palestinian women have been represented by the General Union of Palestinian Women (al-Ittihad al-'Am lil-Mara al-Filastiniva), an official section of the PLO, whose executive members represent the various political organizations that make up the PLO. The second difference comes from the significant spread of education. Since 1948 an increasing number of girls have begun to receive at least a basic education, and personal experience suggests that virtually 100% of the daughters of the urban middle and upper classes have been expected to complete secondary school at the least.

In their daily lives Palestinian women suffer from social harassment and legal discrimination imposed on their sisters in every Arab country. The laws, imposed by several countries that have signed the UN Charter of Human Rights, are: (a) the 'honour' law provisions which in effect condone the murder of a woman by her husband or any male related to her if she is suspected or accused of illicit relations with a man; (b) the divorce laws; (c) the *Shari'a* law of inheritance which automatically accords the largest share to men; (d) the law which forbids a woman to travel outside the frontiers of her country without written permission from her husband or other male guardian. Every country of the *Mashriq* is guilty of imposing at least one, and sometimes all, of these national disgraces. The 'honour' law has been abrogated once, by Abdul-Karim Qasim in Iraq, but it was restored when the regime changed.

Before 1948, Palestinian rural women enjoyed the relative freedom of a mountainous country; the necessity of sharing in the

work of the fields freed them from the veil and allowed them to
visit towns to sell agricultural produce. But after the exile two
opposing trends appeared. One, based on the belief that their own
ignorance had contributed to the disaster, was a determination to
acquire as much formal education as possible. The other was a
nostalgic longing to preserve the old society's structures and habits,
which led to the metaphysical resurrection of the destroyed
villages and urban neighbourhoods within the chaos of the refugee
camps and to a strict enforcement of the old mores. In 1967, when
the Resistance movement began in Jordan, and in 1969, when it
opened up the camps in Lebanon, a new idea began, slowly, to
percolate: that women constitute half the available manpower
resource, one that a small, embattled nation cannot afford to waste.
Women began to participate, publicly, in every crisis, from Wahdat
camp in the 1970 Amman battles to the latest Israeli invasion in
South Lebanon.

No individual can really be 'typical of' or 'represent' an entire
nation, and the women in these conversations are, as individuals,
very different from each other. Their ages range from 22 to 65,
their backgrounds from birth in exile and life in a refugee camp
to the upper reaches of pre-1948 Palestinian society. All but two
have a university education. I have deliberately omitted religious
affiliation, on principle. Nor did anyone consider it a decisive
factor, but in the two cases where references have been spontaneously made to a confessional factor impinging on their lives these
have been left. This is not by any means a sociological study —
the only criterion of choice was an active commitment to the
national cause — but a reflection of a strand of the Palestinian
experience.

May Sayigh[4]

My mother was a member of the Women's Union[5] and very active
and aware politically, so my first education in the struggle came
from my home. I was born in Gaza and became involved as a child
of nine when I joined a political party, or rather, the party joined
me to them, as a sort of mascot, I suppose. I went to university in
Egypt and then married and went to live in Amman where I
joined various political parties. But really I was always looking for
the resistance and I always believed that armed struggle was the
only way to recover Palestine. When Fateh began I joined it, was
trained and became a member of its militia. After the 1970
fighting in Jordan I came to Lebanon and I've been here since then.

I've never felt that there's any difference between the struggle
of men and women, but men don't understand the women's

65

problems: not a single political party has handled it properly or
even understood its seriousness — the parties don't even have a
women's section. After centuries of being treated as second-class
citizens women have so many inferiority complexes, they lack
confidence in themselves, they have no practice in life, life in the
outside world. They need to be gradually prepared to work side by
side with men because without this preparation they find men
superior, and they lose heart. One often sees them at meetings,
keeping silent although they are bursting with ideas, because they
are afraid to express themselves. They don't realize that they have
been absent for centuries and they just give up and go back in
silence to their homes. You mustn't think that it is an insult to
have a union for women as though we were a special, subhuman
category; you must remember that it is the poor women who
suffer. Throughout our history the Arabs despised work and left
it to the Persians and Turks; women were the symbol of their
vanity and allowed to work even less than the men. If Palestinian
women can work now, this is because of the exile and changing
social attitudes. But although our women had to go to work after
1948, and the man often left his family in order to work abroad,
so that the children saw their mother as breadwinner and head of
the house, still, it takes more than one generation to change
centuries of social attitudes. And it also takes a lot of structured
work. The PLO Charter talks of the equality of men and women
and the elevation of woman's role in the revolution. Elevation!
Even the word *(tarqia)* is wrong and suggests that they're going to
teach her to play the piano or do watercolours or something
equally 'elevating'! In fact neither equality nor elevation have been
brought about and there is no single organized programme to
implement. Abu Ammar (Yasser Arafat) thinks women should go
to the bases and fight and live there, but he doesn't understand
that we have difficulty just getting women to leave their homes
alone in broad daylight. One can't jump several stages just like that,
it's as mistaken an idea as keeping women locked up at home. If
she goes to the bases she'll be considered a prostitute. I remember
when we started going to the camps in Jordan, in 1967-68, all the
men used to greet us by lining the streets and chanting, ironically,
'Here come the *feda'iya.*' First of all we need *legal* equality, so
that a man can be imprisoned for divorcing his wife just because
she's a militant, or for beating her because she has joined the
Women's Union. Of course I want women to go to the bases, but
they must do it in their thousands, not as exceptional individuals.
A vanguard that is too far in advance of the general experience will
only delay the advance of the whole; the woman who goes to the
bases now only builds a wall between herself and the others. One
can't really talk of a general situation, because it's different in

Jim Downing

every one of the countries where Palestinians live — in Lebanon, for instance, attitudes have changed since the civil war.

In Palestinian literature the mother has always been the symbol, and played the role, of the land: strong, protective. The son leaves and returns, she is there, the recurring protection. And it is a fact that the Palestinian woman dies very young. Over the age of 40 men outlive the women, unlike what is found in most other societies. This is simply because the women are worn out, overworked and exhausted physically and emotionally. But the younger writers and poets, like Khalid Abu-Khalid, Yahia Badaw and others, now depict two faces of woman: the strong mother, the home and the land, who encourages her son to fight, and the young woman, the beloved, who is herself a fighter and active in the struggle. These are new depictions of woman: to be loved she has to fight actively for her country; the mother is no longer just generous, making coffee and baking bread, but has become the strong one who celebrates her son's death in battle by songs and who goes side by side with him through the nights of terror. In my own poems I try and emphasize that I am a woman, although I don't feel a second-class citizen at all. I feel the Palestine cause is mine and the work is mine.

The GUPW is hewing a road through rock to change the position of women, to help them to live their own lives and to depend on themselves economically. There are three categories in the camps: women with large families and conventional husbands who do not allow them out of the house; the Union is very interested in this category and considers that it is there to serve them in particular. Then there are women who can leave their homes and move about in the camp and finally those who leave the camp and become cadres and instructors. The most emancipated women are the ones whose children are grown up, and the unmarried. There's no birth control programme in the camps because women want to replace the heavy Palestinian losses.

Before the civil war we offered literacy classes three times a week, which were open to women of all ages. Their men were opposed to this and we had to persuade them one by one. The women themselves were very hesitant and we used to persuade them too to spend at least an hour a week learning how to read and write in order to understand the political situation and how to encourage their children to participate in the work of the Resistance. When things get bad and a war breaks out the women rush to classes because they feel enthusiastic and the husbands don't stand in their way during these times.

We've opened kindergartens in most of the camps (not all, because we lack the money) and supply the teachers we've trained and draw up the programmes. We've also opened a couple in Syria, but the need there is less urgent because the state runs free kindergartens itself. In addition we train women to do traditional Palestinian embroidery so that they can earn a living at home. Altogether we've trained about 5,000 in the various Union centres and have organized travelling exhibitions to sell their work in the Gulf and other Arab countries, and in Europe through solidarity committees. We hold political meetings in the camps to explain current events and problems. We don't have a regular publication but have published books,[6] posters and pamphlets. Then there's the foreign relations section which receives women's delegations, organizes conferences here and sends delegations abroad. We have links with Afro-Asian women's federations and are a member of the Women's International Democratic Federation.

The Union-run school, Beit Atfal al-Sumud,[7] was not in our programme, but was a debt we had to pay to the mothers who died in Tell Zaatar. We're trying to honour their memory by creating a new life in the face of attempts to eliminate the Palestinians.

Fatmeh

We're from Qiryat Shaab near Acre but I was born after the exile,
in Anjar. Later we moved to Burj Shemali, near Tyre, because the
Armenians didn't want us in Anjar, although they had come to it
as refugees themselves.[8] Finally we moved to Tell Zaatar, because
my father found a job in one of the factories there. We were ten
children, plus my father and mother; the rest of the family stayed
in Palestine, but my father had fought in the resistance in 1948
and it was too dangerous for him to stay. My brother Omar was
born during the exodus, in an olive grove, and later people sent my
mother a sprig of the olive tree under which he was born, in
Palestine, and she kept it and used to show it to us. At first life
was very difficult in the camp, the rain used to sweep the tents
away and we slept in the mud and in the summer there was no
water. We used to say 'in winter we drown and in summer we burn'.
As children we always joined in the demonstrations on May 15[9] and
after the 1967 war my youngest brother, who was 13, went to
Syria and joined Saiqa. Then, after the battle of Karameh in 1968,
Omar left to join Fateh and after the Resistance opened up the
camps. I also joined and learnt how to maintain and handle weapons
and received first-aid training at a clinic. My father tried to forbid
me to do this and beat me, because by this time he had lost heart
in the struggle and the hardness of the years had discouraged him.
But my mother let me go. I joined the GUPW and went to its training camp located inside Tell Zaatar so that the girls could train by
day and return to their homes at night. Then in the May 1973
fighting in Beirut, for the first time I slept — for a week — away
from my family because we were so busy collecting food and
keeping the fighters supplied. When I returned my father was
beside himself with rage: the neighbours had spent their time
telling him 'Aha! Your daughter shows no respect for you!' I
used to tell them, 'But why? Other girls go out to work in factories
or as servants, why shouldn't one work in the Resistance?' I find
that people have changed a lot since then. During the Tell Zaatar
siege everyone worked and no one stopped his daughter because
everybody felt threatened by the danger and the neighbours
couldn't gossip because all the women — mothers, daughters,
wives and sisters — all worked. And the most traditional women's
work, fetching the water, was often the most dangerous — women
were killed while doing this night after night.
   At the very start of the war my brother was killed in the bus on
April 13.[10] He was 17 and studying for his baccalaureate at a

Catholic school in Ashrafiya. And it was strange, but the priest who taught him came to our home to offer condolences and praise his memory. My mother didn't cry or say anything. I had to go to the Qarantina morgue to identify his body. During the siege I worked with the others making bread for the fighters – every night we made 200 kilos of dough. I also worked in the hospital, which was very difficult because we ran out of medical supplies and only had salt and water to use as a disinfectant. We made candles out of a huge block of wax that we found in a factory, and as long as there was water we washed the bandages, but after that we collected sheets from every house and used them. The situation was terrible. My niece, who was nine, died in the big shelter that was bombed, where so many were killed. And my sister gave birth on the steps of this shelter; there was no room below. People remembered 1948 and said, 'We won't go. This is not our home but we'll die where we are, we won't move yet again.' So when a man was killed the women used to bury him in the house, under the earth floor. In the end the men were dead and the women bore arms. When the camp fell my father refused to go down to Dekwaneh and give himself up to the Phalangists; he went off by the mountain road (which led to areas held by the Lebanese allies of the Palestinians) and died on the way. My mother had to go to Dekwaneh because she had the five smallest children with her — the eldest was eight. She put them into one of the lorries that were evacuating us, but when she tried to get on herself the driver said there was no more room. Finally she reached the Museum (the crossover point in the divided city) and there she waited. The children never came. Later she heard that four of them had died suffocated under the crush of bodies in the lorry and that Sonia, who was four, had scrambled out of the lorry, saying she couldn't breathe, and had disappeared. We never saw her again. I stayed in the camp hospital with the doctors and wounded and the stench. When the Chamounists and Phalangists came they killed some of the wounded on the spot; others were carried out on stretchers. Later Dr Abdul-Aziz and we nurses followed as hostages. On the path down we passed the stretchers and saw the slaughtered wounded, many of them mutilated. The Phalangists began arguing, some wanted to kill us on the spot, others to take us off for questioning. At last they took us to a Lebanese Red Cross office and then somewhere else to be questioned and held. We were saved by an International Red Cross car that passed by; there was a girl in it who knew us from the hospital and she insisted on taking us with her. I reached the Arab University at midnight, having left Tell Zaatar at 10.30 in the morning, and there I met a comrade who told me my family was all right (which wasn't true, but he wanted to comfort me) and who gave me the key to his apartment. I went there and fell down and slept. Now my mother lives in Burj Shemali and I stayed in Beirut and worked first at registering the children of all who died and then in the school the GUPW set up for them and then I married. I'm 27 now and in charge of supplies for the orphans' school, Beit Atfal al-Sumud.

I think that at least half of the new generation has changed in their attitude to women. The Resistance only came to the camps in 1969, it's not yet 10 years, and the road is very long. If a woman doesn't even work outside the home, how can she work in the revolution? She has to persist and persuade her family, but things have changed already, in less than 10 years.

Um Samir

My father knew more about the Zionist movement, back in Haifa in the 1920s, than we do now. As a child I used to sit up at night and listen to him talking to his friends and ask questions and when I was eight or nine I used to join the demonstrations on Balfour Day, without understanding anything. Then Izzeddin Qassam[11] came to the schools to mobilize us. He found the ground prepared in Haifa and organized a group of schoolgirls and we worked for him during the Revolt. I had some training with a rifle but I never fought. Mainly we prepared food and took it to the fighters because the men couldn't move around as freely as we could, and we acted as couriers and collected money for the movement. My family encouraged me because they believed in the cause; in fact as long as we were involved in the struggle no one ever criticized us, although we were in our teens and roamed around quite freely. Even when I went to a village I didn't know and was taken by a guide — a man whom I also didn't know — to the caves to deliver a message, even then no one thought anything of it; on the contrary, the peasant women would salute you if they saw you were in the movement. It was that political work that opened my eyes to the social problems of our country. Time and again we would go to a house to collect money and the woman would say, 'You'll have to come back. I have to ask my husband first.' We would ask why, since we knew she had plenty of money available. 'Yes, but my money can only be spent on housekeeping, and the cause is nothing to do with the house and not my concern.'

In 1947, when the partition plan was passed at the UN, we established the Amin Hospital in Haifa and began working with the Red Crescent Society, in preparation for the war that was coming. Sadej Nassar was the moving spirit in this and in the whole women's movement. She always maintained that a popular *assise* was essential if women were really to liberate themselves; it could never be achieved by a few upper class women doing social work.[12]

Well, the war came. We had very little money in the Women's Union (al-Ittihadal-Nissa'i). I remember we used to train with guns in the backyard of my house because it was the biggest space we could use free. But although we trained, we never used the arms. The situation got worse and worse — lack of supplies, primitive weapons, snipers, terrorization of the civilian population. People go on now about the horrors of the civil war in Lebanon, but Haifa was much worse. The Zionists used to demolish entire buildings with gelignite, with all the people inside, while in Beirut a rocket wrecks one floor but leaves the building standing. There was a lot of individual bravery in Haifa, I remember some acts of outstanding courage, but there was no structure, no organization; the civilians were left to their own resources and the individual fighters acted on their own. Then the Arab armies took over and I took my children to Lebanon. Those of us from the Women's Union who met up again began helping with the refugees. In Tyre we used to find babies washed up on the seashore. King Abdullah wouldn't allow us to continue our work in Jordan unless we changed our name to the 'Jordanian Women's Union', so in 1951 we established the Union in Lebanon. Our largest project was the orphanage school in the mountains, Beit Is'ad al-Tufula, which has 240 children.

There's no doubt that the Resistance has improved the lot of women since 1969. The Palestinian used to be much more advanced in his own country and women were independent and freer than women in Syria or Egypt or Iraq, but after 1948 this changed: in the camps the Palestinian became ultra-strict, even fanatic, about the 'honour' of his women. Perhaps this was because he had lost everything that gave his life meaning, and 'honour' was the only possession remaining to him.

'Abir'[13]

When I was 20 I started working as a teacher in a village near Irbid in Jordan where my family had settled after they were driven out of Haifa in 1948. My parents were pretty backward and I led the ordinary life of most girls around me and was brought up to marry and stay at home, bringing up the children. But I was good at school, came out among the top ten students in Jordan, and decided to go to university. Then my family arranged an engagement for me; I was young and completely unaware socially, but I didn't like my fiancé because he wanted to stop me studying and leave the university. And he kept on trying to impose another personality on me, telling me how to dress and how to do my hair and this and that, as though I had no existence of my own. So I refused to marry him and went to court to get the contract[14] annulled on the grounds that I was being forced into it. When I became a teacher I met others who were members of the Ba'ath party, and one colleague in particular, who was in the Arab Nationalist Movement, had a great influence over me and taught me about the political situation. I became strongly pro-Abdul Nasser and took part in the 1955 demonstrations against the Baghdad Pact and talked to my pupils as much as I could about politics. After the battle of Karameh in March 1968, I joined Fateh and received military training, I spent the battles of 1970 at a military base, sleeping there — at that stage families didn't protest against this. But before it was different. I remember once I returned home after 10 days at a base, stinking, filthy, longing only for a bath and a change of clothes, and my father gave me the most awful scolding. 'Where have you been? In America or what? What do you think you are? What do you think *we* are?' And so on and so on. He used to shout at me but other fathers beat their daughters, locked them up and even threatened to kill them, so I was lucky. But when the fighting was on in September all the girls used to sleep away from their home because it was too dangerous to come home every night, so their families had to accept it. Yet when the fighting ended it was back to the old story, home before eight o'clock at night. In October the Jordanian secret police began their investigations in Amman but they didn't come to Irbid, which remained very revolutionary until the army tanks entered the town after the Jerash battles in the spring of 1971. Then I was arrested and questioned but they didn't find any arms because I had already buried them in the garden. I suppose they're still there and one day some farmer will find them. Then I was demoted and transferred from teaching Arabic literature to secondary school students and sent to a kindergarten. Finally I escaped and went to Damascus which was full of Palestinians who had fled the battles. The PLO arranged with the Libyan government to send teachers to Libya as we all needed work and I went to Benghazi. For me this was a real exile. The Palestinian teachers were scattered and unorganized; there was no real PLO presence and people weren't interested in the problem. I spent a year there but I was miserable, feeling cut off, an exile in an Arab country. After a year I resigned, returned to Damascus and then I came to Beirut, where I got my higher education certificate and rejoined my family who had sold their house in Irbid and moved to Lebanon. I was in a state of acute depression because of the events in Jordan and then the shock of Libyan ignorance; I couldn't pull myself together. In 1973 I joined the GUPW and did hospital work during the attacks on the camps in May. Now I'm running a Union project for the bereaved wives and daughters of Tell Zaatar. In

Damour alone there are 400 families headed by a woman — all the
men are dead. Seventy percent of these women are between 18 and
30 years old and the average size of a family is eight persons. Many
are Lebanese, but all are helped by the PLO, which assumes responsibility for the dependents of anyone who dies for the sake of
Palestine, including those killed by the Israelis in the South. There
are 8,000 widows and fatherless daughters from the Lebanese civil
war alone. The Union programme trains women to earn their
living by teaching sewing, traditional embroidery, accountancy,
typing and secretarial work, languages (English and French) and
social services. We also train kindergarten teachers.

Last year I married my cousin, who is three years younger than
I am and doesn't have a university education, but he is a member
of the movement. I love my freedom and I've talked to him about
it until he has understood what I feel. We've agreed not to have
children, neither of us being very young. I don't feel I can sit at
home looking after an infant, but we may adopt a three- or four-
year old from Tell Zaatar. After all, we got married to live with
each other, to be together, not to found a family, but we haven't
told his family about this because they never liked me. His sister
used to say, 'She's a woman, not a girl,' as though a sexual relation
really changes one's essence, as though a virgin were a separate
species of humankind. In fact, we didn't have a wedding party or
even tell people that we were married; it wasn't their business. But
his family used to go on about me and tell me I was preventing
him from marrying until I told them, 'The truth is that we are
married'. My mother was immensely relieved because she could
tell the neighbours that I had settled down at last.

All of us women are brought up in a certain way and this affects
every one of us. I have progressive ideas but I can't implement
them fully because of my upbringing. I can't be too open in
discussion with men because they may misinterpret what I say,
even though I've received military training and fought in battles.
Men are my comrades but deep down they don't believe I'm really
their equal. Socially we haven't caught up with our political
development — we're all walking on an advanced political leg and
dragging a backward social leg behind, impeded and crippled. I'm
36 and I haven't yet met a man who has really shaken off the old
conventions about women. I feel that an Arab woman has to marry
if she wants to live in society. We can't live freely on our own,
even my brother, who's a revolutionary wouldn't and couldn't
accept my being involved with a man, so in this social situation
you are forced to marry if you want to relax and be happy. One
can't live with someone in secret and if you do it openly everybody else changes in their relations toward you. And the leaders
are hypocritical about it all At public meetings they talk about

liberating women but they really believe, and some of them say it
openly, that a woman does her revolutionary duty by ironing her
husband's shirts, cooking his dinner and providing a cosy and
restful ambience for the warrior.

'Fahimeh'[15]

Six years ago, when I was a student, my family used to object
very strongly when I took part in demonstrations, but their opposition got worn down bit by bit because they were really only
worried about what the neighbours would say. And the neighbours
were given so many subjects of conversation, first by my joining in
demonstrations, then by my being wounded, then arrested, that
at last my family gave up and now they don't worry when I sleep
away from home. Also I'm financially independent now and if I
could find a cheap place I would live on my own.

I first became involved in the women's question in 1974, when
about 50 girl students, who were semi-involved in politics, began
to work on it with the help and encouragement of Dar al-Fan.[16]
But when the civil war broke out in 1975 they decided that social
problems were not important and went off to fight. I think this
was a mistake and that the women's problem is inextricably
related to everything else that's wrong. (For instance, in a poorer
suburb of Beirut, like Shiyah, girls were forbidden to join in the
struggle, simply because they were girls, not for any political
reasons.) At any rate, at the beginning of the civil war we tried to
bring women together to discuss the problem, but this failed. The
war was very difficult for me because I was living in Ras Beirut
and working and sleeping in Shiyah and I couldn't study things or
think clearly. There was danger and fighting and confusion. I was
fighting in a small Trotskyist organization, and the men in it
tried to push me forward: 'Why are you sitting passive? It's your
problem, not ours'. After one year of war Shiyah was virtually
empty, the only girls there were fighters who had left their
families, but who had acted as individuals, not as part of a larger
social transformation. I concentrated on political problems but
this was a mistake. The women's problem is the most difficult one
facing us and it's so difficult that one gives up because one feels
that all the efforts one makes are useless, they collapse under the
inertia all round. We once tried to do something about birth
control — got films from the UN family planning office and a
woman doctor to give explanations. Some of the women agreed
that they were worn out — 'God damn all these children' — but
most were frightened that the pill would harm them or that their
husbands would change toward them. If I could I would found a

sort of popular club *cum* social centre for women in a poor quarter and teach hygiene, literacy, politics and so on, but unless one has a big organization to back one it's impossible. And in the political organizations they don't think about the situation of women, they're only interested in recruiting women as members for their respective organizations. Still, one of the first steps is for girls to become politicized, because then they gradually start thinking about their situation as women.

When the Israelis invaded the South in March 1978, my organization sent me to run a military base there. They began by appointing me assistant to the man responsible for the base and that made the introduction easier because the men got used to me giving orders. They were very liberated but all the same I was surprised when they accepted me so easily — perhaps it helped that it was night when I first arrived and I couldn't see the expressions on their faces. I was in charge of the base for ten days, assigning guard duties, organizing supplies, reconnoitring the terrain, and so on. At first I was frightened of the responsibility, but I forced myself to do more than I really could, to prove myself, because I know that if a woman doesn't show herself more capable and braver than others, no one will respect her. I liked the time in the South so much and was greatly encouraged by my success. In Shiyah the men are very petit-bourgeois and *macho* and find it very difficult to accept a woman over them. Whenever I gave an order to a man I knew he would go home and brood about it all night, even if he said nothing. But in the South it was different. Also, what helped was that we were small groups, never more than 15 and usually less, which wasn't enough for social attitudes to harden. And I was careful about my behaviour. For instance, if someone made a joke, I would laugh a little, not too much, because men take these trivia seriously and might think I was laughing because I liked the man who had told the joke. So my laughter was always balanced and held in rein, and I would never greet an acquaintance too warmly, and all the other little details that matter. Some of the other girls in the South would exaggerate a bit and then there would be trouble; one has to take care and remember that attitudes are deeply ingrained however progressive the political ideas may be. When my organization appointed me they sent another woman to the base with me. They didn't want me to go alone. But there were quite a few women fighting in the South — I know that the Popular Front for the Liberation of Palestine (PFLP) had five there and I heard there were others.

I'm a Palestinian, from Acre, but I work with a Lebanese organization because I wanted to fight, not sit in an office. In 1973, when I was 17, I joined a PFLP workcamp but all that happened was that I got my hands calloused digging and then I returned to university. I didn't want to play at it and to boast of having work-hardened hands; I wanted to be really part of a refugee camp, not just be taken in and out, and then returned to my 'proper place'. And the PFLP is one of the most radical and least bureaucratic organizations. . . . So I work in Shiyah now — any way I consider it's all one and the same cause, there's no difference.

The situation of women is the most difficult of all the problems facing us and it's going to take the longest to solve.

1.   Matiel E.T. Mogannam, *The Arab Woman and the Palestine Problem* (London, Herbert Joseph, 1937), p.70.
2.   Ibid., p.74.
3.   Ibid., p.95.
4.   May Sayigh is well-known as a poet in the Arab world. Her first book *Iklil al-Shawk* (Crown of Thorns), was published in 1968. In 1971, after the battles in Jordan, she published *Qasaid Manqusha ala-Masalat al-Ashrafiya* (Songs Engraved on the Ashrafiya Memorial). She later published *Qasaid Hub li-Ismin Mutarad* (Love Songs to a Name Pursueo) in 1973 and *'An al-Dumu 'wal-Farah al-Ati* (On Tears and Future Joy) in 1975. She is the vice-president of the General Union of Palestinian Women (GUPW).
5.   The Arab Palestinian Women's Union (al-Ittihad al-Nissa'i al-'Arabi al-Filastini) was founded in 1921 and still exists in Lebanon and the occupied territories. It is independent of the PLO and the GUPW.
6.   Including *Tell Zaatar al-Shaheed wal-Shahid* (Beirut, 1977) and Marie-Rose Bulos, *Shahada min Jirah al-Watan* (Beirut, 1974).
7.   The 'Home of the Children of Steadfastness' was set up after the 1976 siege and massacre of Tell Zaatar to provide an emotional and psychological haven for Palestinian and Lebanese children whose families had been killed. It has expanded since the civil war to accomodate 120 children, but financial problems prevent it from accepting all the dozens of applicants.
8.   Anjar is a town in central Lebanon largely inhabited by Armenians who fled from Turkey in the 1920s.
9.   The date of the establishment of Israel.
10. The incident which marked the formal beginning of the Lebanese civil war, when Phalangists ambushed a busload of Palestinians returning to their camp.
11. Leader of the Palestinian Revolt, killed in 1935.
12. Sadej Nassar was the first known Palestinian woman to marry a man of a different religion. She edited the newspaper *al-Carmel*, actively supported the 1930s Palestinian Revolt and was imprisoned by the British. She died in exile in the 1970s.
13. Pseudonym.
14. In Islam the engagement contract has the legal force of marriage, though a girl is considered as engaged so long as she lives in her parents' home.
15. Pseudonym.
16. A cultural club in Beirut.

6. Women and Liberation in Zimbabwe
Jane Ngwenya

Women fought side by side with men in Zimbabwe's recent war of independence and they now play a crucial role in the country's new development. To quote Margaret Nhariwa, a health worker speaking at the 1981 International Women and Health Meeting in Geneva: 'Our Government is aware of this and is acknowledging the worth of women in developing the new country. This is evident in the creation of the New Ministry of Women's Affairs and Development. It is to women, therefore, that our Government entrusts the development of Zimbabwe and its women. In the past women were the workers for development in the rural areas, but unfortunately their efforts were taken for granted and never fully realized or appreciated by the menfolk. We owe the recognition of our worth to the role played by women in the liberation struggle.' (see *ISIS International Bulletin*, No. 20, June 1981)

The following interview with Jane Ngwenya, ZAPU Secretary for Women's Affairs, took place during the Lancaster House talks in London on 19 September 1979 during the build-up to independence on 18 April 1981. It was first published in *Anti-Apartheid News* (November 1979).

AA News: Why is there only one woman in the Patriotic Front delegation to Lancaster House?

JN: The organization chose me as one of the delegates. I don't think I'm there because I'm an expert but I feel honoured that my President felt that I must be included in the delegation.

AAN: What particular problems do women in Zimbabwe face in getting involved in the liberation struggle and in political activity?

JN: Traditionally a woman cannot be involved in things that are done by men. We used to be very submissive. Even in the family – say a family of five — four girls and one boy. The boy behaves like a little king. He will be given every privilege. He will not wash his clothes, he will not wash dishes, he will not clean the house or do anything. The mother plays a very important part in saying 'he must be respected'. So we became submissive with that background. This has remained with women right through. If she gets married — marriage is taken as a profession. Mother sat down at home, or went to the fields with her daughters, but the mother was always a teacher to her daughter — to respect her husband, to respect his parents, and so on. This respect was exaggerated — because the sisters of your husband have a bigger say about you than even your husband, because if his sister should say 'I don't like your wife', you can be divorced. You have to be their servant — including their children. We accepted that we lived under those conditions as part of an African woman's life. Because of that we found it difficult to have any access to education.

AAN: Has this situation been made worse because of colonialism?

JN: I think so, to an extent, because when colonialism came it added to what we had, it helped the suppression. Although of course there were schools where those who could afford it sent their children, but a very, very small percentage of the women went to school. I'm one of those in the very small percentage, although I'm not very educated.

There were certain phases that came in our society that were not there before — for instance, women staying unmarried who went to the towns, staying there and ending up practising prostitution. Those things were not in our society before the colonialists.

In politics, I don't think anyone wanted women to be there. They just didn't think women would be interested. But in my case, the way I got interested in politics is: I did my schooling, did my teacher's course. While I was teaching I happened to attend the African Teachers Association, which was the spokesman for teachers' grievances. I realized that my pay was not the same as that of my counterpart, who was a man: with the same qualifications, we didn't get the same. The second thing was, when we met to discuss things, we practised policies of appeasement, because otherwise, we ended up being blacklisted. And that to me sounded very much like suppression, because there were so many things that we were not satisfied about and which we wanted to correct, but the President of the Teachers Association, and some of the highly educated teachers — they spoke very nice of a very wrong thing. They always said 'No, we must not do this, we must be gentlemen'. To be a gentleman is to always do things that are against you. So I did not want to continue as a teacher, I decided to resign when I got married, I stayed with my husband, I loved him very much, he was the father of my children, but because of this suppression that I had so much feeling about, I used to think, I don't want someone to have control over me on whatever I do. I was not satisfied, I detected that people were not saying exactly what they wanted to say. They were speaking what was not really their language, from their hearts. So I joined politics where I found them speaking about suppression being a bad doctrine, speaking about how they wanted things to be corrected. I got very interested, I was still very young. This was when the first political party, the African National Congress, which covered the whole of Central Africa, was formed. I became a full member and became elected into a branch. I didn't think I was fitted to be somebody who had any views to put forward. I was sort of a student, but when I discussed things with quite a number of men, who were in the majority, I found that they thought I understood what I was talking about.

So in 1960 when the ANC was banned and the leaders were arrested right throughout Central Africa, I was one of those who were also arrested. But I didn't stay long. Three women were arrested — the late Mrs. (?) Mshambi (?) Mrs. Ntshonga and myself. I stayed three weeks. I had a small baby. After three weeks I went home, but then the eyes of the police were on me and my husband was very cross with me. From then on we never had harmony in the house, we never had happiness at all. His family blamed him – 'What kind of woman is this?'

AAN: Was he involved in politics?

JN: Not actively. He talked about things being wrong but he never took any part. So his people were upbraiding me as a very wrong type of woman: 'She's a disgrace, a woman who gets arrested' — but I felt I had a duty to perform in speaking for my people. Sometimes my husband would hit me, very hard indeed, and at one time I had to see the authorities to see if I could be granted a divorce. They said they could not do it because I got married in church, but they gave us a separation, and I went back to my mother. So from there I continued. I got stronger and I was convinced I was doing right.

AAN: Is yours a common expereince for women, with a lot of prejudice from their husbands? It's certainly a disincentive to get involved in politics, if it means the break-up of one's marriage.

JN: I think it is. While I think it made many marriages very unhappy, when women wanted to be active, I found that women themselves were not interested, because the blame I got was mostly from the women. They thought I was very abnormal — 'What kind of woman is that?'

AAN: Does that still apply today?

JN: No, things have changed radically indeed. More women are arrested than men, not because men are not there, but because they are more vulnerable to shooting. Before martial law, before the war

IDAF

came to what it is today, women became more active because
many men were arrested and no man could speak openly, because
he would just be arrested and tortured. So they became a bit afraid
and those who spoke out tended to be women.

The situation is completely changed today. The women understand much much more. When you hear about curfew breakers,
and Africans 'shot in crossfire', they will not say 'women', they
will not say 'women and children', but these are the people they
shoot, because it is the women who go to fetch firewood. They
suspect them of feeding the boys because they have tried by all
means to intimidate them, but they have discovered that they
cannot stop the women feeding the boys if they know where they
are. Now they know that it is women who are very strong behind
the whole thing, they shoot indiscriminately.

AAN: Do you think that men's prejudices have broken down at the
same time?

JN: Yes I think so. If my President had any prejudices about women
he wouldn't have included me in the delegation, but because he
takes me for a person who can contribute equally to whatever I'm
asked to do, I am here. That type of prejudice is diminishing in a

number of men.

AAN: How was the ZAWU formed and what are its aims?

JN: In 1957 when the ANC was formed, women actively participated; in 1960 we were banned and we formed the NDP. Women were very active; we went to the congress, I was elected into the leadership, but at that time there was no women's wing. After the ban of the NDP we formed ZAPU on 17 December 1961. Our President, because of his wide understanding of politics and with his advisers around him, knew we were on a better footing for establishing the women's and youth wing. The women's wing was formally established on 17 December 1961 — the very same day — and the youth wing was formed too. I was appointed National Secretary of Women's Affairs. This was because women were very very active. Many men were arrested and women wanted to know why. When they explained a few things, particularly about the taking of their cattle, things which directly affected them, when they mentioned them — a person just understands.

Our structures are like this: ZAWU has got sections, branches, districts, provinces. Now we have a National Assembly: a new development. We used to have the National Executive which was the Central Committee. With this structure we have been able to organize quite a lot of women, building confidence in them – because when a woman was elected chairman, she would say 'What do I do? I really want to support the organization but if I am elected to that position, what do I do? You tell her, 'you conduct meetings in this way, in that way'. And this has continued to build the women's confidence so much that they are now very active. They have been able to convert a very large number of their educated friends who were driven away because of their professions, because they thought if they were discovered by the government to be active in politics they would be expelled from their duties or blacklisted.

After the banning of the organization women manoeuvred in their own way and tried to organize themselves underground. The regime knew that women, men and youths were active underground but they could not get them because they could never find them. They devised their own means — what means I don't know because I was in detention for many years. (8½ years, from 1964 to 1972, and prison sentences before that in 1960, 1961 etc. I have been in prison five times.)

With the growing of the struggle, women have participated even in the armed struggle. They have organized themselves; they are not only active in that they feed the boys, and get killed and so on, but they now see there is no difference between a man and a woman in Zimbabwe, they suffer the same. So many women have left the country. In Lusaka we have a very large number of refugees, but all those women did not come as refugees, they didn't mean to be refugees, those with children meant to leave them with the party and train to go and fight. But because of the ages and needs of the children and because we are very few to look after the children we have said to those mothers, please, look after the children with us. We have got a lot of programmes for them — knitting, sewing, and some of them are political commissars who continue to educate themselves about the political situation at home. These women are doing fantastic work, many of them have been officials of provinces, branches and districts. So with that we find it very easy to educate each other politically. A few women have trained to go and fight; but they don't train in the refugee camps or even in Zambia. So we are fighting side by side with our men, we are not left behind. While our men are holding guns and deployed outside to fight, women are fighting in another wing of the struggle, because they try to help themselves through self-help schemes. They have trained themselves, they are prepared for a new Zimbabwe. The spirit of unity is so much that it includes thousands, not hundreds and each person feels she belongs to the other person, being women who come from all over Zimbabwe. They are people from Zimbabwe all together. They have made friends, they have come together, they have learned languages together. We have two main languages in Zimbabwe, Shona and Nedebele — and both are spoken very well in the camps without any ill feelings. If you ask a woman, 'How do you feel that this one speaks Shona and this Ndebele?' she will say 'I don't feel anything, she is a child of Zimbabwe'. In the camps we find a spirit of oneness, a spirit of preparedness. We find the women in the camps being very useful indeed for our Zimbabwe, and they are much stronger in their political understanding — I don't want to say that the women at home do not understand but they have not come through the suffering that some of these women have experienced.

7. Women in Namibia: The Only Way to Free Ourselves . . .
Ellen Musialela

Ellen Musialela first became involved in Namibia's liberation struggle in 1964 when she was 14 years old. She later spent seven

years as a nurse in the military wing of the liberation movement,
until the effects of a snake bite obliged her to give up work.
Since then she has been working in the political field and she is now
Assistant Secretary for Finance of the SWAPO (South West
African People's Organization) Women's Council. The Council,
which was created in 1970, describes its aims and objectives as
follows:

'The aims and objectives of the SWC shall essentially be those
enshrined in Article III of the Constitution of SWAPO. However,
the SWC shall, in addition, strive: 1) To achieve equality for
women as well as their full participation in the struggle for national
and social liberation; 2) To develop and deepen political conscious -
ness and revolutionary militancy among Namibian women; 3) To
bring about women's full participation in productive work in
public administration, in education and in the cultural creativity
of our society; 4) To prepare the thousands of female workers,
now engaged in domestic work in Namibia, for productive jobs;
5) To campaign for the creation of sufficient nursery schools and
day boarding schools in a liberated Namibia so as to facilitate
women's full participation in productive work; 6) To inculcate in
the Namibian child a sense of justice and a revolutionary respect
for women; and 7) To develop an internationalist spirit in the
Namibian woman by enabling her to work in solidarity with all
militant and progressive feminine movements, thereby strengthening the world-wide anti-imperialist and anti-colonialist front.'

This interview was given in London to the Women's Committee
of the Anti-Apartheid Movement and is reproduced here from
Anti-Apartheid News (March 1981).

AAN: What particular problems do women face in exile, in the
refugee camps and in the armed struggle?

EM: I think I should start from the very beginning, to say that it
has been proved that no revolution will triumph without the
participation of women. The SWAPO Women's Council was created
in 1969 at a Congress held in Tanzania, to enable women to participate fully in SWAPO and in the armed struggle. At that time there
were very few women who were active. Up to 1974 when our
women started to come forward in their thousands, we were still
faced with a lot of problems. Inside Namibia itself it is very hard
to communicate as women. The apartheid system that we live
under does not allow women to move freely. You have to have an
explanation to move from region to region. We are the people who
are left in the villages, and you know that the work of the woman
in Namibia is just to look after children, to bear them and to bring
them up. Women also have to look after animals in the villages,

while our men are taken away for long months — 18 months at a time — for the rest of their lives.

So when women came out into exile, we were like a body without a leader. In 1979, SWAPO decided that, as we felt we had organized ourselves, it was time to call a Congress. The SWAPO Women's Council had its first Congress from 20-26 January 1980. We elected a Secretary, who has two assistants, and a deputy — Gertrude Kandanga, who is inside the country. She was arrested when she was trying to leave Namibia. Immediately after the Congress, we felt it was our duty to continue to mobilize. We have to make our women understand the need to participate fully in the armed struggle — not by saying that we should go to work in the kitchen, or carrying guns for our men, but participating to such a degree that today there are Namibian women commanders. Some women have sacrificed their lives on the battlefield; some are very good at communications, reconnaissance and in the medical field. Of course, you also find that women in the camps are taking a very active role in our kindergartens, in our medical centres, as nurses, as teachers, and in productive work.

Our women, in the battlefield especially, are faced with a lot of problems when it comes to sanitary towels. It's the number one problem. Also things like panties and bras, the things that women can't do without. It's very important that women from the outside world sympathize. I saw with my own eyes when I went to the battlefield in May, how women were forced to use grass during their periods, and had to go without panties. We also need warm clothing, shoes and blankets. On the same visit I saw small children sleeping in the open without warm clothing. Nevertheless their spirit remains high. With the assistance of our friends in the outside world, the Namibian struggle will continue.

Because women have chosen to fight side by side with men on all three fronts of the struggle — diplomatic, military and political — you find that they are accorded great respect by men. It's obvious that men, especially in [the context of] African traditions, have customs which hinder the progress of women and look upon them as weak. But today you find that our men in the camps don't look at women just as women, to be separated out to do the cooking. But work is divided up among groups irrespective of sex, whether it's gardening, cooking or any of the work of the camps. If you look at the leadership of SWAPO today, you find that both men and women are coming up to be members of the Central Committee, the Executive Committee. Women are starting to appear at the international level, in campaigning for SWAPO. Inside the country also, women are playing an active role; women like Ida Jimmy, Gertrude Kandanga and Rauna Nambinga. Women are harassed because of the role they have taken as mothers, to hide our

IDAF

combatants, giving them shelter and food. We feel proud that despite the traditional barriers between men and women, women have started to understand that we have to fight together to fight the system, because we are oppressed as women, and we are oppressed as blacks — both men and women.

AAN: How has the political consciousness of women changed as a result of their participation in the struggle?

EM: When women first started to come out, in the early 1970s, you would rarely see a woman expressing herself. Inside Namibia, the enemy has made a point of depicting women as less than nothing, just something to be pushed into the kitchen and stay there. This has made our women think that, even if they are talented, they shouldn't show their talent. But when women started to come out, when we started to mobilize them, to prepare them to participate in any front they are called to, you find their consciousness has deepened. They don't feel that to take arms to go and fight, to die, is just a waste of time. They feel proud. When I visited the battlefield in May, I saw them sleeping in the open, in the cold, sometimes they didn't have enough food. I asked them, 'Comrades, why did you come here? Why did you leave Namibia?' They said, 'We wanted to be trained, to go back and fight, because that's the only salvation, the only way to free ourselves.'

So you can see that their consciousness is very high. Their consciousness has been alerted to watch out for the enemy. In reconnaissance, you find that our women are very active. They are the people in the forefront, bringing in information to our base commanders.

AAN: What kind of solidarity can women in other countries give to women in Namibia?

EM: It's very important for women in other countries to stand with us as women. As mothers, we should understand that it's our children, whom we carry for nine months, who suffer and die. It's important that women help us by writing petitions to the South African Embassy and to their own government. We want our political prisoners released, especially Ida Jimmy, Gertrude Kandanga and Rauna Nambinga, and many others whose names we don't know. It's important for women to protest, as women, that these kind of barbaric acts, by which South Africa harasses women, should stop.

It's important that women here in the West should support women from the liberation movements in South Africa and Namibia. We tell them our problems, because we are the people who feel the pinch, who have been affected by apartheid.

When we went to the United Nations Women's Conference in Copenhagen (1980), we were very disappointed by the women from the West. I don't mean the solidarity committees, although it's up to them to put pressure on women to understand that it's we who feel the pinch. These women from Britain, West Germany and America were trying to force us to restrict ourselves to equality, development and peace, on the grounds that if we went outside these topics we would be trying to bring in politics. But we can't see how we can otherwise talk about equality, because in Namibia both women and men are oppressed as people: we don't vote; we don't control our natural resources; we don't have any say. This is very well known. We can't talk about development because we have been pushed out of our land — we don't have any land to develop. Even if you are inside the country you are pushed into the bantustans. We can't talk of peace because our country is at war. All these things have to be understood, so that women in the West appreciate the importance of solidarity with the women in the liberation movements and in the struggle.

AAN: Can you say something more about the conditions of women in detention?

EM: I'll start with Gertrude Kandanga, the Deputy Secretary of the SWAPO Women's Council, whom we elected at the Congress in her absence. She was arrested when she was trying to come out to the Congress. Since then we have been trying to find out where she is in Namibia, but we have very little news. What we do know is that conditions for prisoners in Namibia are very bad, whether for men or for women, we go under the same conditions. People should understand that in detention in a South African prison, you don't sleep — the light is on for the whole 24 hours, and they disturb you. This has resulted in many of our people coming out of jail in a disturbed and confused state. The conditions under which people are living in jail, whether women or men, I'm sure they have last been seen in Nazi Germany. It's up to women here to protest for their release. We ourselves cannot get information from the South Africans; there are many prisoners who have disappeared.

AAN: Can you comment on the dangers that women face of being raped by the security forces?

EM: In Namibia today the situation is very bad. I'm not trying to exaggerate, but our country has been placed under martial law. You find the South African Police patrolling in the streets, and their work is to shoot on the spot, rape, and commit genocide, by burning villages, and destroying food. This has resulted in many of our women leaving their villages and crossing into Angola for shelter. Our women are raped, whipped in public, tortured almost to death — some of them have been killed during torture, some of them have been thrown into jail without trial. Even those women who have left Namibia in the mass exodus with their children are still followed by South Africa, bombed and killed. South Africa announces they have killed SWAPO freedom fighters when in reality they have killed innocent people who are not armed, people who are running away from their own country.

AAN: What kind of health and welfare services exist in Namibia under the apartheid system, particularly as they affect women — childcare facilities, maternity facilities, nurseries and so on?

EM: I think Namibia is the worst country I have seen. The South African government has completely ignored the health of the people. That's why the people of Namibia have taken up arms, because of the way we have been treated. If you go to Namibia today, you will find that there are still people who don't know what a hospital is, what a doctor is. This has resulted in many deaths of children before they reach the age of five. From the time that the child is in the mother's stomach, the mother won't receive any care, won't go to an ante-natal clinic for examination, up to the time that the child is born in the village. Maybe she'll be lucky and the child will be born in a hospital, but the facilities are so bad that you find that in the so-called maternity hospitals, women still sleep on the floor, they are given dirty blankets, the children are not provided with enough clothes.

When it comes to the welfare of the people, that has been

forgotten about. Centres for the disabled, clinics for the under-
fives — these things don't exist in Namibia. Malnutrition, measles,
whooping cough — all these diseases of children just continue.
Nurseries — I have never seen a nursery in Namibia.

When it comes to contraceptives, these are not known. This has
resulted in many deaths. A woman will have as many children as
she can, because she doesn't have any means of spacing them.
There's no place where our women can go to be advised on spacing
their children. In Namibia children are very much needed, because
we are underpopulated. But it's useless, because each year you will
find a woman will have children, and they won't grow because
they die of malnutrition, they die from all kinds of diseases.

It's only now that South Africa is trying to deceive the world.
I'm trying to point out to Western women, especially feminist
groups, that I think they have a role to play. Because the West is
dumping medicines in the Third World, including Namibia. Women
who decide that it is better to space their children go to a doctor
for advice. Those women will be stopped from giving birth — these
days they are using Depo Provera on them, without telling them
the truth about what they are doing. It's a form of genocide; the
South African government has that dream, of making sure that the
black population remains low. They are using Depo Provera both
in South Africa and in Namibia. Women here should look into this,
and fight against the companies that send these medicines to
Southern Africa and sterilize our women.

8. Women's Lives in El Salvador
Miriam Galdemez

This article was first published in the British feminist magazine
Spare Rib (No. 06, May 1981), with the following introduction:

Introduction

Vividly expressive, humorous and passionately committed to the
struggle of her people, Miriam Galdemez is a tiny, vital woman
whose roots lie deep in the El Salvadorean countryside. Today

she is working in Europe representing the Revolutionary Democratic Front (FDR), the major opposition force which has widespread
support in El Salvador.

Miriam recently made a brief visit to England for International
Women's Day. Jenny Vaughan and Jane MacIntosh met her and, as
she talked, the day-to-day lives of El Salvadorean women and their
double struggle against the elite who control El Salvador and against
the *machismo* of many of the El Salvadorean men, came alive.

'For women in the countryside the day starts very, very early.
Even before the sun has risen they get up from their rough bundle
of a mattress and, trying not to wake their husbands or step on
their children, go outside their little shack and start grinding up
maize into flour for *tortillas*. These are the little pancakes that
everybody eats for breakfast, lunch and dinner. You get really sick
of *tortillas* I can tell you! Grinding the maize is really hard work,
because it's still done by hand, and it gives you muscles like rock.

By the time she's finished the children and her husband will be
up. If the children are old enough she'll send them off to get some
water, but if not she has to go herself. Water is one of our biggest
problems, because only about 30% of people in the countryside
have access to safe drinking water, so they're always getting sick.
Diseases from bad drinking water are one of the biggest killers in
El Salvador.

Once she's got the water the family breakfast on *tortillas* and
coffee, then, if its harvest time, everybody goes off to work on
the big plantations picking the crops. Children usually start work
at about 10 or 11 years of age, but often they start even earlier,
because harvesting means money and every family needs as much
as it can get.

If there's no work on the plantation, and often there isn't,
because they only need people for a few months of the year, there's
still plenty of work for her to do! She looks after the animals; goes
down to the river to wash the clothes; collects firewood for
cooking; looks after the family's few crops; cooks the dinner;
maybe she weaves to make cloth or sews clothes, things like that.
Sometimes she'll go and see friends and chat or if a woman is
giving birth she'll go and help with the labour, sometimes . . .'

Miriam smiled, but her eyes clouded with pain. 'Sometimes
women have to give birth on their own. I remember once, when I
was still quite young, I was walking along the river bank, when I
saw a woman cutting her umbilical cord herself. She'd given birth
then and there! Just as she finished her kids came tumbling back.
Well, I went home with her and, do you know, she cooked the
dinner and sent the kids off to play before she lay down!

Sounds incredible doesn't it! But you see, El Salvador's got hardly any hospitals or doctors and most of them are in the capital and cost a fortune. There was a census in 1971 which said that there were three doctors and 17 hospital beds for every 10,000 people. You can imagine how many women die in childbirth and how high the infant mortality rate is as a result. Women have an average of six to eight children but often have twice as many pregnancies.

But that's not all you know. The women we've been talking about are what we call *minifundistas*. That means they live with their family on a little piece of land called a *minifundio*, which is what the peasants got left with when the big landowners took over all the best land for their plantations. That was a really terrible period in our history. But many women don't even have a *minifundio* to live on and so they lack even the security of a home and family around them. They have to make their living as migrant labourers.

I think this is the hardest life of all: when she has to travel, caring for her children all the while, from the cotton harvest down on the coast to the coffee harvest up near the volcanoes of the central plateau. It's a terrible life and it's getting worse because there's less and less work available as agriculture gets more mechanized with so-called development. I think this is one of the reasons why women are getting more politicized and joining one of the popular organizations or the guerrillas.' Miriam's words reminded us of the many women in different countries in Latin America who migrate from the countryside to the city to become domestic servants or *empleadas* for well-off families. We asked Miriam whether this happened in El Salvador as well.

'Definitely! Peasant women have always done this because there's so little work in the countryside. Even more are migrating now because the repression in the countryside is horrific. Some find work as *empleadas* and, unless they're very lucky, end up exploited as workers and as women. Its just expected that an *empleada* will service her boss and the sons of the family sexually as well. If she refuses she loses her job. Its the same for many nurses and secretaries, they are forced to give into the sexual capriciousness of their bosses or the directors of the hospital to keep their jobs.

There's another area where women who come to the city try to find work and that's in the free trade zone areas that have been set up. These were supposed to help us develop, but the only thing that develops are the profits of the firms because they don't have to pay taxes and trade unions are illegal. We found out that some 70 % of the firms in these areas are North American owned — another reason for the USA's concern. Women work in the pharmaceutical and textile factories — making things like Maidenform bras!

91

But there are still many women who can't find any sort of work — especially if they're illiterate, which lots of women are. But they've still got to eat and so they fall easily into prostitution and all its evils: beatings, illness, endemic syphilis. But what can they do? They can't go back to the countryside because of the situation there. They're stuck.

Government soldier failing to impress an onlooker

The social structure in El Salvador is inhuman. It's important to say this because, yes, *machismo* is a real problem, but nothing's ever going to change until we have the basic necessities of life: economic security, housing, health and education. At the moment most people don't have either. And we're never going to get them until we change the whole power structure in El Salvador. We must join with our men who suffer too, as well as fight for our specific rights. That's why we set up the Association of El Salvadorean Women (AMES) on International Women's Day last year — to make sure women could do both these things.'

We asked Miriam to explain more about the social structure in
El Salvador, for as well as telling us more about women's lives
these were facts that had been missing from our TV screens and
daily newspapers.

'The El Salvadorean elite — the oligarchy — is tiny. Its just 2%
of the population but these 60 or so families own 60% of the land
— and it's the best land. The land where all the cotton, coffee and
sugar cane is grown for export. It goes mainly to the USA and
West Germany. Of course the oligarchy keeps the profit, or, to be
precise, they share a profit with the firms who buy their crops —
another reason for US interest! Well, they have no intention of
giving up anything, land, power or privilege.

It's always had the military in its pockets and its own para-
military forces like ORDEN, who have terrorized the peasants for
years — nothing's changed, things have just got worse. We've tried
every democratic means of change. Some people thought it might
work as late as last year when they backed the present government
of Napoleon Duarte which tried to implement a very small land
reform. Really this was just a strategy to try and buy off the
peasants and justify the repression of the Left which was thought
up by the US State Department.

But when they tried to take the land from the oligarchy — well,
that was when El Salvador blew up! The military and the paramili-
tary went on the rampage. Peasants were murdered; whole villages
were destroyed; workers suspected of being Left-wingers were
knocked off. The Roman Catholic Church has estimated that over
13,000 people died in the year that followed. As for the government — well, lots of people left and joined the FDR. Duarte stayed,
but now he's just a puppet of the military. The land reform has be
been abandoned.'

But what, we asked Miriam, about American intervention?
Wasn't she frightened of it? 'Of direct military intervention? Yes
I dread it. It will be a bloodbath and the people who suffer will
be the poor, the dispossessed. All this stuff about Russian and
Cuban intervention is a lie; an insult. We are fighting to bring an
end to the day-to-day suffering of the people, not because any
outside force is telling us what to do. Look at the lives of the
women I've told you about — wouldn't they make you want to
fight?

Nobody has seen any Russian sub-machine guns or tanks in El
Salvador, but they've seen plenty of US ones. Tons of military
arms that are being used to kill the people. Green Beret para-
troopers who are already inside the country. We are also fighting
US imperialism which has dominated our country and has backed
the oligarchy because the oligarchy does its dirty work. What
people don't know is that the US has been intervening in El

Salvador for years: training army officers in techniques of counter-insurgency; spying; imposing programmes of population control and sterilizing women without their consent; dumping dangerous drugs which kill us. Many things. Had it not been for the US my people would have been at the door of their liberation many years before now.

We were all silent when Miriam finished speaking, a shared anger stopping our words. After a time we began to speak again, as Miriam told us about the participation of women in the war: 'The late 1960s and the 1970s saw the growing participation of women in the guerrilla armies and in the popular organizations. They have always been closely linked to the guerrilla forces, but they based their work in trade union struggles; struggles for housing and water — popular struggles that really related to people's day-to-day needs. Women have taken to the streets in protest at the repression: organized strikes for improved living and working conditions; produced an enormous amount of political propaganda. Their courage is immense, because in El Salvador today these activities are answered with a bullet.

Women have joined the guerrilla armies too, but not in such great numbers. Many women still believe that the armed struggle is a matter for men and there are still many men who cannot accept a woman fighting alongside them. There's a long way to go before women pick up a machine-gun as easily as a casserole! But things are changing. Many of the women in the guerrillas — often at top level — are fighting through discussion and general assemblies to incorporate more and more women into the army. In one of the liberated zones the people in charge of civil engineering, campaign hospitals and weapon production are women.

Women have suffered terribly too, through repression. Now it's common practice to stab pregnant women in the stomach to make sure they are not carrying arms.'

In this sort of situation we wondered what the role of the Association of El Salvadorean Women (AMES) was. Miriam explained that: 'AMES was set up for two reasons: one, to provide an organization through which women such as housewives, nurses and secretaries could participate in the liberation struggle; and two, to provide all women with an organization which would fight for the specific rights of women: for the right to maternity and an end to forced sterilization; to safe family planning; to free child-care; to education and training.

We believe that our liberation from a *machista* society won't come until we achieve our national liberation, for it is an integral part of this, not separate. But we believe that women's liberation — establishing her own rights, carrying out her aspirations — is going to be done much quicker than in other countries such as

Network

This woman carries a white flag for safety while she goes shopping.

Cuba. Cuba has begun to look, a little late, at the specific situation of women. Nicaragua is going more quickly and we think we will go pretty fast too.'

Finally we asked Miriam what women in Britain could do to support the women of El Salvador: 'Women must get their organizations to condemn US intervention in El Salvador and to demand recognition of the FDR. What I'd also like is for women to donate the price of a packet of tampons or sanitary towels to the Solidarity Campaign here which can be used to buy protection for the women in the guerrilla armies for often they have to fight using nothing. Both these things would help us tremendously.'

Part III:
The Experience of
Armed Struggle

Asian Women and Political Repression

Freedom has changed the face of the world
It rules the mind, the heart and the person
It dispels the mist hanging over the mountains
the valleys, the shores, the fields, the factories
and the cities, and the heads of us, women.

Now we are no longer
just giving birth to worker soldiers.
We too are worker soldiers.
No longer just wives of people's heroes
We too are people's heroes,
And when the fortresses of obsolete time are smashed
And workers' power stands proudly in our land
We shall no longer only tend the graves
read the prayers and weep for the dead,
We shall be a part of the foremost ranks.
Sugiarti Siswaldi

Published in *Quest*, a feminist quarterly, (Washington D.C.)
vol IV, No 2 Winter 1978.

9. Four Years of Armed Struggle in Zimbabwe
Nyasha and Rose

The following two interviews have never been published before. They were obtained in Zimbabwe in February 1980 by Margaret Ling of the International Defence and Aid Fund for Southern Africa (IDAF). The interviews were arranged by Julia Zvobgo, former representative of ZANU (PF) and now an MP in Salisbury's House of Assembly. We are grateful to the Research and Information Department of the IDAF for permission to reproduce their material.

Nyasha

Nyasha was 17 years old when she decided to cross the border into Mozambique to join the freedom fighters. The year was 1975, and she was a secondary student at a mission school near Umtali.

'The thing that really pushed me to join the armed struggle was the rule that said black girls were not allowed to be air hostesses, or bank accountants, or to be trained for public administration. When I was very young I made up my mind that I wanted to be an air hostess. When I was in Form IV I applied to be an air hostess and they said there was no room for blacks. It really puzzled me. I went home and started thinking about it. I had a friend with similar problems. She wanted to go for nursing but blacks didn't qualify unless they had a super first grade. It was easy for white girls to go for nursing or even for a degree. Then I heard it said that if the armed struggle was successful we would have the same education as the whites. So I really couldn't wait a moment to complete that Form IV and join the armed struggle.'

The Journey
'The final thing that moved me to go to Mozambique was the curfew. Blacks were not allowed to go out after 6 o'clock. I knew by rights I was a Zimbabwean yet I hadn't the pleasure of moving in the country as an indigenous person. After the curfew was set

99

up our teachers were moved too and started politicizing us — they told us what happened in 1964 and 1968, what happened when the whites came into our country. These were black teachers, but there were white teachers too — missionaries — who knew that these things were wrong. They told us that our education system and the white education system were different. And really I knew that I had to do something about this.

And just imagine how this spread in a school of over 1,000 students. It started with the head boy and a few boys, they were advised to go to Mozambique where they could have a really political course and be trained as guerrillas, to defeat not the whites, but the system. After they left no one could trace them and I thought there was a chance I could go too without any trace. So I and 10 friends organized our journey. We had a map and we knew where Mozambique was and we knew where Villa Pery was, the town we were going to go to. After we had made our arrangements we found 30 other girls who had also made their arrangements.

In our lessons that day our teachers knew we were interested and called us and said we could go to Mozambique at any minute. They said "We are not forcing you to go but if you really want to fight for the country, let's go". So with our geography master and 65 students we planned our journey. We couldn't move during the day, because of the curfew, so we started at 7 pm. As soon as we left the school some other students discovered that we were out and followed us. In the end about 200-odd students left from that one school.

We started walking. It was over 100 kilometres from our school to Mozambique, via the Cashel Valley. We wanted to go to Mozambique because we knew that it was now an independent country under Comrade Samora Machel and that he was prepared to help us. We knew that as soon as we got into Mozambique we were going to get support and shelter and everything. So we started out on our journey.

The only problem we met was that some of the students fainted because they were not used to walking such long distances. They had to remain behind on the way, and I understand that they were taken by the police, interviewed and put into prison, some for three years, for trying to go to Mozambique.'

Training
'When we got to Mozambique we were received fairly well, despite the fact that the Frelimo government at that time wasn't very well established. We were taken to a camp, where we stayed for two months without seeing our Zimbabwean comrades who were fighting in the bush. We started our training as soon as we got to the camp. It was very hard and difficult because we had no shoes

and we were expected to run for kilometres to keep our bodies
fit for the coming years we were going to face in the bush. The
food was very little. We ate maize boiled with salt and we were
given just a cup for the whole day yet we were expected to do
military training. Anyway, we had very good political lessons. I
will never depart from ZANU (PF) because the orientation I was
given was so moving. So under these circumstances we did what we
were required to do and we always had such high morale. That's
one thing I can't understand even now, the conditions were tough,
but still we had such high morale. We were taught the basic things,
so we could hurry to the bush. There was a great need for
soldiers at that time.'

On the Front Line
'Life in the bush was very difficult, especially during the first few
days, your first experience. You would carry a single blanket,
and some 10 to 12 tins of beef, some dried vegetables, dried meat,
a bottle of water, some pants, some bras, cotton wool or pads and
an extra pair of shoes, an extra pair of trousers, a jacket, a cap and
a hat. Apart from that you had to carry war materials. You had
to carry your own gun, either a rifle or sub-machine gun. If you
were given a mortar you would have to share it because you
couldn't carry the whole thing alone. So it was quite a heavy load
for one person.

We didn't have transport to take us from the border to the front,
so we travelled the whole journey by foot. It was very difficult. I
remember at one time we had to travel about 130 kilometres to
the next new base which had been established at Nyadiri Mission.
We did the journey in four days. We were very lucky because at
one stage one of our supporters gave us a lift.

The masses at Nyadiri were very afraid because that was the first
time our comrades had been in the area, and the security forces
had been there. It was April 1976 and I was 18 years old.

We established a base and then returned to the border. On our
way back several girls fainted because by then we had no food.
When we reached the border we were armed again with war
materials and sent back into Zimbabwe, this time right up to
Mount Darwin. People in Mount Darwin had experienced war since
1972 or so, so they really knew what we wanted them to do. We
had two serious contacts with the security forces. Somehow
information had leaked out that our group contained female
comrades, and so they really harrassed us. We were 9 girls and
14 boys.

During the second attack we lost two of our male comrades when
the security forces dropped a bomb — what we call carpet-
bombing. Our comrades were hit by fragments and passed away.

IDAF

We buried them there, and we left the place.

As time went on we spent longer periods inside Zimbabwe. In May 1976 I was transferred to Manica province, and went to Zimunya township, Umtali. I knew the place, and it was easier for me to make contact with families, relatives and fellow-people from the village. They came to see and talk to us in our camps, gave us food and everything. By then I was a section political commissar.

We enjoyed staying in Zimbabwe more than in Mozambique. In Mozambique we were attacked, there were diseases, and this and that. But when the security forces heard that there were comrades in an area inside Zimbabwe, they seldom attacked. We were safer and happier here than in Mozambique, and to me and to most of the other comrades it seemed that to be at home at the front was best.'

Chimoi
'I was a guerilla until June 1976. That's when I was taken to the rear for a six month political course at Chimoi in Mozambique. We studied dialectical materialism, historical materialism, logic, space and time. Political students are the vanguard of our revolution, so we knew that it was very important to have our political lessons.

Later I did research in the Department of Education and Culture, from where scholarships were obtained for some of us to go to Tanzania. I studied in Dar es Salaam for a further six months, learning techniques of textbook writing and how to deal with children, studying research work in education, adult education and the like. From there I came back to Mozambique before Chimoi was attacked. I witnessed the Chimoi attack. That was the hardest time of the whole revolution. I had never seen so many dead people in my life. I fell in a pit and I couldn't come out for three days, while the attack lasted for two days. It was a very big camp, four square miles or more I think, The Rhodesians bombed the whole camp and captured some comrades. They took war materials, they poisoned our food, they killed our cattle, our goats, our chickens. The largest number of people who died were school children because they were too young to have arms, and had to be defended. And in a war like that where you could see more than 100 planes at one time it was hard to use anti-aircraft machine guns. Their planes were so fast. It's fantastic that we managed to shoot down eight planes in that attack, because we had very simple weapons — sub-machine guns, rifles and anti-aircraft weapons. We lost some of our central committee members, and our general staff members and our military commanders. I would say there were 800 comrades who died at that place. We had our medical centre there and most of the patients died because there was no attention.

After the attack we moved to a base 30 kilometres from Chimoi. Four months later the place was bombed so we moved to Pungwe. After only two weeks that too was bombed so we moved again to a place now called Mavudzi. There we had security. From that time to this there haven't been any attacks on Mavudzi, although they have made several attacks on our operational camps in the border area.'

Women comrades
'During 1979 I went back to the bush in Manica province. By now conditions were a little bit better. We could use cars and buses, and comrades were spread all over the country. We had quite a large liberated area on the Mozambique border where we could stay for months without even hearing a helicopter, doing nice projects and programmes.

There is one thing I want to say: we women were never given anything different from the men. If a man is carrying a gun and his equipment, his female comrades must do the same. There isn't a division, although sometimes we would be given small privileges. If we were very tired they might give us a better place to sleep, or if the conditions were really tough, for instance if it was raining. Sometimes when we were guarding the camps the men would give us first preference to guard early and they would guard later. But usually we would go together.

We weren't able to wash often, so that when we were menstruating things were difficult. We wore jeans or those heavy uniforms, and just imagine, with your periods it's not comfortable. Anyway, things come and go, we still had to proceed, so we had to manage. With time you get used to the whole thing.

Usually it was the men who did the cooking, because the food was cooked in very big drums. The girls did the washing and other lighter things. Some people had very bad health despite the fact that they had managed to cross the border, and such comrades would be given lighter jobs to do. But all the female comrades who were physically fit would have the same treatment as the boys. We would build homes together. Girls were able to construct the roof of a building nicely. They would say they wanted us to build a barrack, and the commander would tell us that he wanted it up in three days, and we could do that. We would go into the bush with our axes, cut our trees, cut our grass, come and dig our holes and construct our barracks. At times we were mixed so that the girls and men worked together, at times we were separated.

Love and Marriage
'Some comrades were married in the bush. But it was very hard to stay with your husband because of the division of labour. Say you were in the education department and he was in the military department, you couldn't stay together. You just had to separate, until perhaps, on a good day, you could meet.

If you wanted to get married you had to do it properly. You would go to the political commissar and say you would like to get married. He would take your details, your name, home, parents and so forth. Because your parents would like to know how you got married, that was very important. Then they would ask you whether you were sure you wanted to get married. They would give you time to consider and then, two weeks or so after your requisition, they would come and say 'O.K., we've approved of your wedding, you can get married'.

Having babies in the bush was practically impossible, though some comrades did. If you were working in the office in Maputo or were in Chimoi or overseas, there would be a house, beds, this and that. If you were stationed in Maputo and were having a baby that was just by chance, you couldn't go to Maputo for that purpose. If you were in the bush you had to stay there and do your work. If you had a baby in the bush you had to go to a town or elsewhere for about three-and-a-half months. Our support groups would provide us with baby clothes and everything. After

that you had to leave your baby at a nursery school and go back
to the bush. If the mother had complications or a caesarian section,
she would be given a lighter job. She could work in the security
departments or manpower and planning, education, social welfare
or transport. Those departments operate in the rear, not at the
front.

At first women didn't like leaving their babies in the nurseries
but as time went on they saw that the facilities were good. There
were beds, cots, blankets, toys, enough meals — porridge, fruit
and everything. The kids were healthy and the mothers were pleased
to leave them there. The supervision was good and the comrades
were very patient with the children. So after three-and-a-half
months you would leave your child there and go back to your job.
If the child is a girl we like them to mingle with boys as much as
possible, so that a child doesn't grow up with the mentality that
she's a girl.

We had access to contraceptives in the bush. People brought them
back from overseas and I'm glad because really I wouldn't like to
have had a baby in the bush. We have adopted what we want from
Western culture into our revolution and we are aware of the fact
that people have sexual feelings in spite of the dangers of the
struggle. It was possible for us to get abortions especially from
doctors who came from Europe. We had to face the reality of the
conditions we were in.

Our attitudes to contraception and abortion changed during the
years of the struggle. The girls have really adopted a new way of
living after what they've seen in the bush, from the contacts
they've had with other people from European countries, from the
books they've read and from the kind of orientation they've
received. They are quite different from the people who have
stayed in Zimbabwe. If a person doesn't want a baby or if you
can't manage to keep a baby you should not stop someone having
an abortion just because it is not part of our culture.

Some of the male comrades did not like contraceptives because
they thought it was murder, but really it was our duty and we
female comrades were ready to defend it. We told them how
necessary it was to use contraceptives, and that to be sent back to
Mozambique for five months to have a baby was a setback to the
war.

We still have to convince our masses, our mothers and fathers
about this sort of thing. We have been doing this for the last five
years of the struggle. I really have to convince my mother that even
if it is a European thing I should still use it to protect myself. A
lot of the mothers are now educated and they accept this. My grand-
mother wouldn't accept it but my mother and her generation will
accept it, I think.

The Future

'Physically I'm not very strong, I've had ulcers and this and that, but I feel I want to be an engineer, because I'm good at science and I'm interested in it, and I would like to develop my talents. I would have to get a B.Sc. and then I would go in for chemical engineering. That's my field.

The position of women has really changed through the armed struggle because now we have equal positions and equal education with men. If a man is dull, a man is dull. If a girl is intelligent, she is intelligent. Each one according to his ability and contribution, that's how we are treated.

I think this a great march forward because now I don't have to go for nursing only or teaching or accounting or typing. I've got a wide choice, I can go for engineering if I'm fit and strong. It's not seen as a male job. I can be a bus driver if I want, I can be a pilot if I want. Now I can be anything I want.'

Rose, A Chimbwido

By the end of the war, the term *mujibha* had become quite a familiar one to supporters and observers of the Zimbabwe liberation struggle. The *mujibhas* were teenage boys and children who acted as 'eyes and ears' for the freedom fighters in the operational areas. They passed on information about the movements of the regime's security forces, carried messages and served as guides.

The *mujibhas*, however, had their female equivalent — the *chimbwidos*. The *chimbwidos*, most of them girls in their teens, played an equally vital role as a support network for the guerrilla forces. Those working in the towns used their earnings to buy provisions for the fighters. They prepared food late at night and carried it out into the bush to escape detection by the police and army. They did laundry and obtained supplies.

Rose, who came from the Charter district, west of Umtali, had wanted to go to Mozambique. Family circumstances didn't permit this. Instead, she had worked for three years with guerrilla forces operating in her home area, from 1977 to 1979.

'I joined ZANU before my Dad died in 1972. At that time I was in Form III. In my family there were four girls and two boys. I wanted to go to Mozambique because I enjoyed seeing the comrades and going to their meetings. I had some friends who had gone to Mozambique. And the situation in this country was too hard. I tried my level best to get to Mozambique but I couldn't find anyone to give me advice about how to get there. I was still young, I didn't know anything. And I couldn't leave my Mum alone to join my sisters and brothers in the bush. So I stayed at home and finished my schooling.'

What Did You Do in the War?
'I was one of the *chimbwidos*. We were helping our brothers and
sisters — cooking for them, giving them clothing, doing the washing
and everything. We used to do those things in such a way that the
authorities didn't find out. We used to go in the evenings, at
about eight o'clock, to the comrades' bases and to their meetings.
We would collect their dirty clothes and do the washing and the
ironing. And the next day they would come and collect their
things. We were doing a job for them.'

How Did You Manage to Avoid Being Caught?
'With the clothing you couldn't tell that these were the clothes of
comrades because they wore the same clothes as other people.
And with food, we used big tins to put the *sadza* and meat in,
covered them and carried them to the bases. We would tell the police
or the security forces that we were going to the fields, because our
fields were far away. There were few soldiers in that area, it was a
liberated area.

   We got the food from Salisbury. The money to pay for it was
ours. I wasn't in a job but my mother was working so I would tell
her what the comrades needed. They would write a note listing
what they wanted — cigarettes and matches, beer, food and other
things like clothing and blankets. So it was easy for us.'

*Did Most Families in your Home District Support the Comrades
in this Way?*
'Yes, everybody. Everybody supported them, because the
soldiers were harassing people. The comrades would warn us not
to use this road or that road because of landmines, don't walk
around in the evenings because we will be moving around and we
might shoot you if we think you are a soldier or an auxilliary. We
were told to come to the comrades' bases. In the morning we used
to go with tea for breakfast, by one o'clock they would need
something for lunch, and dinner around seven. It was nice in the
liberated areas. I and other people liked it.'

10. Women and Revolution in Eritrea
National Union of Eritrean Women

This is an extract from the booklet *Women and Revolution in
Eritrea* which was published in June 1980 by the National Union
of Eritrean Women (NUEW). The Eritrean people's struggle for
independence from Ethiopia has been going on for over 20 years,
headed since 1970 by the Eritrean People's Liberation Front
(EPLF). The NUEW describe their role as follows:
'The National Union of Eritrean Women which held its founding
Congress in the liberated areas of Eritrea in November 1979, is one
of the mass organizations of the EPLF. The founding Congress
centralized at the national level the various democratic women's
associations in Eritrea and abroad which had been militating for
some years under the vanguard of the EPLF. The successful conclusion of the Congress last November represented a significant
step in the development of Eritrean women's struggles and consistent efforts by the EPLF to raise the political consciousness and
organizational ability of women. The formation of the NUEW will
undoubtedly accelerate the development of the Women's Movement
and their active participation in the ongoing national struggle
against colonial oppression and feudal exploitation. The NUEW
(based in Rome) centralizes at the national level regional unions in
Eritrea, Ethiopia, the Middle East, Europe and North America.'

Women are Double-Exploited

Eritrean women constitute half of the population, and hence an
indispensable component of the workforce both in rural and urban
Eritrea, and they suffer the same class exploitation and oppression
as men, as members of the toiling masses under colonialism and
feudalism. Moreover, Eritrean women suffer additional exploitation
and oppression by virtue of their sex.
   In rural Eritrea, where agriculture or nomadism are the main
means of livelihood, women are generally excluded from any
direct ownersip of land or other property. This is despite the fact

that women play an important role in social production. For while men till the land and thresh grain, women weed the farm and participate in harvesting and all the other tiring chores are left to them. Indeed, a typical day in the life of peasant women in highland Eritrea clearly illustrates her miserable lot. The peasant woman gets up before sunrise to grind grain, prepare breakfast and lunch. After feeding her family, she joins her husband in the farm. After a full day's toil in the farm, the woman goes ahead of her husband to gather firewood, cook dinner and begin another cycle of back-breaking household work.

And yet, despite her decisive contribution to social production, she has no right whatsoever to land ownership. In highland Eritrea and in all forms of land tenure the woman is excluded from any direct land ownership, the father or husband has the full rights of user (ownership) and in the privately owned lands, the right to bequeath it to his heirs, who are almost invariably his sons or male relatives.

In the lowlands of Eritrea and particularly among the pastoralists, women are totally excluded from ownership of property and participation in social production and are relegated to domestic work.

The condition of the Eritrean women workers is no better than their peasant sisters. They are generally paid less than half of their male counterparts wage for the same job. They face layoffs for reasons of maternity or illness with no compensation. In the foreign capitalist plantations and farms, women agricultural workers are viciously exploited. Working mostly as seasonal labourers, their working hours are longer than 12 hours and their wages very low. A large number of women are also employed as domestic workers in the homes of foreign capitalists and the Eritrean bourgeoisie and upper petty-bourgeois classes. Working hours for most domestic workers run from 15-18 hours a day, and wages can be as low as US $5.00 a month. As domestic workers, the women have no rights. The employers have all the power over them, firing and cutting their wages as they please.

Political and Social Suppression

Because of their economic position, Eritrean women hold an oppressed and down-trodden place in the political, social and cultural life of the society.

They are conditioned and given opinions by the prevailing oppressive ideology and the social norms which denigrate their role while consecrating male supremacy and chauvinism. The prevailing feudalist and bourgeois ideology inculcates in the woman a false or subservient consciousness deluding her into succumbing and accepting male supremacy as intrinsic in his biological makeup, as something natural and immutable. Her perspective of her own social status is thereby limited within the framework of subservience to man, within the confines of immutable subordinacy to man.

It is sufficient to cite a couple of the hundreds of proverbs, sayings and songs which were current in the oppressive society to have an insight into the prevailing thought:

> 'Just as there is no donkey with horns, so
> there is no woman with brains'

> 'Where is the gain if one marries a woman,
> to give birth to a woman.'

This oppressive ideology was reflected (and reinforced) by depriving women of political and social rights enjoyed – however incompletely – by the men of the society. And so, although the Eritrean masses as a whole are subjected to political, social and cultural oppression at the hands of the Ethiopian occupiers and the local exploiting classes, the patriarchal system further denies Eritrean women even the limited role that men play in the political life of the society.

The limited decisions regarding the affairs of the village, the family, and the children are made by men with no consultation with women. In the village assemblies, where issues of concern to the entire village, such as the question of land distribution, land sale, disputes etc. are discussed and resolved, only men are allowed to attend. Women are considered incapable of contributing to social discussion, as expressed by the saying 'If women gather, they overcook the meal'. To this must be added, the oppression of women within the smallest social unit – the family. Male dominance here reigns supreme. Female members of the family are discriminated against and all the privileges, even if within the context of a colonized society, accrue to the males. Schooling and any training which would enhance the social status of the young members of the family are almost always reserved for the male while the girls take apprenticeship in domestic work in preparation for a married life as a diligent housewife. On the question of marriage, a girl does not have any right on the choice of her husband.

In brief, deprived of ownership of the means of production, generally excluded from social production, viciously exploited when able to work, and burdened by the back-breaking stultifying drudgery of private domestic slavery – such was the wretched condition of Eritrean women in colonial society.

Militant Tradition of Eritrean Women

Eritrean women, the most oppressed section of Eritrean society have never stood aside from the anti-colonial and anti-feudal struggle of the Eritrean people. There is indeed no instance in the history of our people in which Eritrean women submissively re-signed themselves to class oppression. The tradition of throwing ground, hot pepper into the eyes of aggressor troops, which Eritrean women have successfully employed against the Ethiopian aggressors is of long standing, dating back to the early years of Italian colonialism in Eritrea.

In the 1940s, peasant women played an active role in the anti-feudal peasant uprising in Western Eritrea. With the rise of working-class struggles in the 1950s, the women workers were also drawn into the struggle. Under the sham federation period, the working people, including women workers of the textile and other factories waged militant patriotic struggles. In particular, between 1956-58 several strikes and demonstrations organized by the working men and women took place in all the major Eritrean towns in protest at the systematic erosion of their political rights, the suppression of the General Syndicate of Labour Unions and against severe economic exploitation. The general strike and demonstration of 1958, in which several thousand men and women workers partici-pated, paralyzed the entire country for four days.

In the student movement which also intensified and developed in the late 1950s women students took an active role. Although a very small percentage of Eritrean women were able to attend school, they participated vigorously in the numerous demonstrat-ions over the years and many have faced imprisonment.

Women and the Armed Struggle

The beginning of the armed struggle in 1961, was a turning point in the Eritrean people's struggle. In the early days of the armed struggle, the major necessity of the liberation fighters was food and shelter. In this, peasant women displayed their patriotic zeal by providing food and shelter, and information about the enemy movements to the liberation fighters. In the cities, working women began organizing themselves to raise funds for the front. A typical example is that of the women workers of an incense factory in Keren, who in 1967, out of their own initiative decided to contribute 10% of their monthly income to the front. Abroad, particularly in Sudan, patriotic Eritrean women played a very active role in supporting the liberation fighters financially as well as nursing and sheltering wounded fighters.

Today, Eritrean women play an active role in the national liberation struggle. With the active support and leadership of the EPLF, they have set up and are consolidating their own mass organization – the National Union of Eritrean Women (NUEWmn).

The National Union of Eritrean Women mobilizes Eritrean women so that they can realize their role and participate in the political and armed struggle 'against colonial aggression and for social transformation'. It gives high priority to raising the political consciousness of Eritrean women so they can grasp the source of their oppression and the road to emancipation. Since over 95% of Eritrean women are illiterate, which hampers their political development, the NUEWmn also fights illiteracy among women. The NUEWmn is a source of fresh recruits for the EPLF's people's army. From among its most conscious members, women are also chosen for the people's militia.

Tens of thousands of workers, peasants as well as urban pettybourgeois women have already become members of the organization. NUEWmn branches have been set up throughout the liberated areas in the cities under enemy occupation as well as in many countries abroad. In the cities under occupation the women's organization functions in strict secrecy. Women workers are organized in cells in every factory and workplace alongside their men comrades. Cells of women students and intellectuals are also established. In the liberated countryside, the NUEWmn functions openly with branches set up at village level.

Organized, politicized and armed, Eritrean women are dealing heavy blows to the Ethiopian aggressors and Eritrean reactionaries. In the occupied cities the NUEWmn, in close co-ordination with the National Union of Eritrean Workers, takes an active role in support of the EPLF's armed actions. Women who work at or have access to, important enemy military and economic installations have participated with EPLF units in numerous heroic missions aimed at destroying the enemy's installations or seizing important supplies needed by the Front. For example, organized workers, the overwhelming majority of whom are women, of a certain textile factory in Asmara took hundreds of thousands of dollars worth of urgently needed supplies available in the factory, packed them in the factory trucks and drove them safely to the liberated areas.

In the countryside, peasant women are playing an increasingly active role in the struggle to defend, consolidate and transform the liberated areas. In close co-ordination with the National Union of Eritrean Peasants, the NUEWmn struggles for the implementation of the EPLF's programme of land reform and setting up of people's power. The NUEWmn carries out vigorous propaganda among the poor and landless peasants on the necessity of the land reform. The NUEWmn also wages systematic struggle against the backward feudal culture and ideas that oppress the women and severely hamper their participation in political and social activities.

A large number of women workers, peasants and students have joined EPLF's people's army. Assigned to all the different departments of the EPLF after six months military and political training, the overwhelming majority of EPLF women fighters have displayed outstanding revolutionary zeal and heroism.

As members of the Eritrean People's Liberation Army, Eritrean women are resolutely fighting as combat leaders or regulars and have shown unsurpassed heroism in hand-to-hand combat, blowing up tanks with hand-grenades and capturing their occupants. Unhindered by natural problems, they are facing all the hardships of a guerrilla fighters, running up mountains and valleys carrying their guns and amunitions, hunger, thirst etc. ... and many have lost their eyes, legs or other parts fighting for the glorious aim of dignity and liberation. There are also those who have lost their lives in combat, those heroes who will always be remembered by their people with great pride, those who have made history for the liberation of their people. All these feats of heroism that Eritrean women are demonstrating in practice are tearing apart the reactionary feudal myth that 'women are weaklings'.

The EPLF considers women's participation in social production as an indispensable requirement for their liberation. The EPLF political programme calls for: 'A broad programme to free women from domestic confinement, develop their participation in social production, and raise their political culture and technical levels,' which is already being implemented. In the EPLF base area, women fighters are engaged in agricultural production and cottage industry. Others work in the machine shop, wood works, electrical shop and weapons repair departments on jobs previously 'reserved for men'. Others are working in the salt mines in the liberated parts of the east coast.

Women fighters are also performing outstanding services in the the medical department, in the departments of education and information, in the department of culture and social welfare. In fact there is not a single department in the EPLF in which women are not actively engaged.

As a result of the struggles waged by the oppressed masses in which women played an active role, changes in the status of women are taking place. In the areas where land reform has been successfully carried out, women, who have always been deprived of land ownership, have received an equal share. Barred from participation in the village assemblies for centuries, women are now taking an active role in the people's assemblies in the liberated areas. Girls are attending the schools set up by the EPLF in the liberated areas, on an equal footing with the boys. Even old women are overcoming the fetters of the feudal society and are learning to read and write and are vigorously participating in political discussion and activity.

The backward feudal culture which has enslaved women is giving way to the new democratic culture of the masses. Forced and child marriage are fast becoming a thing of the past. The male supremacist attitude towards women is being replaced by women's self-confidence and men's respect and admiration for the heroic role of women. The NUEWmn is now working actively to create public opinion among the masses against the dowry, and for marriages based solely on comradely love between man and woman.

The changes taking place in the role and status of Eritrean women are truly significant. From a handful in 1974 the number of women fighters has climbed to thousands. Today (1979) women fighters make up 30% of the EPLF army. 11% of the delegates to the historic First Congress of the EPLF were women. The national democratic programme adopted by the First EPLF Congress has put down women's liberation as one of the key goals of the Eritrean revolution.

While these changes are significant, they are by no means sufficient. The task of organizing, politicizing and arming the women, of realizing their full participation in the revolution and achieving their emancipation is a long and arduous process. The EPLF is working actively to arouse the inexhaustible potential of oppressed Eritrean women and is fostering and training a number of capable and conscious women's cadres from all nationalities. But what is more important, the EPLF is dealing heavy blows to the reaction ary Ethiopian occupants and is overturning the old semi-feudal colonial society, thereby striking deep at the roots of women's oppression. In the final analysis, it is the total destruction of the

oppressive and exploiting society and the establishment of a
people's democratic regime that will open the way for the total
emancipation of Eritrean women.

11. Women and Revolution in Oman
Omani Women's Organization

This article is taken from a special issue of the publication *News
from Oman and Southern Arabia* (No. 36, November 1980) on
'Women and Revolution in Oman', edited by KROAG (the
Committee for the Revolution in Oman and the Arabian Gulf).
The article outlines the role of women in the more recent years of
the Revolution and includes extracts from documents passed by
two Congresses of the Omani Women's Organization (OWO), held
in 1975 and 1979. It is introduced with a brief outline of the
background to Oman's liberation struggle, summarized from the
above publication.

The background to Oman's present liberation struggle goes back
to the mid-19th Century when the country's economy was dis-
rupted by invasion from the British who have virtually held Oman
under colonial rule ever since. First attacks on British hegemony
were launched during the reign of Sultan Said bin Taimur
(1932-70) and, from 1965 up to the present day, three phases of
the liberation struggle can be identified.

The first phase, 1965-68, was marked by heavy fighting led by
the separatist Dhofar Liberation Front, who made considerable gains
during that period. The beginning of the second phase in 1968 saw
a change of policy indicated by the Front's adoption of a new name,
People's Front for the Liberation of the Occupied Arab Gulf
(PFLOAG). Uniting with popular opposition in the whole of the
Arabian Gulf, their aim now was to liberate the whole of Oman,
guided strictly by the principles of 'scientific socialism'.

By 1974 a number of liberated areas had been established in
spite of constant retaliation from the British, increasingly backed
up by Iran and the USA who were also eager to protect their own
interests (mainly oil). That year also marked the third phase of the
Revolution when, under mounting pressure, PFLOAG decided to
split into autonomous units, and in Oman the present People's

Front for the Liberation of Oman (PFLO) was formed. At the end
of 1975, after prolonged resistance, the PFLO were finally forced
to evacuate the liberated areas and today they are mainly gathered
on the borders of the People's Democratic Republic of Yemen where
they are organizing and carrying out political education and rebuilding programmes.

From the beginning, women became spontaneously involved in
Oman's liberation struggle. However, their active participation
alone didn't eliminate traditional prejudices against women and, by
1975, the formation of a women's organization was long overdue.
Qaboar has encouraged elitist women's groups, while persistently
attacking OWO, for instance, attempting to have OWO expelled
from the General Union of Arab Women.

For a long time the extensive participation of women in the revolution had required a regular women's organization to pursue new
aims, to find ways to attain these aims, and also to consolidate the
achieved results. A women's organization was considered to be
important in the mobilization of women for the following reasons.

Firstly, there existed a number of special obstacles to women's
integration in the Revolution in the form of traditional prejudices
of women's inferiority, their worthlessness as human beings, their
poorer abilities and their limited position in society in general.
These prejudices were widespread among both men and women.
Furthermore, pregnancy and parturitions place women in a
particular situation involving specific problems, and as the child
minding and housework is still taken care of by women, then the
weight of this sphere also becomes a specific woman problem.
Women in the liberated areas had already tried to solve one of
these problems spontaneously by organizing collective child-
caring so that women took turns looking after the children. It was
natural to try to spread such ideas deliberately as it could be
done by a women's organization. At the same time it was also an
important political task to consolidate the advances made by
women, to fight for further advances, and also to ensure that
women's participation in the Revolution is never restrained either
in level or in time. It was important to learn from the experiences
of the revolt in the Green Mountains (1957-59) when men forced
by circumstances, allowed women to bring them food and information, but at the same time retained the traditional view of
women as inferior individuals.

At its 1974 Congress the Front, therefore, decided to form the
Omani Women's Organization, OWO. In preparation for the
founding of OWO six months of political discussions were carried
out. A preparatory committee and various sub-committees were set

116

1976

Solidarität mit dem nationalen
Befreiungskampf des Volkes von Oman
unter der Führung der PFLO

Solidarité avec la Lutte Nationale
de Libération du Peuple d'Oman
sous la Conduite du FPLO

Solidarity with the National Liberation
Struggle of the People of Oman
under the Leadership of the PFLO

up to arrange political meetings for women. Moreover, the sub-committees visited women in their homes, explaining to them the importance of OWO, the importance of women playing a vital role in the Revolution, and the importance of women participating in the work of the women's organization. Only in this way can women become conscious of themselves as an oppressed group so that they can fight against this oppression. The sub-committees started new literacy classes and political education and encouraged women to participate in other activities outside the home. The preparatory committee also held several meetings to evaluate its own work and the work of the sub-committees. Analyses and resolutions were worked out and distributed for discussion before they were submitted to the first general congress.

In June 1975 OWO was officially formed and held its first Congress. On this occasion the organization adopted a working programme to comply with the obvious needs. The analysis and agenda

117

of the Congress are illustrated by the following passages from one of the documents passed by the congress.

> The liberation of women cannot be achieved through men making concessions to women, but through constant organized struggle by women on the economic, social, and political levels. The liberation of women is not indicated by the percentage of female workers or employees in government departments or corporations, nor by the number of employees or secretaries in Ministries, nor by the number of educated women or university graduates. The liberation of women is fulfilled through the effective contributions of women on the productive, social and political levels. . . .
>
> It is clear that an understanding of the significance of the woman question coupled with an understanding of the importance of the participation of women in the national struggle is a first and essential step towards women's emancipation. The main task of women's and of other organizations is to explain to all women their basic human rights, how they can fight for these rights, and what major role women can play in reconstructing society. . . .
>
> The concrete tasks of OWO are summarized as follows:
>
> 1) To enlighten and mobilize women around the woman question and women's liberation which cannot be achieved except through the liberation of the entire society from colonialism and its puppets in the area; 2) To educate the broad masses of women in a patriotic spirit and to include these masses in the ranks of the Omani revolution under the leadership of the PFLO, 3) To educate women and eliminate illiteracy by opening literacy centres in areas populated by illiterate women; 4) To organize weekly courses on social and political issues; 5) To change women's situation by mobilizing them to join in mass activities, and in the struggle against the British and Iranian colonial presence in Oman; 6) To struggle against the incorrect ideas that women's only role is marriage and the production of children.
>
> We are working to establish a special agitation department for women. Its first task is to meet the specific problems of the less educated women, to raise their consciousness, and to lead them towards participation in the revolutionary struggle. The other task is to mobilize women to make demands in their capacity as women and to defend the right to for instance, maternity and child welfare programmes, the reduction of housework etc. We have made the basis for this work and hope to develop it in the coming period. . . .
>
> The Organization of Omani Women is at present working to train women cadres who can lead the Omani women's movement as a whole, and form a women's vanguard. It will in no way compromise women's demands for equality with men. Nor will it allow anyone to pacify

women, or to stop them after the completion of the liberation struggle. We are well aware that traditional ideas remain in the minds of many people for a long time — even after a transformation of the social system. We are building a cadre force in order to lead women towards their liberation, so that they will reach the end of the road and not stop half way.

The Role of Women Today

Women in particular were affected by the general demobilization in the ranks of the PFLO following the military setback at the end of 1975. This resulted from the fact that women primarily had played a prominent role in the military field of the liberation struggle, as they on the ideological and organizational levels had suffered from the lack of experience and education. Many men had received education and political experience when they worked in the Gulf States, i.e. before they joined the Front, while women had their first education and political experience when as young girls they joined the Revolution. The military setback therefore removed the most important basis of women's position in the liberation struggle. At the same time women had only a limited possibility of playing a prominent role in other fields of the struggle due to the lack of skills in reading and writing, political knowledge and experience; and consequently many women in the border area were demobilized. They left the People's Army and the Schools of Revolution to get married and then relapsed into their traditional role.

In the light of this development, the existence of OWO has been of vital importance since the evacuation of the liberated areas. OWO has tried to implement the working programme arising out of its first Congress in the border area, and as this represents an important part of the general rebuilding programme, it has been given high priority by the PFLO. Since the setback, OWO has worked hard to engage women in its activities. OWO has emphasized that women have to play a prominent role in those fields in which the practice of the Front is concentrated today, that is the ideological and organizational fields. This is only possible if women engage in educational and political activities, so that they develop their capabilities and raise their consciousness on issues concerning women and politics in general. The primary obstacle to such an engagement is the traditional role of women where they are stuck with housework and child-care. In order to overcome this problem OWO has organized child-care in connection with the various educational activities. Moreover, OWO has organized education for those women who lived in the refugee camp near Gheida, and were not able to attend the ordinary education

programme in the town because of their large families. The PFLO
has also tried to ensure a better educational level for young girls by
introducing a law that forbids them to marry before they have
finished secondary school.

OWO has continued the work with literacy classes and political
and cultural meetings which was started in the liberated areas, but
was never consolidated because of the offensive of the Iranian
invasion troops. OWO also stresses the value of visiting women at
home and discussing their specific problems. These visits are an
important part of the continuous mobilization work, but have been
very difficult, because the families in the border region are disper-
sed over a large area and because OWO until recently has not had
any means of transport at its disposal.

OWO has also taken the initiative in building up a centre for
women in Al Gheida which represents a great step forward in the
mobilization of women. Isolated women will be able to attend
educational, cultural and political activities, and simultaneously
the children can be looked after at the same place. The number of
activities will be increased and include, for instance sewing and
typewriting and there will be a maternity and child welfare clinic.
All this will make it more attractive for women to join the centre.

The Second Congress of OWO

Under the slogan: 'Struggle for Liberation, Democracy and Social
Progress' the Omani Women's Organization held its second Congress
in June 1979. The Congress evaluated the work of the organization
since its foundation in 1975 and laid down the lines for its future
work. Moreover, the Congress discussed the general situation of
the Omani Revolution, and the perspectives of the progressive
movement in Oman and in the entire Gulf area. Below, the structure of OWO is briefly described, and then follows a summary of
the most important decisions and resolutions passed by the Congress.

The Structure of OWO

Any Omani woman over 15 years of age, who accepts the programme
and internal regulations of OWO, can become a member of the
organization. The members are under an obligation to share in the
activities of the organization, and work to improve and develop its
practices. Members are organized in local branches which elect their
own leadership.

The highest authority of OWO is the *General Congress* which is
held every three years. Here, delegates of all local branches meet

and discuss the political line and practice of the organization and lay down the general lines of the future work. The Congress elects the President of the organization and the 14 other members of the *Central Council* which is the highest authority of OWO between the Congresses. The Central Council meets every half year. It elects the members of the *Executive Bureau*, which meets every three months. The Executive Bureau directs the work of the organization between the meetings of the Central Council, and undertakes the implementation of the decisions and resolutions passed by the Congress and the Central Council. The Executive Bureau is composed of seven members including the President of OWO.

The Objectives and Tasks of OWO

The second Congress of OWO passed a number of resolutions on the future objectives and tasks of the organization. Here follows a summary of these (*8, 9, 10, 11*):

OWO divides its objectives and tasks into three levels: the local, Arab, and international level.

At the *local level* the general objectives of OWO can be summarized in the following points: to struggle for an independent Oman without foreign military bases and troops; to fight for the democratic rights of the Omani people, including the right to organize in trade unions, the right to strike, the right to express freely one's opinion and criticism; the right to arrange peaceful demonstrations, and the right to move freely in the entire Oman, to fight for a legal system based on internationally approved rules of law, including the right to a defence, the right to appeal, and prohibition of all acts of torture, incidental arrests, ransacking of houses, and infringement of Omani citizens and their property; to fight for women's emancipation on all levels, that is the political, economic, social, and matrimonial levels, including the right to participate in political and social activities, the right of employment and education, the right to choose one's partner freely, and the right to apply for a divorce. Moreover, OWO demands a reduction of the bride-price, and prohibition of humiliation and corporal punishment of women, to fight for special privileges in connection with pregnancy and parturitions, and for the establishment of nurseries and kindergardens all over Oman; to combat illiteracy and spread education and the national culture among Omani women; to train female cadres to lead the struggle of women,

Concretely OWO will continue its work to preserve the progressive social laws gained by the Omani women through their extensive struggles and sacrifices in the revolution. The OWO will continue its work to eradicate illiteracy among women and take further steps to develop women's skills through technical and political courses. OWO will also carry on political and cultural meetings in order to raise the political consciousness of women and to preserve the national culture. The organization will expand its publication activities by developing its monthly magazine, and by preparing publications on the struggle of the Omani woman and her role in society. Besides, OWO will continue its efforts to build up the above mentioned cultural centre for women.

At the *Arab level* OWO considers its most important task to be the strengthening of the struggle of the Arab nation against imperialism and Zionism, and against all conspiracies aimed at liquidating the Arab revolution and the Palestinian struggle. Concretely, OWO wants to strengthen its relations with other Arab women's organizations, and to participate in Arab women's conferences, in order to spread information about the Omani Revolution and to exchange information and experiences in general and thereby promote the cause of the Arab woman and the Arab nation. OWO wants to strengthen the General Union of Arab Women because OWO considers it to be the sole legitimate representative of the Arab women.

At the *international level* OWO considers its work to be a contribution to the struggle of mankind against imperialism, facism and racism, and also a contribution to the struggle of women all over the world. Therefore, OWO wants to develop and consolidate its relations with all democratic organizations in the world, especially all international democratic women's organizations including the Women's International Democratic Federation.

The Congress especially greets Yemeni women, Palestinian women, Iranian women, Bahraini women, Eritrean women, and Sahara women.

Part IV:
After the Revolution

Dora Tamana

You who have no work, speak.
You who have no homes, speak.
You who have no schools, speak.
You who have to run like chickens from the vulture, speak.
Let us share our problems so that we can solve them
   together.
We must free ourselves.
Men and women must share housework.
Men and women must work together in the home
   and out in the world.
There are no creches and nursery schools for our
   children.
There are no homes for the aged.
There is no-one to care for the sick.
Women must unite to fight for these rights.
I opened the road for you.
You must go forward.

Dora Tamana

Quoted in *To Honour Women's Day*, booklet published by the
International Defence and Aid Fund for Southern Africa in
co-operation with United Nations Centre Against Apartheid,
August 1981.

12. Mozambican Women After the Revolution
Anabella Rodriguez

Anabella Rodrigues was only a child when the first woman joined
the Mozambican Liberation Front's (FRELIMO) guerrillas during
the war for independence from Portugal. At 16, she left her
school and family and joined FRELIMO to teach soldiers how to
read and write. Today, six years after independence, Rodrigues
is a member of the national secretariat of the Organization of
Mozambican Women.

Over 500 years of colonialism the Portuguese took a great deal
of wealth out of this southern African country in profits from
cashews and cotton produced by forced or poorly paid human
labour. But they added little to the development of modern
agriculture or industry. When Mozambique became independent
in 1975, most people were still illiterate peasants. living by the
customs and taboos of traditional society. Faced with the overwhelming problems of an impoverished country, the Mozambican
women's movement has had to take a different course from
the women's movement in Western nations.

Candice Wright, who here interviews Anabella Rodrigues, is a
member of Liberation Support Movement and has been involved
in solidarity work with liberation movements in southern Africa
for 15 years. The interview which includes a short introduction
took place in early 1979, when she spent five weeks visiting
Mozambican factories, schools, clinics and communal villages. It
has already been published in *Newsfront International* (No.238,
August 1980) and *Third World Magazine*.

'We have received delegations from capitalist countries where the
development of women has taken a feminist line and it is difficult
for them to understand our reality,' Rodrigues told me. 'They
say that integrating women into a sewing co-operative is not really
a movement toward emancipation. They feel that real
emancipation is having women as *responsibles* in the ministries,
factories and mass organizations. We agree, but we must begin by

putting a woman into a sewing co-operative and not a leadership position when she does not yet know how to read and write. During the armed struggle this was not a limitation. Illiterate women led detachments of soldiers into combat. But now in this more compli - cated time of national reconstruction, literacy is essential!'

Candice Wright: Why was independence a difficult time for the women's organization?

Anabella Rodrigues: After the creation of the transitional government in September 1974, FRELIMO entered the whole country and formed dynamizing groups in residential areas and workplaces. The Organization of Mozambican Women had a part in these groups. There was great enthusiasm among women but our organization wasn't prepared to solve new problems that came from the influence of colonial and bourgeois ideas. At that time there were many opportunities. In some provinces wives of former Portuguese officials infiltrated our organization and became *responsibles.* In our offices women were learning how to cook desserts with eggs when they had no eggs at home or to crochet doilies for tables when they had no tables.

In November 1976, FRELIMO called a conference to reorganize the women's organization. Representatives came from all the provinces, not only those who had served in the armed struggle, but women from the factories, public services, residential areas and the new communal villages attended and created a programme for the organization. Until then our members were from the women's wing of the armed forces but we now began to recruit among peasants and working women.

We educate and mobilize women, preparing them to join FRELIMO which is a Marxist-Leninist party. FRELIMO recruits members from the mass organizations where people have had collective political education and experiences. The party co-ordin- ates with and supports the women's organization but we determine our own programmes and activities.

CW: How does illiteracy affect your work?

AR: It is very difficult to find women to be *responsibles* because of widespread illiteracy. Since 1977 we've eliminated illiteracy among the national and provincial *responsibles* but in the country's 99 districts most are still illiterate. We have organized three month national literacy courses with women attending from all the provinces. For the first time women are leaving their villages to come to Maputo, the capital of their country. Here they exchange ideas with women from other provinces and realize that we are really part of a nation. In addition to learning how to read and write, women see films and hear news broadcasts for the first time. This cultural and political experience is very important for them.

CW: What is the Organization of Mozambique Women's programme for women?

AR: Our main work is organizing women in communal villages because this is the basis of economic development in Mozambique. We have organized mobile brigades which go into communal villages for a month and organize the work with the women. We help in public meetings with the discussion of women's problems with both men and women. There are many Mozambican languages and the majority of women don't know how to speak or read Portuguese, so our brigades translate information about the women's organization and also national and international news into the local language.

This year we will establish two nutrition centres, one in the north and one in the south of Mozambique, to teach peasant women how to organize family life in the countryside. We will teach child-care, sewing and care for houses and livestock.

CW: Do you also organize women in the city?

AR: We've set our priorities and begun our work among the women in the countryside. Although they live under difficult conditions, they are the backbone of the organization. Their material conditions and consciousness are improving, while women in the cities are affected by our work only in the sense that we are changing the way they think about their roles. In the cities petit bourgeois women working in public services say they agree with FRELIMO and the women's organization, but they are not putting this into practice in their lives. They only want to finish work and go home to their families.

Because of widespread illiteracy, we need the help of these women to organize the administration of the co-operatives and our offices. We are beginning to work with women in public services and we expect that within two or three years the situation will begin to change.

CW: What is the role of the sewing and handicraft co-operatives?

AR: It is important to put women in sewing and handicraft co-operatives where they have a role outside the home. The co-operatives organize women in collective work, making it easier to give them political tasks, literacy classes and cultural activities. We also started these co-operatives because clothing is so expensive. Traditionally men do handicrafts but we have integrated women into this work.

We have many difficulties because we lack transport and money We do get some support from the Party but we must also raise funds for our work. When these co-operatives are in a good economic situation, they will give 30% of their funds to the Organization of Mozambican Women.

CW: Are women a significant part of the work force?

AR: While we have no statistics on women in agricultural and industrial work forces, we know that the majority of women are still in domestic situations. Most factories are located in Maputo, Nampula and Beira. In the past, most women who worked in factories did so out of necessity. They were single mothers or had been left by husbands who went to work in the South African mines. The majority worked in cashew, garment and shoe factories. Since Independence many more women have been integrated into the factories but the process of bringing women into the workforce is just beginning. Unemployment and under-employment are the main obstacles, and only economic development will make it possible to eliminate them.

We are also organizing in the factories. It is necessary to make women understand that they must participate in the decisions of the factory Party cells and production councils. And with this political work it becomes possible to solve other social problems. For example, here in Maputo it was possible to create day-care centres in seven factories.

CW: Do women still work primarily in unskilled jobs?

AR: Women are now asking factory administrators for training in skilled jobs. At a textile factory in Manica province, for example, women operate machines where before they had only packaged clothes. The Organization of Mozambican Women requests that factory workers' councils begin integrating women into courses for skilled work. The state-owned factories co-operate more than the private ones. For example, at a privately owned cashew-nut factory in Gaza, no women are hired even though most cashew workers in Mozambique are women. We have been trying to change this since 1977. This factory is exceptional, because many private factories say they want to make a contribution to the Revolution and take up the initiative in making changes.

We are integrating women into courses for professional training. When the Ministry of Labour offers a course, places are reserved for our organization to send women. In the last two years about 300 women have participated in these. They are now working in jobs never before done by women in Mozambique — as electricians, taxi and tractor drivers, shoe-makers, carpenters, car-body painters and mechanics. Because of the general mobilization in the countryside we find more initiative to involve women in new jobs there. For example, on the state farms near Maputo, women are taught to be tractor drivers. This was done at their initiative, not the Ministry's.

CW: Are there any efforts to solve the special problems of working women?

AR: There are many social and economic problems that are not yet solved. In the factories women are not given the opportunity to be away from work to care for sick children for any long period of time. In the past they were allowed to do this but this policy was abused. Now women are allowed two days a month away from work to care for family problems. After giving birth a woman may be away from work for 60 days.

Because the shops used to open from 7 a.m. to noon and 2 to 5 p.m., women who worked in the factories could not get to the stores during lunch hours or after work. So in 1976 shop hours were changed to 9 a.m. to 1 p.m. and 4 to 8 p.m. This gives working women the opportunity to shop. But often there are shortages of staples. Domestic women line up early to shop, so little is available to working women later in the day. Forming consumer co-operatives (which distribute goods equitably among members) has been one solution.

CW: Are the traditions oppressive to women changing?

AR: It is easier to eliminate the colonial, bourgeois influences that were imposed on us and identified with the enemy than to eliminate generations of tradition from within our own society. Among the hardest traditions to eliminate are the initiation rites, polygamy and *lobolo* which are based in the economic organization of traditional society. *Lobolo* is the dowry a man must pay to a woman's family when he wishes to marry her. He must buy the Woman because she is part of her parents' labour force and it transferred to the labour force of the new family. Polygamy brings wealth and social importance to a man, because his wives provide labour in his fields and also produce sons for that labour force. There are no laws agains polygamy, but FRELIMO does not give responsibilities to men who continue traditions which subjugate women.

There's a big difference between the communal villages and the areas that are not yet organized. In communal villages production is collective and women receive the same wages as men for the same work. In Gaza, women are beginning to understand the oppression of the polygamous family and want divorce. They are part of collective production, earn a salary and can now take care of their own lives. But in areas like Cabo Delgado, many of the men served in the armed struggle and now live in other provinces. In some areas we find 1,750 women and only 300 men. How can we combat polygamy in this situation? Polygamy is not good for our society and the emancipation of women, but it is not possible to eliminate it until the economic basis of society is reorganized.

CW: Are women protected by law against abuse and discrimination?

AR: Women have problems with men who beat them, desert them or do not provide for the children. There are also problems with divorce and abortion. If the women's organization cannot solve these, the women can go to the Ministry of Justice which is guided by the Constitution, which gives women the same rights as men. This year FRELIMO will develop new family laws.

One issue is the minimum age for marriage. Many young girls who are 13 and 14 years old marry men who are 30 to 50 years old. Divorce was allowed in colonial times but it was much easier for men to get divorced than women. Women would have to pay a large fee and meet many conditions. Another custom is that a woman whose husband dies becomes the property of another man in the husband's family. Members of the women's organization participate in tribal justice and in solving cases over dividing property and custody of children, taking into consideration the traditions of the province. We are calling meetings for women to find out what they want in the family laws, but I don't think all the traditional problems can be solved by law.

CW: Do women have access to birth control and the right to abortion?

AR: In the countryside, women are pregnant every year and have many children. We need both contraceptives and people who can teach women about them. We must also work with men who think that having many children gives them social importance. Since nationalization of health services, doctors and nurses have been teaching women about birth control and women have been enthusiastic about this.

We have received letters from women who have had an IUD in place for six months but because of the husband's objections have

returned to the hospitals to have it removed. Husbands do not yet understand this right. Sometimes women don't tell their husbands they are using a contraceptive and he becomes upset because he is no longer fathering children. Because of traditional education many men and women don't accept the idea of birth control.

Women do not yet have the right to have abortions except in special circumstances. The abortion issue is more complicated and has not been discussed. Now there are many women and young girls having abortions clandestinely. With the discussion of the family laws it will be possible to discuss and resolve this problem.

CW: Is the cultural role of women changing?

AR: In each province we are organizing cultural centres where women form groups for singing and dancing. Traditionally some of the dances were only for men. The *Makwayella* is a popular one danced only by men who have been to the mines in South Africa, but now women are dancing it too. We are also teaching them theatre, painting and sculpture which traditionally were not done by women.

In the factories we have organized soccer games among women. They are very enthusiastic about sports, and women of all ages now play soccer. Our goal is not to create famous women athletes but to provide women with ways of expressing themselves outside their roles of wife, mother and housekeeper.

CW: How has the social role of women changed?

AR: At Independence many women attended meetings but did not speak out, particularly in the presence of men, about our problems — the economy, sabotage in the factories or the enemies at our borders. But during the recent regional and national assembly women contributed for the first time to the discussion of our country's problems. Also, many more women than we had expected have joined the Organization of Mozambican Women as a result of our campaign for new members. The role of women varies from province to province depending on the economic situation. In provinces which were liberated during the armed struggle, women are active; and in the communal villages, women lead in collective production.

CW: What is the response of men to these changes?

AR: Early in the struggle, it was clear that public opinion was in favour of women going to literacy classes, party meetings and doing tasks for the women's organization. But many men were unhappy with this and would beat their wives if they tried to participate. Some were beaten so severely that they had to be hospitalized.

But the position of men is changing. Some men want to be Party members but they never speak to their wives at home. Their wives are only slaves to them. After work they come home to drink wine with their friends or go out to the soccer game. But now when they want to be Party members, they are confronted in public meetings about how they treat their wives. Those who mistreat their wives are not accepted. To become active in the Party, they must study and put into practice women's emancipation. It's easy to say *Viva a emancipation*, but the development of the Revolution makes it obligatory for people to transform their mentality.

Last year in Cabo Delgado province, I was in a popular meeting with men and women to discuss women's problems. The men were asking important questions about the division of labour. Some of them were angry at our suggestion that both husband and wife should take responsibility for the children. Many found it difficult to accept that now their wives were working in the agricultural co-operative, the situation in the family had to change too. If a woman is going to carry water, a man must look after the children or do some of the cooking while she does this. The important thing is not that women begin as work brigade leaders or directors in ministries but that we become part of collective production. This will give us a salary and economic independence. And we will broaden our view from the family to our role at work and in our country.

13. Building a New Life for Women in South Yemen

Aisha Moshen and Noor Ba'abad

The following is a revised and expanded version of interviews
carried out by Maxine Molyneux in December 1977. They first
appeared in *Feminist Review* (No. 1, 1979), together with a third
interview and an introduction to the political situation in South
Yemen, officially known as the People's Democratic Republic of
Yemen. In her introduction Maxine Molyneux explains that the
women interviewed are members of the General Union of
Yemeni Women, a mass organization of the Yemeni Socialist
Party (previously the National Liberation Front, abbreviated here
as NLF) and hence tied to both Party and State structures.

Since independence in 1967 'the State has intervened in a
number of ways to confront the more oppressive traditional and
religious practices', establishing a new secular Family Code which,
among other things, 'abolished divorce by repudiation, limited
polygamy to exceptional circumstances, gave divorced women
custody rights over children, and outlawed both early marriages
and marriages without the consent of both parties'. There has also
been a major attempt to erode *purdah* restrictions and encourage
women's entry into all areas of public life. At the same time, however, there has been no serious attempt to redistribute the burdens
of domestic labour; the GUYM is 'not permitted any degree of
autonomy in programme and practice' and 'there is little, if any,
sustained discussion of such questions as the relations between
the sexes, the persistence of ideologies of women's inferiority, the
problems of familial oppression, or of female sexuality'.
(*Feminist Review*, pp. 7-8). Clearly the emancipation of women
still has a long way to go.

Aisha Mohsen: the Women's Union

Now in her late twenties, Aish Mohsen is the daughter of a Yemeni
migrant worker in Britain and was elected first President of the
General Union of Yemeni Women (GUYW) at its 1974 Congress.

She held this post until the end of June 1978 when she was dismissed and, along with several others, was also expelled from the Central Committee following a failed coup attempt by the then President of the PDRY, Salem Robea Ali.

Maxine Molyneux: Could you first tell me what the main objectives of the Women's Union are?

Aisha Mohsen: The Union is trying to help the state by encouraging women to participate in economic production. It tries to get women, especially housewives, involved in these activities by, for example, training them so that they acquire skills. In this way both the women and society can benefit.

MM: What is the political status of the Union?

AM: The Women's Union is a mass organization of the NLF, directed by its Central Committee. As such, its work consists in mobilizing support for the aims of the Party and the state. The mass organizations elect representatives to the Supreme People's Council, our Parliament. We now have six delegates there. In general, the Union acts according to party directives; the Family Law for example, although relating to the interests of women, was promoted initially by the Party in accordance with the wishes of women. But of course we in the Union are consulted about legal matters concerning women. All mass organizations have the right to suggest laws and modifications in the law. The final decisions as to whether to change a law or not are taken by the Supreme Council.

MM: Could you give me a brief account of the history of the Women's Union?

AM: Well, although the Union was founded in 1968, its activities as a national organization really date from the Conference held in the town of Seyun in 1974. This gave the Union a proper organizational structure and official representation in all six Governorates.

MM: What was the Union doing in the period before 1974?

AM: From 1968 onwards we were involved in the literacy campaigns and in discussions concerning the Family Law. As you know, this was very widely debated in public meetings all over the country, so that people's opinions could be taken into account. The women were always more extreme – more radical – than the men, by the way! But there was no real leadership then, and only three branches of the Women's Union were in existence – in Aden, in Lahej and in the Fifth Governorate [the Hadramaut region]. We used to try and hold open meetings with women, although not many came because of *purdah*. But with the revolutionary changes in the countryside after 1971 more women became active.

MM: So what is the organizational structure of the Union now?

AM: At the Seyun Conference where delegates from all over the country were present, we were able to elect a 35-member Central Council. From these 35 we then elected a seven-member General Secretariat of the Union. Each of these members heads a committee with specific responsibilities; the seven members comprise the Head of the Union, the Secretary for Internal Relations; the Secretary for External Affairs, the Information and Cultural Secretary, the Social Secretary, the Financial and Administrative Secretary, and then lastly, the Economic Secretary. This structure forms the model for committees at lower levels of the Union, for example at regional and district level. It is only this year that we have been able to develop the structure at the local level and we now have 193 committees all over the Republic, 32 of which are in the First Governorate [Aden area].

MM: You said that the Union's main objective is to encourage women to enter social production. How exactly do you do this?

AM: In the first instance, by training them to acquire some technical expertise. As part of International Women's Year we set up technical training centres in all the Governorates to train women to be mechanics for cars, tractors, refrigerators, air-conditioners, televisions, radios etc. We also trained women to type and to use sewing machines. In 1975 there were some 1,500 women involved in training centres and most of these women have taken up jobs in the same projects in which they were trained. The centres were residential and the courses would run for periods of up to a year. The training would generally take place in the mornings, and the afternoons would be given over to activities such as military training, literacy classes, music, handicrafts, political education, cultural circles, and the like. This experiment still continues.

MM: I understand there was some opposition to women going to these centres?

AM: Yes, they had to be suspended in some governorates this year because of traditional obstacles. Some families forced the centres in two of the governorates to close. We have tried to get them reopened but conditions are very difficult there, because of illiteracy and ignorance . . . and people spreading gossip about the women in the centres. Anyway, this is one of our projects. In addition the Union puts up part of the capital, i.e., 10% to run two factories in Aden — the perfume factory at Maala and the foam-rubber factory at Sheikh Othman. But we are not entrepreneurs! Our aim is to try and influence policy in these two projects and to make women's employment easier. Most of the employees of the perfume factory are women. The state owns part of the capital, about 50%, the Union owns 10%, 40% is privately owned. Participating in these projects helps to strengthen our own budget too; but it won't be a long-term involvement because we don't want to become capitalists.

MM: Apart from this, where does the funding for the Union come from?

AM: We get some state subsidy and some income from the membership, but the state ought not to continue giving us this subsidy because we are a mass organization and should depend on ourselves. Our aim is to be financially independent, but at the moment most of our income comes from the state and from the Party.

MM: What is the subscription from members?

AM: A worker pays 100 fils a month [about 30 cents] and a housewife 50 fils.

MM: What is the membership of the Women's Union?

AM: 14,296.

MM: How do these break down according to social classes?

AM: Nine hundred and fifteen are women workers employed in factories, workshops and so on; 528 are agricultural workers, members of co-ops and state farms; 253 are employees of different government ministries. There are some graduates from universities and secondary schools, and the rest are housewives and older students, mostly from secondary schools, i.e., 14 to 16-year olds.

MM: So most of your members are younger women?

AM: The majority are between 20 and 30. Hardly any are over 30. It's very difficult to change an old woman.

MM: Thirty-one is old?

AM: Our hopes lie with the children of the revolution, the ones we have given the benefits of education.

MM: And how do you recruit your members?

AM: Membership is on the basis of residence; women come to the offices of the Popular Defence Councils which have been established in each residential area, to discuss their problems, participate in campaigns, and so on. There is always a representative of the Women's Union there; usually she is the Social Secretary, so she naturally comes into contact with women. She helps on questions of divorce, marriage, bad neighbours, social problems.

MM: Is she really a social worker?

AM: Exactly, a social worker.

MM: So you don't have representatives and recruiting campaigns at the workplace?

AM: No, we leave that area to the trade unions and the Party.

MM: Of over 100 women industrial workers I have interviewed, only a handful were in the Women's Union and active participation of women in the trade unions and in the Party is very low indeed. So how are women's interests in the workplace guaranteed?

AM: We are trying to encourage more women to enter these organizations at the workplace. This will be easier now that there is the example of women standing for elections and women being able to vote for the first time ever. Before, women were completely excluded from political life, so it is very new for them. But even so, of the ten women who stood in the Aden area for the 1977 Local People's Council election, eight of them were elected, which is very good.

MM: Were they members of the Women's Union?

AM: Yes.

MM: What are the main campaigns of the Union?

AM: The two most important were, first, the campaign to gain support for the Family Law and, second, the campaign against illiteracy.

MM: What about the veil and the *sheidor* [full length covering]? Are you campaigning against these?

AM: The veil and *sheidor* have started to disappear with social development, by themselves. The veil is not an obstacle in the way of the women's struggle, because before, during the struggle against the British and against feudalism, women struggle, even though they were wearing *sheidors.*

MM: Is there any specific campaign mounted by the Union or by the state directed at men to encourage them to change their attitudes vis-a-vis women? After all these can't have changed automatically.

AM: Yes, in the Party there is. The existence of women in the Party and in the Supreme Council and the Local Councils is proof of the high esteem in which women are held in the PDRY. There *is* a campaign in the Party to reform attitudes. Then there is also a campaign at the mass level *through* the Party.

MM: Do you have any views on the women's liberation movement in the West?

AM: I'm not sure what you mean.

MM: It might be said that, generally speaking, the women's

movement in the West is identified with two principles which are
at variance with those of the Yemeni Women's Union; a large
degree of autonomy from existing political organizations, and some
commitment to the belief that men collude in and benefit from
the oppression of women.

AM: Women should not make it their most important aim to
oppose men, because in capitalist countries men are also
oppressed. The oppression of women cannot be ended unless oppression in the whole society is eliminated. Men and women are
oppressed by the capitalist classes so they should join in their
struggle against these forces.

Noor Ba'abad: Women and Social Change

Noor Ba'abad is on the Executive Committee of the GUYM and
occupies the post of Head of Cultural and Information Affairs.
She is married and in her late twenties.

Maxine Molyneux: I'm interested in the decision of the Yemeni
Women's Union not to campaign actively against the veil but
rather to leave it to die out by itself.

Noor Ba'abad: There was a campaign against the veil in 1972.
During the peasant uprising and the land occupations there was
an important process of radicalization among women as well, and
one of the popular demands called for the end of the veil. In fact
it was one of the most popular slogans.

MM: So if it was a popular campaign why was it subsequently
dropped?

NB: Well, in those days it marked a real advance for women. The
demand is still raised occasionally but there is no need to push it
strongly because objective processes will destroy the veil. Through
the 1972 demonstrations against the veil we achieved our aims —
that is, to make it possible to overcome the veil. In our schools,
for example, girls don't wear the veil or the *sheidor*. Khaki uniforms
have been brought in for offices and factory workers. In addition
there has been a mass media campaign to reduce the effect of
family opposition and to get them to accept what we are doing.
Already you can see the veil is gradually being used less, and the
sheidor is gradually being replaced by a coat.

MM: What kind of discussions, theoretical debates, and political
arguments are going on in the Women's Union at the moment?

NB: The main task now is achieving literacy for women and
liberating them economically.

MM: Are there any particular texts on women that you read and refer to?

NB: Nothing special. Rather it is part of Marxism in general. There's no special instruction for women. Of course, Engels' *Origin of the Family* is very important for us.

Literacy class

MM: Is the question of women's subordination discussed at all at the Party School?

NB: Not as a separate subject, but in general our political and ideological line is to be aware of it; in that sense it is part of the programme.

MM: In its drive to encourage women to participate in production does the Women's Union express any preference for the kind of work women should do?

NB: We don't want them to do work in heavy industry or to work as carriers of heavy loads. We are encouraging our women to have a technical training; as you know, this is why we have set up the Training Centres.

MM: Female circumcision is a traditional practice in some parts

141

of your country. Has this been abolished?

NB: This custom affects both boys and girls and the degree to
which it was practised varied from governorate to governorate.
With regard to women it was an expression of their shame; with
boys the custom continues and this is excellent. But as it is a
degrading custom for girls and not a proper one, it has begun to
decline.

MM: But is it not illegal to practice clitorodectomy?

NB: There is no law against it.

MM: What about prostitution?

NB: As you know, under imperialism prostitutes could be found
in the ports of Aden and Mukalla. But few Yemeni women accepted this degrading custom, less than 1% in fact. It was the imperia-
lists who organized it. The government has discovered the class
basis of prostitution, and has arranged alternative work for these
women. [There is a tomato-paste factory at Fyush, outside Aden,
staffed by ex-prostitutes, and co-operatives under the aegis of the
Women's Union have absorbed some of them.]

MM: How do you think women can achieve their complete
emancipation?

NB: We cannot speak of liberating women without making them
participate in social life to convince them of their role in society.
In our constitution we have included a commitment to the
principle of women's liberation. It is women's right now to work
in factories. By encouraging women to work in factories and to go
to school we will achieve the right orientation. The state has also
abolished the existence of women as a special stratum. No text in
the laws or constitution discriminates against women. If a woman
wants to work in any sphere no one will stop her.

MM: What kind of emphasis, if any, is placed on the role of
ideological struggle in the effort to emancipate women?

NB: Our ideological struggle is our Party line and the Party's
policy affects all strata of society. But we have our own ideological
activities in the Union — information programmes, courses, radio
and television, newspapers, mimeographed papers, posters, political
and social lectures. The experience of work itself is important plus
the experience of the other socialist countries, for example, the
Central Asian Republics or Cuba.

MM: Do you have any knowledge of, or views on, the women's
liberation movement in the West?

NB: Yes, we know about their struggles concerning work, wages,
children, and other things. Our society is, however, a backward

one; while our tactical struggles are different, our aims are the
same.

14. Iranian Women: The Struggle Since the Revolution
London Iranian Women's Liberation Group

The first of the following pieces is an extract taken from a booklet
of the same title, written by the London Iranian Women's Liberation Group. It was published in spring 1980, almost a year after
the Group brought out their first publication *Women in Iran: the
Part they Played in the Revolution.* The Iranian Women's Liberation Group was set up in May 1979 following a conference on
Iranian women which was held in London at that time. It was felt
by the conference organizers that, after the Revolution in Iran
and the emergence of a women's movement there, it was necessary
for Iranian women in other countries to get together and form
groups to help in consciousness raising and becoming aware of
their rights — or lack of them — in Iran. They were also needed to
help and support the struggles of women's groups in Iran and to
educate the public towards a better understanding of the
situation of Iranian women.

Apart from holding regular meetings, the London Group's main
activity has been the publication of a number of newsletters in
Persian. It has also established contact with the major women's
organizations in Iran and has been exchanging publications and
information with them. Finally, it has organized a photographic
exhibition called *Behind the Veil* and obtained and shown a film,
shot by French Feminists, of the massive women's demonstrations
which took place in International Women's Day, 1979.

The second piece, 'The Revolution That Failed Women' was
written more recently by Manny, a member of the Group. This
article was first published in *The Leveller* (13-26 November 1981)
and is reproduced here with their and the author's permission.

The Revolution in Iran was carried out by a unity of forces among
all the diverse interest groups and sectors of society who were
opposed to the Shah's dictatorship. However, with the coming to

power of Khomeini and his fundamentalist/opportunist followers,
it became evident that the new regime, far from being a broad-
based one, was only promoting a strict Islamic morality, often at
the expense of ignoring some of the basic demands made by different sectors of society. Among these were the minorities' demands
for autonomy, notably the Kurds, the demand for redistribution
of the land among the Turkamans in the North and other regions.

Generally the masses who brought about the Revolution and the
Shah's overthrow, wanted a genuine change in the structure of
society. This included a substantial redistribution of wealth and the
establishment of a governmental apparatus that would be fairly
immune to corruption and plundering of natural resources. Also,
a stop to the importation of the worst aspects of Western culture,
namely commercializing of every aspect of life and the replacement
of spiritual and human values by purely materialistic ones. Since
these were the only Western values introduced by the previous
regime to the Iranian people, a rejection meant rejecting the West
altogether, and who was better placed to lead such a movement
than the Islamic fundamentalist who could offer the attractions of
a society modelled on the egalitarian and moralistic early Islamic
community of Muhammad and his followers?

Thus the irony of large numbers of women revolutionaries who,
in opposing the previous corrupt regime, rallied behind an ideology
that could be totally retrogressive for them. It is difficult to
estimate exactly the role and the extent of women's participation
in the Revolution but there is no doubt that it was very substantial.
Starting with the early waves of demonstrations in Tehran and other
cities where large numbers of women took part, it was followed
by strikes that also included a lot of women especially in areas
such as telecommunications, hospitals and factories with a majority
of women workers.

In the final February insurrection in Tehran women were very
active either as a back-up force in helping the wounded, distributing
food, setting up barricades in the streets and preparing 'molotov
cocktails', or actually taking up guns and taking over the police
stations and other strategic points. When the local committees
were first formed to take over law enforcement, women were also
involved and some actually participated in the armed guard duties
at night.

However, soon afterwards it became evident that women were
not going to achieve further emancipation through the new regime
and instead the inadequate rights and concessions granted by the
previous regime could be reversed.

The women's movement that emerged soon after the Revolution
was in response to the negative attitude of the regime to women's
particular problems. It was also carrying the general struggle against

dictatorship and for democracy and freedom a step further for women by focusing on their specific demands, such as the right not to wear the veil and maintaining the family protection courts, by now threatened with closures and a reversal to the Islamic laws on marriage and divorce.

The height of the women's movement was the events of International Women's Day and the following few days. A number of small women's groups had sprung up during and after the Revolution. They helped to organize a rally that was to celebrate International Women's Day for the first time for 25 years. However, the day before, a statement by Khomeini had denounced this day as a Western phenomenon and emphasised the need for the *chador* for women. These pronouncements enraged a lot of women, already worried and dismayed by the new authorities' attitude. They subsequently took to the streets the next day, swelling the ranks of the demonstrators.

Altogether 20,000 women took part in Tehran, some of whom went on to occupy the Ministry of Justice and passed a resolution demanding equal rights with men in family affairs, in jobs, and society at large. Also the right to choose their own dress was raised. Further demonstrations on the following days were met by much hostility and physical attacks from some reactionaries and religious fanatics. Eventually the religious leadership retreated by denouncing these attacks and confirming women's right to choose their clothing and praising their contributions to the Revolution.

Thus women had raised the first opposition to Khomeini's regime, and a partially successful one at that. Next was the turn of the national minorities who started the opposition to Khomeini through their demands for autonomy and official recognition of their religion where it was different. Most prominent among these were the Kurds in the West and the Turkamans in the North East, both groups being Sunni Muslims, as opposed to the majority Shi'ite population.

Meanwhile, the economy was in ruins. Following the strikes and the Revolution, which brought the industry to a standstill, a lot of rich businessmen and capitalists fled the country, taking away large sums of money and abandoning their business. This was especially so in the building sector which was heavily invested by foreign companies as well as large-scale agricultural developments. However, the government has taken no major steps to regenerate the businesses and subsequently there has been massive unemployment. As has been the case with many other countries, the section of the population most vulnerable to this change has been women. In this case, in addition to the customary male chauvinistic attitude that women's place is really at home — therefore the men should have priority over jobs — the puritanical religious attitudes have also helped to justify the sacking of women from offices and some other workplaces on the grounds that they are not prepared to dress according to Muslim traditions. In fact Khomeini's statement on this issue have helped some employers to cut down on women office staff to help their economy drive.

In reaction to all this, an unemployed women's group was formed that was quite active in the demonstrations and the occupation of the Justice Ministry in April 1979. A significant number of women, veiled and unveiled, took part in this occupation that lasted a few days and ended with a promise from the Labour Minister to consider the occupants' proposals regarding unemployment benefit, re-employment of the sacked workers and so on. But, of course, most of the grievances were not dealt with adequately. The new labour laws that were drawn up did not do away with discrimination against women, either in their lower pay or poorer conditions. Women were still barred from most jobs in the building industry and other heavy, skilled craft jobs.

Generally, though, in recent years, women have entered the job market in large numbers, mainly in the bigger cities. There are now industries that are run mostly by women, such as food processing, electronics, textiles etc. Also in offices, banks, and government ministries, clerical and secretarial jobs are mainly performed by women.

The new regime shows no commitment to improving conditions of women workers. This is of course in line with its ideological stance that a woman's place is at home and not outside. The first group of women to be hit by this drive for segregation were the women announcers and speakers on the radio, and especially television. It was regarded as un-Islamic for the female face to be viewed by all those eager males! Next was the turn of women lawyers whose practices and positions within the judiciary system were being curtailed, although this time there was a strong resistance. A women lawyers association was immediately set up which started a vigorous campaign against these discriminations. They were supported by various Left and progressive parties and organizations. But, due to a lack of any industrial power and the fact that the Ministry of Justice is still being run by a group of *mullahs*, they have not had much success.

In spite of all the pressures that were being put on women to go back to their homes and withdraw from the public sector, it was realized very early on that in some sectors, such as the medical profession and the industries that were heavily reliant on women, their contribution was absolutely vital. Hence these women had to be exempted from the same kind of pressures. For instance, the directives sent to hospitals on how the women employees should be dressed were often totally ignored or rejected, and there was nothing that the authorities could do about these.

Another sector that has come under attack from the new regime, following its segregation drive, has been education. In small towns and villages where there is only a mixed school, girl students have often been effectively barred from attending, as not enough resources have been available to separate the schools properly, and the boys' education is regarded as having priority over the girls'. At the same time, the Ministry of Education has been sending directives to girls' schools prohibiting them from accepting married girls, whilst lowering the age of marriage to thirteen.

Darwin's theories have been deleted from school text books and any form of sex education has been banned, not that there was much of it. Physical education and sports in general have suffered the biggest blow. The sight of young women in tennis shorts is obviously too offensive to the traditional Islamic morality. So is that of women in swimming costumes. Over the summer, women who were trying to escape the intolerable heat by going to swimming pools and the sea had to accept the limited resources offered by the separated pools and the shortage of women life guards. The spectacle of segregated beaches and a divided sea was satirized in many of the Left-wing papers.

By the end of summer opposition to Khomeini, and in particular to the ruling Islamic clique, was growing. With a worsening economy and a new form of dictatorship setting in, there was a lot of disillusionment. In spite of a severe clamp-down on the Left and press freedom, while radio and television would only broadcast the regime's propaganda, the new Constitution that was to be put to a referendum did not seem to have a great chance of being voted in. Women's position in this Constitution was implicitly much worse than in the previous one, in spite of all the praises and tributes made to women as mothers — the only function accredited to them. With a strictly Islamic Constitution this was inevitable.

To reduce the disunity and growing conflict in Khomeini's own camp, as well as generally, and hence improve the chances of a 'yes' vote for the Constitution, Khomeini used his political shrewdness once again and came out in support of the students seizing the American Embassy. Anti-imperialist feeling had been as genuine and almost as widespread as the anti-Shah feeling among the masses. After all, the Shah had been reinstated and supported through direct involvement by the Americans and the CIA. Initially it was the power struggle between the clergy supporting Khomeini on one hand and his appointed government of bourgeois Muslims on the other that culminated in the Muslim students' action, with the former trying to force the latter's hand over their continued link with America. However, afterwards, everyone jumped on the anti-imperialist bandwagon, including ministers like Ghotb-zabeh and Bani-Sadr whose background and political motivations should have disqualified them from any such claims.

Women, and other exploited strata of society, such as the national minorities and the working class in general, would benefit by preventing the government from strengthening itself through further links with America, and in generally heightening the Revolution by highlighting anti-imperialist feelings. The drawback, though, was that the support the Muslim students and Khomeini were receiving was strengthening the hands of the reactionaries. The whole saga was used also as a diversionary tactic to disguise the ineffectiveness of the new regime in dealing with the vast problems of post-Revolutionary Iran. The various women's groups had to come out in support of the anti-imperialist demonstrations, but their cries about the repressive laws and regulations that were imposed on women were often ignored.

Since the Revolution, most of the left and progressive groups and parties had formed their own women's group. They range in their size and level of activity, but the largest single group is the National Alliance of Women whose branches in the provinces are mainly formed by Fedayeen supporters (Marxist-Leninist), but in Tehran there are Mujahidin supporters (Muslim Socialists) as well as other left feminists. They have been able to extend their activities beyond the publication of a regular paper and a monthly magazine to organizing some literacy classes and health clinics for women. Other groups, however, who have been more directly associated with a Left group have found it difficult to go beyond publishing their paper. Apart from the problem of resources, the main difficulty has been the attacks and the pressure that is put on these groups by the Muslim reactionaries and fascists to whom the idea of Left-wing feminists is even more intolerable than just the godless Communists. This has meant that these groups have had to operate even more clandestinely than the Fedayeen or other Marxist groups, thereby having a more limited chance of success.

After months of attacks on women's rights and the emergence of the new constitution, a committee was formed consisting of the representatives of all the women's groups, called the Women's Solidarity Committee. Its initial activity was to organize a conference on women that was attended by an estimated 23,000 women. The resolution that was passed demanded equality in jobs, in law and other spheres for women and it was publicized in the press. The committee's next activity was to organize a rally to celebrate International Women's Day. This rally was very well attended, 7–8,000, most of whom were women. Other rallies were also organized by some women's groups.

In response to the women's movement that emerged soon after the Revolution, the Islamic regime tried to set up its own alternative Muslim women's group. The only noticeable activity, of this group was a paper called *The Muslim Woman* edited and run mainly by men! This paper printed a lot of articles by Bani-Sadr one of the prominent Muslim ideologues and an economist who became the President.

The approach used by this paper, and the Muslim ideologues in Iran in general, is very similar to that of fascists, in elevating motherhood and emphasizing the need for family authority, sexual discipline and generally religious morality. They seek to divert women's militancy from a path that will result in any real emancipation and instead control it to further their own political means. The thousands of women, clad in their black *chadors* — the veil — who regularly come out in the streets to back Khomeini's dictatorship against the Left or any progressive demands in general, while at the same time defying their traditional role of staying at home to care for their husbands and children, are the best witness to this.

Another tactic used by the Muslims, again not dissimilar to the fascists, is to employ a distorted scientific or a traditional basis for the justification of the kinds of emphasis that were mentioned earlier. For example, the assertion that 'The family is the fundamental unit of a Muslim society' is then followed by 'nothing should endanger its stability and, therefore, sex outside marriage is a totally corruptive factor' and supported by an assertion that men's level of sexual urges and needs are much higher than women's and this is because of certain sex hormones in men's bodies whereas there are no sex hormones in a woman's body!' Another example that demonstrates this tragic conditioning is when, soon after the Revolution, in a television interview with Bani-Sadr, a young girl dressed in the Islamic fashion, covering her hair with a big scarf etc, asked him if it was true that women's hair is supposed to emit certain rays that arouse men sexually and that is why in Islam women are asked to cover their hair. His answer — a man who had spent the last 20 years of his life in the West and obtained a Doctorate degree from a French university before coming back with Khomeini to win Iran's Revolution — was simply 'Yes, it is true'!

However, in spite of all the propaganda and the pressures exerted on women, whether physical force or simply rules and regulations, they have still displayed a degree of militancy and been involved in the general struggle to such a degree as to be quite unparalleled, especially in the Middle East. This has been partly due to the nature of the Revolution and the struggle that took place during the year leading up to it, and partly due to the ineffectiveness of the present regime in dealing with any of the economic or social problems that resulted from it. Looking back on the news of the past year where women were also — or solely involved in a struggle makes this quite evident. The examples of girl students taking over hotel buildings when faced with a lack of accommodation or girl graduates in the education corps — who are supposed to be given jobs as short-term teachers in villages but have been denied it — occupying the Ministry of Education offices and staging sit-ins till their demands are dealt with have been fairly abundant.

In summing up the events of the past year, one can see that on the one hand the Revolution has been a setback for women but on the other, with the unleashing of the revolutionary and militant forces in women — as well as generally — avenues have been opened to them that never existed under the Shah's overwhelming and absolute dictatorship. Whatever gains women make now — such as the right not to wear the veil — are theirs to keep, as they are not handed down by a benevolent king, and the confidence they have gained through the recent struggles will also be hard to eradicate. However, what happens in future is still not clear, since the diverse forces in Iran are still engaged in a power struggle whose outcome is not only dependent on their own strengths and tactics but also the influences that the imperialist forces — American or Russian — will eventually evolve. There is no doubt that the more secular and socialistically inclined the future regime, the better are women's chances of gaining equality and some degree of real emancipation.

The Revolution That Failed Women

Manny
Oh women till when so silent?
Till when burning and bearing
Try, like the tribal women,
Don't wear the garment of slavery.

Zand Dokht

In 1953, the Shah was restored by a CIA engineered coup. To the ally of America and gendarme of the Gulf, as was intended, Iran's economy had to be totally 'modernized'. Because of the international need of capitalism and its dependency on Gulf oil, the Shah created a dependent capitalism in Iran. Along with this came wealth for the middle classes, wealth but no democratic rights. The working class got jobs but very little else. Women too received

Mitra Tabrizian

Monireh Gorji is the representative of Iranian women in the Assembly of Experts, the temporary parliament set up to debate and draft a constitution for the Islamic Republic of Iran. Mrs Gorji was married at 14 and has three children. She has studied Islamic religion and travelled to other Islamic countries.

'Men and women are equal,' she says, 'but they have different duties and consequently have been given different rights. For instance, a woman, as a mother, is responsible for rearing her children and therefore is entitled to financial support from her husband. This right, given to women, creates a kind of security for them.

'The chador is a traditional outfit — by itself it is not important. But it is essential for a woman to cover herself (only the face should be revealed) in order not to excite men sexually. That is to say, women should have respect for themselves if they are to be respected by men and not treated as sexual objects. To some extent this applies to men as well, who should not dress so as to draw attention to their bodies.'

Since the Revolution, women have been executed in Iran for adultery. And there has been one report, which Mrs Gorji denies, of the execution of a 14-year-old unmarried girl. 'Islamic law is clear that an adulterer should be stoned to death. But to be so condemned there should be four male witnesses, which makes adultery difficult to prove. If revolutionary committees make irrational decisions it is not the fault of Islamic law.'

According to Islam, a woman cannot be a judge or even a reliable witness. 'Muhammad has said that judgment is a very hard task,' says Mrs Gorji. 'A woman is too sensitive, emotional and soft-hearted to be objective enough to judge. This has nothing to do with a woman's intelligence but has something to do with her kindly nature. This is one of the characteristics of being a woman, which, if destroyed, destroys the nature of woman. One must not rebel against one's nature; to do so would be to stand against God's will, and this is something an Islamic woman can never do.'

151

a share of the boom, but only as tools to suit the State's needs.

The Shah gave women the right to vote in 1964, The industries' demand for cheap labour had opened the job market to women. Skilled labour was needed, so education was encouraged, and women were accepted in technical colleges and universities. In later years, some factories, hospitals, and government offices got their own nurseries. Powdered milk was given free to children in the countryside, and children at school were given breakfast. Family planning was introduced, with free contraceptives, and abortion became legal.

Consumer goods like washing machines, televisions, dishwashers, Japanese electric rice cookers, poured into the country. The most banal aspects of Western life and imperialistic culture, with all its consumerism, were injected into women's lives. Most of the cinemas began showing semi-pornographic films, and advertisements on the television used women more and more as sex objects. Violence against women rose to an incredible extent. Women were attacked in the streets, were raped in their cars, on their way to work or shopping, and everybody was advising women to be home by nine p.m.

Iranian social life was topsy-turvy, and Tehran had become a sick and diseased society. Ironically, working-class boys and girls enjoyed the growing relaxation in their social life, frequenting the cafe and cinema, and discarding the veil, although most of them later joined Khomeini and supported him against these middle-class values. Women too, working outside or at home, benefited in some ways from these reforms, but they too did not ultimately defend them. They helped to bring Khomeini to power.

Women under Khomeini's Regime
When Khomeini created his Islamic Republic in 1979, he relied on the institution of the family, on support from the women, the merchants, and the private system of landownership. The new Islamic constitution declared women's primary position as mothers. The black veil, symbol of the position of women under Islam, was made compulsory. Guards were posted outside government offices to enforce it, and women were sacked from their jobs without compensation for refusing to wear the veil. The chairman of the Employment Office, in an interview with the government's women's magazine (*Zan Rooz* No. 777) said, 'We can account for 100,000 women government employees being sacked as they resisted the order of the revolutionary government, when it was demanded of them to put the veil on'.

Schools were segregated, which meant that women were barred from some technical schools, even from some religious schools, and young girls' education in the villages was halted. Lowering the marriage age for girls to 13, reinstating polygamy and *Sighen* (temporary wives), the two major pillars of Islam, meant that women did not need education and jobs, they only needed to find husbands.

The Ayatollahs in their numerous public prayers, which grew to be the only possible national activity, continuously gave sermons on the advantages of marriage, family, and children being brought up on their mothers lap. They preached that society would be pure, trouble free, criminal-less, (look at the youth problem in the West) if everybody married young, and if men married as many times as possible (to save the unprotected women who might otherwise become prostitutes). The government created a marriage bank at a time when half the working population was unemployed, whereby men were given huge sums — around £3,500 — to get married. Another *masterpiece* of the revolutionary Islamic government was to create a system of arranged marriages in prisons, between men and women prisoners, to 'protect' women after they leave prison.

Because abortion and contraception are now unobtainable, marriage means frequent pregnancy. If you are 13 when you get married, it is likely that you will have six children by the time you are 20. This, in a country where half the total population are already under 16, is a tragedy for future generations.

Women prostitutes were executed under Khomeini, who said that the cause of prostitution is woman's lust for sex. Any woman, however, who disobeys her father or brother, doesn't wear the veil, demands education and a job, is called a prostitute anyway. When 15,000 women demonstrated in Tehran against the compulsory wearing of the veil on International Women's Day 8 March 1979, Muslim men harassed the women, shouting 'You want to come out unveiled, you want to be prostitutes! If you want my prick, come on, I'll fuck you', and holding out their pricks.

Khomeini's representatives at the United Nations conference in Copenhagen last year defended the execution of prostitutes and homosexuals by saying that 'We only shoot a few of them.' They also said in an interview, 'If we were going to execute all the women prostitutes, we would have to shoot a million women.' An Iranian woman from the group told us, 'They mean us too.'

Religious morality demands that all pleasures and entertainments be banned. Wine, music, dancing, chess, women's parts in theatre, cinema and television — you name it, Khomeini banned it. He even segregated the mountains and the seas, for male and female climbers and swimmers.

But compulsory morality, compulsory marriage, and the compulsory wearing of the veil did not create the Holy Society that Khomeini was after; but public lashings, stonings, chopping of

hands and daily group executions sank Iran into the age of
Barbarism.

Why Women Did It

Why do women, workers and unemployed, support this regime
which has done everything in its power to attack their rights and
interests? The power of Islam in our culture and tradition has been
seriously underestimated by the Marxist Left, and it was through
this ideology that Khomeini directed his revolutionary government.
The clergy dealt with everyday problems and spoke out on human
relationships, sexuality, security and protection of the family and
the spiritual needs of human beings. It was easy for people to
identify with these issues and support the clergy, although nobody
knew what they were later to do. When Khomeini asked for
sacrifices — 'we haven't made the Revolution in order to eat
chicken or dress better' — women (so great in the art of sacrifice)
and workers accepted these anti-materialist ideas. (Numerous
workers' strikes were ended at his call, and their attention redir-
ected towards the siege of the American Embassy and the main
enemy, American imperialism.)

Women's attraction to Khomeini's ideas was not based simply
on his Islamic politics, but also on the way he criticized the treatment of women – as secretaries and media sex objects - under
the Shah's regime. Women were genuinely unsatisfied and looking
for change. Some educated Iranian women went back to Iran
from America and Europe to aid the clergy with the same messages,
and became the government's spokeswomen. They put on the
veil willingly, defended Islamic virtues and spiritual values, while
drawing from their own experiences in the West. They said it was
cold and lonely, Western women were only in pursuit of careers
and self-sufficiency, and that their polygamous sexual relationships had not brought them liberation, but confusion and
exploitation. These women joined ranks with an already growing
force of Muslim women, to retrieve the tradition of true/happy
Muslim women — in defence of patriarchy.

The most oppressive aspect of the role of these Muslim women
intellectuals can be seen for instance in the case of Safar Zadeh,
a leading poet and also a strong opponent of the Shah. She wrote
poems that praised Khomeini as 'The Leader', 'God's representative
on Earth', 'The Leader of the Oppressed', 'Our Saver'. These
poems were published in the daily press in large thick black letters
with a photo of her, returned to wearing the veil. A new literature
was in the process of being made, a literature of women's oppression and how women should adore it. Z. Rahnavardi is a leading
woman theoretician. She points to Marx and Engels and rejects
their materialist view, saying that they ignore all the spiritual

values of Islam, and also ignore women's vital role as producers of human life and labour. She defends the Qusas Law of retribution — a law which legitimizes the execution of homosexuals and lesbians, women adulteresses and thieves, and degrades and humiliates women publicly (women are put in a sack for public lashing). Rahnavardi says: 'There is no doubt that the laws should contain violence . . . [as] steps for reaching the purified Islamic society'.

Women and the Clergy

The clergy's contact with people in the cities and countryside has always been with women. The clergy's most important role is as administrator of the religious laws and also the economic role of collecting religious dues. Most of them were largely landowners themselves, and as a class they have been reactionary and corrupt.

The economic network created through the clergy's collection of dues plays an important social welfare base of women who are widowed or are ill, handicapped, have husbands away in jail, or are responsible for their elderly relations. (These are the common duties of women in a Third World country, where there is no social security system.) This charity function supports the indoctrination that women are helpless, and must rely on 'God the mighty, the gracious and his Imams'. It is also another reason why the religious hierarchy successfully fights against women becoming wage workers.

The clergy is also intellectually a dominant class. Many women are illiterate and they go to the clergy for help in writing letters or dealing with legal documents. For centuries, women have depended on the clergy in this way.

The mosque is not just a place of prayer, it is also a social club for women. It provides a warm, safe room for women to meet, chat or listen to a sermon, and there are traditional women-only parties and picnics in gardens or holy places. Take away these traditional and religious customs from women as the Shah — with his capitalist and imperialist reforms, irrelevant to women's needs — tried to do and a huge vacuum is left. Khomeini stepped in to fill that vacuum. The reason why Khomeini won was that the Shah's social-economic programme for women was dictatorial, bureaucratic, inadequate (especially in terms of health education) and therefore irrelevant to women's needs. What little the Shah's reform brought to women was just a token gesture. Women dissatisfied with the Shah's reform felt that they had benefited little from him and would not miss it if it was taken away.

The Veil

Perhaps nowhere else in the world have women been murdered for walking in the street open-faced. The question of the veil is the most important issue of women's liberation in Muslim countries. The veil, a long engulfing black robe, is the extension of the four walls of the home, where women belong. The veil is the historical symbol of woman's oppression, seclusion, denial of her social participation and equal rights with men. It is a cover which defaces and objectifies women. To wear or not to wear the veil, for Muslim women is 'the right to choose'.

However, this question has always been raised in conjunction with women's rights to education, health, work divorce and custody of their children. Male leaders have dictated to women for too long, what to do. Reza Shah enforced the veil, his son banned it, and his successor had enforced it. Mujahidin (the Marxist movement in Iran) men, say women should love it and wear it. But I believe in the slogan of the Iranian Women's Movement, chanted in their demonstration before they were banned, 'With veil and without veil, we opposed the Shah, with veil and without veil, we will march to uphold freedom, till the day of our liberation'.

The Future?

Iranian women's struggles since the end of the 19th Century have been harassed, slandered, stifled and banned. Khomeini was the last man who crushed women's strikes in the factory for the right to work, their sit-ins in the universities for women's rights to education, women's press meetings, demonstrations and the new Independent Women's Movement in Iran. But the movements are not remembered for victories or defeats, but for their mass participation and the messages they transmit to the future. The experience and memories of the Iranian Revolution will still linger on into the future.

The position of Left-wing parties in Iran is pretty much the same as here (small, in conflict with each other, and with very little mass support). Out of the numerous small socialist groups that exist even the revolutionary Left supported the war with Iraq and the American hostage taking as anti-imperialist struggles against the 'main enemy : American imperialism. The Communist Party of Iran has put all its weight behind Khomeini with one hand, and blind submission to the Soviet Union with the other.

After Khomeini made the veil compulsory in March 1979 one month after the Revolution, there was little doubt in the Iranian woman's mind that the Revolution was being betrayed. But the Left continued calling it a revolutionary government and supported it. In August last year, *Liberation*, the French radical newspaper carried a feature entitled Women's Groups are the only opponents of Khomeini'. And so it was. It is only since Khomeini began persecuting the Muslim socialists, the Mujahidin, that they have come out to oppose him openly. (1,800 of their members, among them many women, have been executed during the last few months.)

The Mujahidin is growing in Iran. They have socialist views on class struggle and the planned economy, but on the women's question they uphold Quranic principles. Their leader in Paris has created together with ex-president Bani-Sadr, a government in exile. Mujahidin could become a mass movement to overthrow Khomeini. Although their guerrilla activities could go against them they could use the contradiction inherent in Islamic ideology to push for social reforms. But we will not be fools, 'Once bitten, twice shy'. However, their strong identification with Islam seems to be working against them, and a takeover by the army and the Shah's supporters is more possible.

When Khomeini came back to Iran, four million people demonstrated in his support. Today, at most 30,000 demonstrate for him when he calls them to the street. He has been losing his supporters faster than the Shah. A mother of a friend in Paris phoned from Tehran and said, 'My dear girl the situation is grim, really bad . . . well . . . praying and the religious duties are not solving our countries problems, nor feeding our bellies'. She was astounded to hear this from her old, pious mother. This is our best hope, the doubts that Khomeini's government is creating in women's minds. Perhaps for the first time women are questioning the usefulness of Islam.

Sisterhood is Strong — Is It International?
I don't know. Britain is an island anyway. But I have come across numerous historical documents where women have expressed such desires on both sides. Today, most important of all the tasks is the creation of *links* and *dialogue* between the individual feminists, feminists groups, and the Women's Liberation Movement in the West with the struggling women in the east. After the revolution Iranian women asked us to send them any materials on women's struggles from here. We posted them any leaflets and papers we could get hold of. The anti-pornography campaign, the *depo-provera* campaign and the ideas of Women Against Violence Against Women are most relevant to the struggles of women in Muslim countries. Why not make the link? An equal link, based on what we have in common. As women struggling for rights — the right to walk in the streets — our struggles have no boundaries wherever we may be.

In one of the Iranian women's demonstrations, the Muslim women were chanting against other women. 'Neither the East, nor the West. Islam is the best'. Iranian women chanted back, 'Liberation

is neither Eastern, nor Western, but International'. A year ago,
during the International Workshop within the Fragments conference, the participants decided on a Middle East day-school. Can I
here suggest that it is about time we organized it?

15. Women in the New Grenada
Patsy Romain

Patsy Romain is 27 years old, the mother of four children and now
works full time as a member of the National Executive of the
National Women's Organization of Grenada. The NWO is affiliated
to the New Jewel Movement, the political party which formed in
1973 to lead a long popular struggle against the corrupt dictatorship of Eric Gairy. Gairy was finally overthrown on 13 March
1979 when the now ruling People's Revolutionary Government
was established.

During the pre-revolutionary period women played an active
role in the underground struggle, including the production and
distribution of illegal newspapers and pamphlets, as well as in
public protests and demonstrations, and in fund-raising to support
the liberation movement. Many took up arms and, with the
constant threat of direct military invasion, Grenadian women are
now fully integrated into the National Militia. They are also
studying and working in many other non-traditional areas, such
as fishing, furniture-making, welding, dentistry and science, as
well as taking part in all aspects of the island's revolutionary
development.

This interview with Patsy Romain took place on 12 March
1981 in St George's, Grenada, and was first published in *Inter-
continental Press* (6 April 1981).

Question: Can you tell us how the National Women's Organization was formed?

Answer: The NWO was started around 1977. We could not
organize women to have meetings in the open because of fear of
victimization by the Gairy regime. From the different parishes, we
had ten sisters all together. They went out to the different areas

to organize women underground. They would go out speaking in the homes of people they knew. You had to be careful around that time. You had to know who would accept you in their homes, who would not put out the news that you were coming to their home.

We talked about how lower prices would be better for women and their children and husbands. We had pamphlets explaining why it was necessary for a change in Grenada, what the benefits would be if there was a government that was supporting working and poor people in Grenada.

Shortly after the revolution, we had about 13 groups. We now have 46. We also have groups in the sister island of Carriacou.

Q: How many members do you have?

A: At present we have a membership of 1,500. The sizes of the groups vary. Sometimes you find a big village where no group has been formed; sometimes in a small village there is one.

Q: How young are women in the NWO?

A: From 14 years.

Q: The breadth of support among women for the Revolution seems very extensive. How do you explain this amount of support among women so early in the Revolution?

A: Since the Revolution, women in Grenada have seen many benefits coming from it. I think this is one of the reasons you find so many women in Grenada supporting the Revolution.

You have equal pay for equal work. You have free medical attention. You have the lowering of secondary school fees to £12.50, and these will be free from September 1981. You have more scholarships being given. You have women getting their equal rights in this society. You have women getting the Maternity Leave Law. The more benefits women see, the more they support the Revolution.

Q: What are the day-to-day activities of the NWO?

A: The activities of the NWO are to push forward all programmes of the People's Revolutionary Government. For example, the co-operatives, helping to ease the unemployment situation. We have the CPE, the Centre for Popular Education, trying to wipe out illiteracy in our country, which is higher among women.

We also have the community brigades. All around the island the NWO is actively involved in pushing these forward. Also there are a number of women playing an active part in the People's Militia and the People's Revolutionary Army.

Q: What are the long-range goals and projects that the NWO is thinking about?

A: As for this year 1981, we are hoping to open the first day-care centre in Grenada. For the time being there are many pre-primary schools that are being opened by the NWO At present there is a co-operative bakery at Bylands being formed by the NWO group there.

Q: Could you explain a little bit about the co-operative bakery and how it works?

A: At Bylands, I was vice-president of that group and around that time we had a campaign going around 'Grow More Food . It is a campaign that every inch of land in Grenada must be made to produce. It is the 'Idle Lands for Idle Hands' programme to help ease unemployment.

When we looked around Bylands, there were no idle lands. There was a high percentage of unemployment. So we decided that something had to be worked out in another way. We made different suggestions, trying to think just what would work at Bylands. Then the suggestion came for a bakery.

So we informed the co-operative officer at the National Co-operative Development Agency (NACDA) that we would like to have a little talk on co-operatives and how to go about it. He came up and did a feasibility study.

Sometime last year, everything was fixed up. The land was rented and we had the funds from NACDA The bakery has helped to employ ten sisters from NWO in Bylands and four men. The oven will not be run by gas or electricity, but will be one of the old-time brick ovens. It will hold a few hundred loaves at a time.

Q: How does it work with the profits?

A: I must say that the co-operative is not open yet. The building is just going ahead. But the profits will pay back the loan and then the shares will be equally divided among the people at the bakery. So after the loan has been paid back, these people will be the owners of the bakery.

Q: Does the NWO have relations with women's organizations in other countries?

A: Yes. We have relations with many other women's organizations — Nicaragua, Cuba, Guyana, Jamaica, St. Vincent, the United States, Canada. In some cases, when they have a conference, they will invite us to send a representative to speak on behalf of Grenada. Likewise when we have a conference we send them an invitation.

We, the women of Grenada, decided to celebrate International Women's Day on 8 March as it is celebrated all over. We had the NWO groups in all the different villages going out to mobilize the women to come out to that rally. We sent invitations to different countries, asking them to send representatives.

It was a successful rally: many people turned out and we had many visitors. Mrs. Mugabe [wife of Zimbabwean Prime Minister Robert Mugabe] was here. The success of that rally was very good for the the NWO group in Grenada.

Q: You've talked a little bit about this already, but perhaps you could elaborate on the kinds of changes the Revolution has brought for women, particularly in terms of the kinds of jobs they do?

A: Before, women were never considered for high positions. Today, in Grenada, we see women are being placed, for example, in the Marketing Board. We have a woman who is the manager there. At the bakery at Bylands a woman will also be the manager.

Before, women would not take up an offer to learn to be a dentist or to be an agricultural person. They would see such jobs as men's. But now, when a scholarship is offered for a woman to learn to be a dentist, to go away and study and come back to teach the people about agriculture, engineering, mechanics, you see women coming forward and saying that they would like to be trained to do this.

We did not have this before: women were not seen as equal to men in Grenada. That had an effect on women also not wanting to go out there, to be a dentist, because they were always thinking that their place was in the home.

But a lot of work has to be done and is being done to show

161

women that their place is not only in the home, but to be equal, working alongside men. Not fighting against men, but working alongside the men.

Q: What about day-care for the children of women who work?

A: Every place you have your farm co-operatives, you create jobs, and there must be places for the children in day-care or pre-primary schools. We have plans for this. In Bylands, where the co-operative bakery is being formed, we decided that it would be best to also have a pre-primary school in that area to keep the little children while the parents are at work.

Q: Are birth control and abortion available?

A: The Grenada family planning association's responsible for birth control. Right now the NWO is not really controlling that. We are hoping in the year 1981 to push forward, showing women the need for birth control, how it will be good for them, the advantages and disadvantages in birth control.

As for abortion, there is no law in Grenada stating whether women have the right to abortion or not. We haven't worked this out yet.

Q: How have the changes in health care affected women specifically?

A: It has been good, especially after we had the help of 12 Cuban doctors and dentists. In Grenada, there was a time when some of the villages had never seen a doctor for weeks. Right now there is free medical attention in all government clinics and hospitals. This has been a great benefit.

Before the Revolution there were times when there was no medicine at the hospitals and people going to the hospitals would have to buy their own medicine. Today it is better in Grenada. We have dentists. Dentists were very expensive, but now we have the Cuban dentists giving free attendance so that will also be a benefit for women.

Q: Could you talk about the role of women in the militia?

A: From the very first day that the militia was formed, the NWO had the task to get all the women organized into it. We had cases where women said that they were too old to join, so we organized classes for them, so that they could also be part of the militia. In case people get injured, everybody will not be able to go out on the battlefield with guns in their hands, but some should be prepared to dress the wounded. Some should also be prepared to cook food to pass along. Some should be prepared to be able to run with news to different parts of the country. So the militia is not just holding the guns in your hands, but also first-aid, cooking, and news running.

Q: How has the Centre for Popular Education literacy drive affected women?

A: This drive was very successful. We had an emulation period of the first phase which ended last Sunday, the first of March. Unfortunately, women had a higher percentage of illiteracy.

Women also took a very firm stand in going out to help teach the unfortunate. We had a high percentage in that also. In most cases they went to the people's homes, because some people did not like going to a classroom. Instead of going in the open so that everybody could see that they could not read and write, they preferred it at home.

But from April, when we start the second phase, which will be teaching basic arithmetic, English, history of Grenada, and so on, this will be done on a larger scale, where people will come out to schools, night schools, whichever they prefer.

Q: What changes are there now in public school education?

A: The entire educational system has been changed since the Revolution. We have a different kind of system, so as to train teachers better to also teach the children better.

Before the Revolution, boys were taught more of the science work, and girls were taught arithmetic, sewing, cooking, and so on. This has been changed. They show the girls that they should do and can do the same amount of subjects as the boys.

16. Women in Nicaragua AMNLAE

On 19 July 1979 the Sandinista Front for National Liberation (FSLN) guerrilla army marched in Managua, the capital of Nicaragua. Thirty percent of the FSLN soldiers were and still are women. Their victory hailed the downfall of Anastasio Somoza, the last in line of the Somoza family which had ruled Nicaragua for 40 years. It also signified an overthrow of the power of the United States which, through its support of rulers such as Somoza, had effectively controlled the country for over 100 years, and which continues to control other countries of the region such as El Salvador.

The role of the women's organization in this struggle was vital, and continues to be very strong today. In 1977, women got together to denounce repression in the concentration camps, the mass murder of peasants and the rape of peasant women. From this, an organization was born: AMPRONAC (Association of Women Confronting the National Problem). After the war AMPRONAC was re-formed into AMNLAE (Association of Nicaraguan Women Luisa Amanda Espinoza), named after the first women martyred in the FSLN, and a working class woman. The name represents an identification of the women's movement with working class ideas. AMNLAE has a distinctive organizational structure, largely based on the promotion of Work Committees composed of two to five women. These are formed in factories, large plantations, rural communities, markets, hospitals, educational institutions etc. and act as points of liaison between AMNLAE and women in the various sectors.

The following interviews with two members of AMNLAE are an edited version of tapes kindly made available by Marilyn Thomson of the Nicaraguan Solidarity Committee in London.

I. There is a generation of peasants living in the city and the majority of them are women who have been forced into sub-employment, concentrated mainly in the service sector; in domestic work, a few in industry and a small group who receive technical or professional training and are working in their own specific field. But AMNLAE is at present working to try and integrate more women into production. In 1977 a study was carried out in the marginal areas and shanty-towns of Managua, working-class areas, and it was found that 40% of the women there are heads of families.

Jenny Matthews

Workers take it in turns to guard their factory against counter-insurgency attacks.

The reason why women became involved in the political struggle was because of their consciousness of themselves as workers and the direct effect of the economy on them. Because of their responsibilities to their children, working-class women were forced to work and became militantly involved in the political struggle. The migration of families from the countryside to the cities was followed by a constant movement back to the countryside by their *compañeros*. Many people don't move straight to the cities but live in the shanty-towns on the outskirts and, in better times, return to the countryside for maybe three months during the harvests. This movement of men between the cities and the countryside meant that women were often left to their own devices in the city, resulting in a high number of single mothers. Sometimes these women might be completely alone because their *compañeros* had forgotten about their children and started a new family elsewhere. Left on their own, they are forced on to the streets to supplement any wages they might be earning. In this way some women fall into the trap of prostitution or take up any type of work, on top of the double-shift of housework. Many women have developed a combative spirit because they have had to assume the economic as well as the domestic role, and also the double, social parental role.

Q: The mass organizations and trade unions don't seem to have special programmes for women. Can AMNLAE meet this function?

A: This problem is one that will be changed with the new direction of AMNLAE. We are suggesting that the small separate structure which AMNLAE has created for women, separate from the rest of the mass organizations, in different neighbourhoods, will now be used to integrate women more into the mass organizations. In the cities, the Work Committees in every neighbourhood will stimulate the participation of women in the CDS [*Commite de Defensa Sandinista*]. In the countryside, where the AMNLAE structures exist, we are going to promote the participation of rural women workers from the coffee or cotton sectors, or wherever they work, in the ATC or UNLAC, which are the two organizations in the agriculture sector. The ATC and the UNLAC will receive instructions through the central committee, the *Secretaria de Masas*, to respond to the problems and the demands presented by women workers. We have already had one experience of how this will work, in the countryside. There was a group of women workers on the state sugar farms who requested assistance from their trade union because they had nowhere to leave their children while they worked. The union took up their demands and found a place for the children. They requested training from the Ministry of Social Welfare for the women who were going to look after the children and they looked for financial assistance from the state and the community. So we can see that, even if at present in the organizational lines of the trade unions there is no particular position on women, they are capable of taking up the demands of AMNLAE. This is official now and should be adopted, which will mean that the most urgent and immediate demands of women will be met through the trade unions and the CDS.

Q: Does AMNLAE have a view on the way in which women should be trained in the future? Will this be outside the traditional occupational roles of women?

A: AMNLAE is concerned that women should be trained for jobs that were previously reserved for men, but we must work within the process and start off with the needs of our Revolutionary process. We cannot just take up the training of women without taking into account the economic situation of the country. Otherwise we could be training these women in areas where later they won't be absorbed into the labour market because there is not enough demand. So we have to start from the point of the most immediate need of the Revolution, and from there look at how women can be integrated. For instance, we know that INRA has been organizing training in the use of tractors and harvesters, but to date no women have gone through these courses, only men. So, through an AMNLAE committee in Leon, engaging in discussion and information exchange with rural women, we intend to promote the idea that they are capable of working on other things, not just in the harvest, and we are going to try and get a group of women on to these training courses. But these are the most immediate needs of INRA within our Revolution, and we must respond to those needs rather than starting from our own perspectives, which are also very valid but won't always fit within the process.

Detail from a mural in Managua.

Q: Does AMNLAE see adult education as a way of training women?

A: Women are mainly being trained in the area of *promocion social*. Through INRA and the Ministry of Employment for instance, women, who make up a third of the workforce, have been trained as health workers, child-care workers for the SIR (*Servicio Infantil Rural*) and in promoting the Soya programme.

Women have been trained in these three areas through INRA and, though I don't have information on the training courses run by the Ministry of Employment, these are in the more traditional areas.

Q: Has AMNLAE discussed the question of women's salaries in relation to those of men?

A: Yes. After the victory, an article in the Employment Code was changed because it discriminated against women in pay. During the dictatorship not only were women being paid less but in the harvests, where women worked alongside men they were paid as part of a family wage given to the man. This was one thing that was changed immediately after the triumph. The reformed article of law states that women must be paid independently for their work and at the same time receive the same pay. However, this code is not being implemented in all areas. For instance, in the private sector, where revolutionary organizations don't exist, these reforms are almost certainly not being implemented. We don't have information on the private sector but I think there are differentials. In the state industrial sectors there is very little difference between men's and women's pay.

II. Since the victory of the Revolution, AMNLAE has worked on the question of women and our principal task has been to ensure the participation of women in the different areas necessary to consolidate our Revolution. We began working at a national level trying to develop the organization to meet the needs of women in different sectors and allow them to participate actively in the tasks of the Revolution that were necessary at the time. We participated in the voluntary work sector to help raise economic production. AMNLAE formed women's brigades and worked in the coffee and cotton harvests, as volunteers in the hospitals, cleaning up neighbourhoods and in the markets. With other mass organizations, we participated in the National Education Conference in which women were given a particular say in the content of children's education. We participated widely in the literacy crusade where we worked as literacy teachers and students. As the Revolutionary process has been developing we too, as a women's organization, have defined and developed our area of work. Faced with the threatened aggression against our country from abroad, and the call of the government to defend our country, we in turn called on women to participate in the popular militias. The participation of women in the militias has been very extensive and we were also able to form a reserve women's battalion. This was real victory we had to fight for, as there was no official plan to have a women's battalion. Yet we women had actually

Jenny Matthews

Communal washing area built since the Revoluation.

demonstrated that we knew how to fight and die for our country with guns in our hands. So we made our demands to the Revolutionary government and there are now two women's battalions, and we are working toward the formation of a third and training women in armed combat. We have also developed a range of activities to meet the country's need for defence. We carry out promotional work to try to involve more women in the militias. At first we had a spontaneous response, without any need for us to recruit. But since then we have responded to the call of the *Frente Sandinista* and AMNLAE has taken this call to specific sectors of women. We do this by organizing activities and meetings to explain the needs of the country, why women must be involved, and why we must increase the level of participation in defence.

Q: How are women participating in the mass organizations?

A: Nicaraguan women have traditionally participated in the struggle of the people and through this we have developed our participation in the Revolution. Prominent in AMNLAE's beliefs is our concern that women should win their emancipation and liberation in practice. Women should fight the discrimination and marginalization of their position that the corrupt dictatorship left us with, and what interests us now is that women are overcoming this within the mass organizations in which they are working. One of our specific tasks as an organization is to ensure that women are involved in trade unions and that they put forward their demands as women and make their presence felt by their active involvement in all the problematic areas that the trade union is working on. It is in our own interest to ensure that our demands as women are being met. The new AMNLAE line is that we should concentrate on promoting the involvement of women and their demands within the mass organizations and that they in turn should feel identified with the organization of women, as we are fighting for their demands at all levels. We are not particularly concerned to have a separate women's organization but that women should be involved at all levels: politically and socially, that peasant women take on more responsibilities within their trade unions and that all women should take up distinguished positions within our Revolution. We also want to see housewives leaving the four walls of their houses and getting involved in work through the CDS. We are not interested in women's passive involvement, we want an active, belligerent integration.

Q: Did AMNLAE have problems as an organization because women were more attracted to other organizations?

A: Women had too much work to be able to take on positions of responsibility within many organizations. So they had to choose between, say, trade union work and AMNLAE, or work with the CDS and participating in the militias. AMNLAE's role should be to promote women's participation, not necessarily to organize women just as women, with their own particular demands, but to meet the needs of the Revolution. This is our guarantee of obtaining our demands and emancipation. We must therefore work toward women's emancipation within the organizations that women are involved in, thus winning the right to equality in society as a whole. AMNLAE has started to implement this form of work and we feel that it is the correct way for us to develop. Women identify with AMNLAE and see it as the organization that looks after their interests, as an organization which is working to overcome the different levels of marginalization that we still have in our society. We women are products of ideological changes and we women, the interested parties, must deepen our involve-

ment in society as a whole. This is a long-term process but we are
making advances as women distinguish themselves through their
own achievements. There are women who still uphold *machista*
attitudes, but we are making gains as women distinguish themselves in different fields, not just in the women's organization.
From the professional women to the unskilled worker, the peasant
woman and in the community, when women start to become more
active in whatever field they are involved, then they will be able
to make their demands felt. The main thing is that AMNLAE has
tried to support the activities of the Revolution while at the same
time putting forward women's demands. Women should be integrated into the mass organizations, the women's situation cannot
be viewed in isolation from the social context and the demands
of the country.

Part V:
An Autonomous Women's Movement?

Delhi Street Song

I watch from my glass-paned door
The streets are filled with movement,
The city hums with life.

> Sister, don't you see it?
> The strut of the servant boy,
> his *lungi* stiff with dirt?
> Girl, can't you feel it —
> the pride in the old man's eye,
> a grandson in his arms?

I only sit behind this window
She can't unlock her garden door.

> Brother, won't you notice
> the daughter-in-law's soft weeping,
> smell the kerosene-stained hands?
> Son, you mean you didn't hear it,
> your grandmother's lone sighing,
> the rub of the rope-hung fan?

I must make the family's living,
I can't dream of foreign lands.

> Uncle, was it you who felt desire,
> Took her body with your gold-ringed hand?
> Heard her whispers in the curtained room?
> Father, did you hear her praying?
> Memories waning, find her
> mumbling to a darkened shrine?

I don't know the women's language,
Daughter, I can't hear some mother's words.

> When the vendor sells his *tikki*, brother,
> do you hear his prices clear?
> When the curry's off the fire, father,
> can't you smell it from afar?

I am just my mother's darling, sister,
He is woman's pride and fear.

>Do you see her clearly, sister,
>face hidden in the sari's end?
>Feel the pinching in the buses,
>hear the 'brother's' taunting words?
>Will you follow in her footsteps
>walking minced, avoiding stares?

>Am I not my mother's daughter, sister
>Can I hold my head up high?
>Does our father hear our voices?
>Can we do anything but cry?

We are not just female servants, sister
and I'm damned if I'll just die
Joined together there is power, sister —
No one hears the victim's sigh

Arlene Zide

From *Manushi*, No 4, Dec 1979–Jan 1980.

17. Why an Autonomous Women's Movement?
Paris Latin American Women's Group

The following extract is transcribed from a much longer discussion which took place among a group of Latin American feminists in Paris. It first appeared in French and Spanish in the bulletin *Latinoamericanas* (No. 1, February 1979). The meeting in Brussels referred to was the first gathering of Latin American women's groups in Europe, in September 1978. Lausanne refers to a solidarity symposium which was later attended by all the groups represented in Brussels.

G: It was after the discussion in Belgium that we saw the importance of reaching a deeper understanding of what we mean by the term 'autonomous women's movement'. What are the priorities or are there any priorities in Latin America? Is the feminist struggle in Latin America different from the struggle here?

AM: In other words we need to discuss, on the one hand, what our understanding of an autonomous women's movement is and, on the other, what the possibilities are of having an autonomous movement in Latin America.

G: Do we believe that an autonomous women's organization is the best form of organization for uniting ourselves and developing our objectives?

AM: All of us here think the answer is 'yes' — that's obvious. But the question is 'why'.

G: What is an autonomous movement? Autonomous in relation to what?

AM: Before we start talking about an autonomous movement, we should discuss why it should be women-only and not a mixed movement. I personally think it's because women have always been oppressed and exploited which means, purely at the level of oppression, that they haven't had a chance to express themselves freely, or consider other women as capable beings, people worth talking to. They haven't discovered the implications of talking with other women because, at the centre, there have always been relationships of rivalry and competition — a form of communication devoid of solidarity . . .

G: . . . based on their domination by certain privileged sectors of society, i.e. men, who also dominate language. A definite ideology is spread through language, a conception of life used by men to negate women. Part of our struggle is also to discover and rediscover language and communication.

AM: That's right. For me it's a question of rediscovering words, the words of women, and it's very difficult. It's hard enough for us to speak amongst ourselves . . . doing it in a mixed group would be impossible, with men looking . . . (laughter) . . . or participating in our discussions. I think we need to go through a process of maturation, of discovery and evaluation.

N: Then, following on from what you've said, it's important to consider how autonomy can politicize certain problems which have always been seen as private problems, experienced by every woman in isolation. Through autonomy and the fact of being first able to join together in solidarity with other women, we have made a private problem into a political one. At the same time, men aren't going to give up their privileges willingly; and it's up to us to denounce those privileges which form the basis of our oppression, by uniting ourselves in a specific women's struggle in the same way that other oppressed groups have done or are still doing, for example, black people in the United States. It's in this sense that I think autonomy is important, where groups aren't mixed.

AM: I think we have got to recreate our own language, our own discourse, completely different and of a different nature from that of the *macho* male. His has been the sole discourse we have used so far, since it's been the vehicle of all human history. This means, in the final analysis, that all hierarchical conceptions, all existing power, is tied to objective conditions, both in terms of the economic situation and the infrastructure. In other words, it's tied to the power relations which men establish with the opposite sex. Our discourse cannot reproduce these power relations or this hierarchy.

G: But we're not at a historical level where we can speak the same language and so, if we don't have a language to affirm our identity, we'll establish a relationship of unequal strength, something which we don't want to reproduce.

N: Everywhere we hear that of course women must organize autonomously and all political parties recognize the fact, but in reality they say 'no' to an autonomous movement because they

say that the liberation of women will come with the total liberation of society. This is perhaps why we have also to explain
how, on a political level, an autonomous women's movement also
touches the whole of society. Comrades, men in general, say 'once
we understand the women's question and want to fight with
women, they won't let us'. But the fact that the Women's Movement isn't mixed doesn't imply that there aren't any male comrades supporting the feminist movement. That's marvellous . . .
great.

AM: For me, a woman who becomes politically conscious of being
a woman is a feminist. What feminism does is to develop our
consciousness of oppression and exploitation into a collective
phenomenon, capable of transforming reality, and therefore
revolutionary.

G: In Belgium many of our women comrades were horrified
as soon as we started talking about autonomy because, on top
of seeing autonomy from a political party as an invalid form of
organization, they thought that talking about an autonomous
movement was almost like saying that our struggle was marginal
to others. In fact this conception directly contradicts what we
believe. For us, an autonomous women's movement is what gives
us the possibility of stating our own demands, which we know
touch all spheres of society. We can only fight inside society when
we ourselves are secure enough to propose an alternative; fighting
for our own demands that are united and go hand in hand with
the process which is happening in society, namely, class struggle.
In Belgium we asked those who thought it was a mistake to have
an autonomous women's movement (and that was how they put
it): do you consider that organizing ourselves as women for our
own demands — which go beyond the family, beyond all classes
and the ideology of this system — we are in any way going against
the movement towards the destruction of bourgeois power and
the power of the state? We believe that our struggle does not
contradict the process of class struggle, because our oppression has
been so deep and is so rooted in the system that, fighting in this
way, we're neither to one side nor outside but, through a militant feminist practice, working right within the revolutionary
process.

N: I think many political parties are afraid of losing control of
our struggles. Some facts are clear: first of all, some women change
positions, taking one stand in women's meetings and another in
front of comrades from their organizations. This was the case in
Brussels where certain positions were taken, only to change in
Lausanne. In Brussels, a certain number of women comrades,
through the dynamics of discussion, were beginning to accept that

autonomy was important because they could see it for themselves and felt freed from the political oppression of their organizations. In Lausanne, however, where there was a mixed audience, the problems which had seemed so clear and had led to quite a number of conclusions no longer appeared so clear and even discussing them revealed quite a bit of insecurity. Therefore, I think that the women's struggle goes beyond the seizure of economic power because it implies ideological changes which political parties don't usually consider amongst their immediate objectives.

G: Talking about economism, I think we can add an example from the Belgium meeting when we were analysing the situation of women in Cuba. We looked at it in the framework of the 1975 Family Code presented to the Communist Party Congress which said: 'Socialist morality doesn't condemn sexual relations outside marriage, but it is against promiscuity', meaning sexual relations which aren't based on love and responsibility. It condemns the kind of 'moralistic' attitudes that force a young woman who gets pregnant to get married and have the child. Abortion is free and there are means of contraception for avoiding extreme situations. *At the same time, we recognize that the goal of sexual relations is procreation*, the difference being that the woman or couple can choose the right time and conditions for having children without having to practise abstinence' (emphasis by the editors of this bulletin). This is no more than a bourgeois morality, proclaimed by a state which calls itself socialist. For us, this shows how structural economic changes just aren't enough. Marxist analysis itself tells us that more than economic changes are needed for the transformation of society. It also requires ideological changes in the superstructure, which are more difficult to achieve and will only happen later.

AM: It's important to clarify (a thousand times if necessary since this is addressed to people on the Left) the weight that ideology has on our oppression, and to expose the economistic bias which we all have as a result of misreading history. This applies to most militants on the Left, both in Europe and in Latin America. To believe that by switching from one mode of production to another we destroy, not only women's oppression but an entire conceptualization of the world, of the state, of power, women, children, education, is to follow what's called in sociology the 'Theory of Reflex'. In fact, it is to castrate Marxism by reducing it to a very crude form of economism in order to avoid calling into question, first of all, the power, hierarchy and vertical structure of our political organizations (for ideological changes also affect political organizations); and the power which our dear, male comrades have held throughout history. 'Mr Marx' could not have produced what

he did if his wife had not done what she did. This has to be said.
And when Marx said in an interview that he considered the main
virtue of men to be strength and of women to be weakness,
this we cannot ignore.

18. The Anti-Rape Movement in India
Vibhuti, Suhata, Padma (Forum Against Rape)

This is an edited version of a paper presented at the National
Conference on a Perspective for a Women's Liberation Movement
in India, held in Bombay (November 1980). The original paper
was introduced as follows: This paper will critically examine
and assess the current anti-rape movement in comparison with
other women's movements in India which have, at one time or
another, mobilized mass support. It is an analysis and account of
the anti-rape movement in terms of its genesis, the extensive
momentum it gathered in a short time and the issues confronting
one group in particular, the Forum Against Rape, Bombay.
Through such an analysis we hope to show that while autonomous
women's movements are necessary, their relevance is limited and
they need to actively and concretely link themselves to wider
radical political movements.

The Background

In the last 20 years, there have been sporadic attempts to organize
and mobilize women, mostly around specific issues and, therefore, by their very nature they have been neither sustained nor
extensive.

The 1960s saw increasing activity amongst trade unions and
political parties in attempts to organize women. A few Marxist
trade unions took up workplace issues and economic demands
made by women, often on a separate platform, in areas where
women predominated. This trend, however, slackened by the
early 1970s. The current, more generalized, resurgence of interest
in 'the women's question' can be traced back to the mid-1970s
and the impact of the Women's Movement in the West on individual

179

women and some women's groups in India. The explosive economic and political situation of 1974 gave rise to women's groups organizing around specific issues: dowry and Eve-teasing [sexual molestation of varying degrees on streets, in buses etc., for example wolf whistling] in Hyderabad, Bihar and Gujerat; price rises and corruption in Bihar, Gujerat, Madhya Pradesh [MP] areas around Bombay; drought in Maharashtra, and so on.

The nature and experiences of women's groups during this period allows for them to be classified as follows: 1) Those which developed as a conscious response to the need for women to organize together in the foreground [within/as part of?] of a broad political movement which also expressed the aspirations of women as human beings; and 2) women's organizations which developed in relative isolation from the broader political context.

The Shramik Sanghatana [Toiler's Organization] in Shahada, North Maharashtra, is an example of the first type. It comprised landless labourers and poor farmers and was formed in the early 1970s. Along with its other activities, the *Sanghatana* took up the issue of the rape of tribal, landless and labouring women by rich farmers, the police and *goondas* [hired henchmen]. Campaigns against wife beating were also organized, and the 1973 droughts saw the beginning of active participation from women. Five years later, a separate women's organization, the *Stree Mukti Sanghatana* (Women's Liberation Organization) was formed. The *Shramik Sanghatana's* all-male leadership, as well as its isolation from other movements, including other women's movements, played a role in the long gestation period before an autonomous women's organization could emerge.

Totally different in class composition and genesis were those women's organizations which emerged during the middle class mass unheavals in Gujerat and Bihar in 1974, and the Anti-Price-Rise women's organizations in Maharashtra, Gujerat and Madhya Pradesh in the same year. The former emerged from the spontaneous participation of women students and middle class housewives but was short-lived. The latter emerged as a result of initiatives taken by women leaders of the CPI, CPI(M) and SP, and took up the issues of price rises, food adulteration etc. and so gathered momentum very quickly. But, despite press publicity as well as the initial enthusiasm it received, this movement too, petered out. The probable reasons for this were the exclusively middle class leadership of the movement with almost no participation by working class women; secondly that the thrust of these movements was around the distribution of essential commodities and their consumption, and not their production. It believed in the myth of the possibility of proper, fair and just distribution within the framework of a total lack of control over production.

The *Stree Mukti Sanghatana* (SMS) and the *Purogami Stree Sanghatana* (PSS) emerged as a result of discussions of 'the women's question' in 1976, mainly around Bombay and Pune. Their composition was almost exclusively upper-middle class, and their impact remained narrow. Neither related meaningfully to a wider political movement which could involve the mass of working class women, and any attempts made to relate to working class women (eg. by founding creches) failed. They can best be described as a cultural–educational forum, and have been functioning as such for five years, a remarkable achievement given the political context in which they emerged.

Other women's organizations such as the Progressive Organization of Women (POW) from Hyderabad, *Stree Sangharsh* and *Mahila Daxata Samiti* in Delhi have taken up other issues, such as the practice of dowry, dowry deaths, sexual molestation of women, work conditions, etc.

Yet again, completely different from any of those mentioned so far, is the *Chipko* movement — a spontaneous agitation of Gharwali women against deforestation and other 'development' practices.

This has developed into a women's movement agitating for basic economic and ecological demands, with as yet ill-defined political foundations. Attempts to co-ordinate actions have been few. One such was a workshop for women activists held in Bombay. Two important consequences were: a) a newsletter called 'Feminist Network'; b) the emergence of *Manushi*, a journal about women and society.

Genesis of the Anti-Rape Movement

An important question to bear in mind, given the variety of women's organizations outlined above, is why did the anti-rape movement gain momentum more quickly than any other issue-oriented campaign or movement?

An examination of the conditions and circumstances operative in the late 1970s throws light on this issue. For many middle class women the Emergency and its practice and consequences was the first time they had seen the oppressive machinery of the State in action. Many began to question the powers given to the police and State authorities in the control of people's lives, heightened further by their role in the caste and communal riots and atrocities committed therein. Increasing instances of rape by the police were coming to light, assisted by press coverage (which reduced its significance to a 'civil liberties' issue). In this context, it was hardly surprising that when the facts about the rape of Mathura by two policemen came to be known, there was a national outcry.

Briefly, Mathura, a young girl, was raped by two policemen behind the police station. After agitations by inhabitants of the area, a case was heard in court which found the accused guilty. However, an appeal was made the this resulted in a revoking of the verdict, and the two policemen were set free. Prominent lawyers took up the case, as did the national press; women from all over the country reacted angrily, and the anti-rape movement throughout India was launched.

Women came out in large numbers in opposition to the Supreme Court judgement, staged rallies, demonstrations, submitted petitions to MLAs and the Prime Minister, and generally alerted the public not just to Mathura's case, but the incidence of rape and its treatment by the law generally. The initiative for this activity was mostly taken by middle class and upper-middle class women, women of higher educational backgrounds, some cf whom were influenced and inspired by feminist movements from Western countries.

From amongst the number of organizations formed to fight

rape, it was the Forum Against Rape in Bombay that sustained and expanded its activities to include investigations around specific rape cases in the area, offering support to the women, although limited in its scope. The Forum began as an *ad hoc* body, and despite its heterogenous composition in terms of economic, social and political backgrounds of its members, it has remained active for ten months. Like many other urban women's organizations, its membership was and is of women of middle class status, mostly educated and well informed about the WLM in the West. Further, most of the women have a value system/life style that reflects the cosmopolitan urban values that are part of an imperialist heritage, and consequently divorced from traditional Indian ways and customs. Our meetings are conducted informally, and below we will list specific activities we have been involved in, bearing in mind the necessity to be detached and objective despite our involvement with the Forum.

Major Action Programmes of the Forum

The Mathura Rape Case: This was the cause of bringing the Forum into existence. Two public meetings were arranged, attended by hundreds of women; petitions demanding the reopening of the case were signed by thousands who also demanded changes in the existing rape law. At this time, Forum meetings attracted 50-60 women on average, and International Women's Day saw the Forum mobilize women to agitate for the reopening of the case, infusing activists and other women with enthusiasm.

The Rape and Murder of a woman in Ghatkopar: The Forum actively investigated and publicized this case of a woman worker murdered on the Ghatkopar Industrial Estate; it also organized a demonstration at the Estate in which trade unionists participated. Following this, the Forum persisted in ensuring that the employer gave compensation to the mother of the murdered women.

Gang Rape of a 15 year old construction worker in Turbhe: She was raped by a man and three policemen. The Forum did a considerable amount of mobilization and activity around this case, demonstrating outside police stations; visiting the villagers persistently, performing plays, skits, songs to create a supportive atmosphere for the raped woman, who later was housed in a welfare institution due to lack of family support.

'Red Rose' boycott: A ban on the film 'Red Rose' was demanded for its anti-woman message, and the Forum called for a boycott of all films that degrade and insult women.

By this time the Forum Against Rape had expanded its activities, and was now called the 'Forum Against the Oppression

183

of Women'. Protests against police atrocities against women were made; political parties that perceived rape as a law and order problem were denounced; and finally, the Forum organized a national conference for women activists on various issues that concern and oppress us.

Issues Confronting the Forum

An important discussion for us has been our structure: should we be registered, and if so would this give rise to bureaucracy within the Forum? The far Left as well as women activists have provided a sophisticated critique of the hierarchical relationships operative in society, as well as organizations formed to change that same hierarchy. In practice, however, a subtle form of bureaucracy exists even in those organizations that have rejected hierarchical modes of organization.

Why does competition exist amongst us, the very manipulative forces that we wish to destroy? Is it because of our treatment as inferior beings in a male world which leads us to assert ourselves in the only space available i.e. with other women? How are we to end the oppressive atmosphere in our own groups which has resulted?

Further, if the Forum intends to become a mass organization (and we suggest that this is not only relevant but imperative to its existence), how are the barriers of class and culture to be bridged?

More specifically, certain political demands that we have made, e.g. calling for State intervention in the banning of 'Red Rose', raise problems. Knowing that the State uses such weapons in silencing radical and progressive movements, should we be asking for such a ban? We suggest that our strength should lie rather in mass mobilizations, creating public opinion against reactionary and anti-woman films.

Issues Facing Autonomous Women's Organizations

Generally, the process of development of any mass women's movement seems to take the following course: the minority of women participating in class struggle activities become increasingly aware of the contradiction between their newly realized power in the struggle for the betterment of their conditions of life on the one hand, and their subordinate position as women both at home and in society. These realizations, coupled with struggles that have developed against wife beating, have drawn many women into struggling against women's oppression. This has

FORUM AGAINST OPPRESSION OF WOMEN

NATIONAL CONFERENCE – BOMBAY, NOV 1-4 '80

led to their involvement in the class movement, possessing a different, new dimension and perspective which, in turn, contributes to redefining the goals of the class movement.

How does the pattern of male–female relationship change during and after the struggles? Initially, women's participation in a struggle which is considered to be mainly the concern of men, is regarded lightly, she is merely an appendage. But this changes. We have seen how women have challenged (and still do) certain dominant ideas held by men, as well as fighting against wife beating and violence against women — so far considered to be a private affair, and 'natural'. We have also witnessed the challenging of various stereotypes and authorities, by women, and the results of these challenges.

In India, where the women's movement is just developing, we must learn from the experience of Western feminists and socialists to avoid the twin dangers of separatism on the one hand, i.e. cutting off the Women's Movement from an overall movement for the total transformation of society, and on the other hand, we must be careful to not get sucked into the framework of the existing Left, thereby losing in the process our goals and our autonomy.

Can the women's movement in India sustain itself in isolation from the wider political movement of the oppressed masses? In India, where: a) the extent of women's economic dependence on the man in the family is great; b) a very small proportion of the workforce is female; c) cultural values have oppressed women and tied us to the family; d) State security is impossible given the historical development of capitalism; e) the 'women's question' and 'class question' are closely linked — it is obvious that the women's movement would have to develop on a trajectory quite different from that in the West.

We need to look for ways whereby we can make links with trade union movements as well as the struggles of oppressed groups eg. *dalits*, *advisasis*, and the working class movements. (We also suggest that we set up broad, women's organizations which take up issues shunned by the unions.)

In conclusion, class struggle is inevitably linked with the women's movement. Unless autonomous women's groups link themselves actively with wider political movements for radical change, we will at best have minimal impact.

19. The Need for an Independent Women's Movement in Mauritius
Muvman Liberasyon Fam

This report (published in a shortened version here) was put together in 1980 by a group from the Women's Movement of Mauritius, *Muvman Liberasyon Fam* (MLF), which came into existence in 1975. After giving a brief background to women's struggles in Mauritius the report goes on to describe the origins and development of the MLF and some of its achievements. The Movement's priorities and chief demands are outlined in its manifesto which states; 'Women's liberation means freedom for humanity. When women fight against domination and exploitation they free not only themselves, but also men who are caught up in their role as dominators. In other words, it can be said that women are like the working class who are fighting for their own freedom — a historical role to free humanity as a whole.

Muvman Liberasyon Fam believes that: Women should have the right to work and the right to join unions. There should be equal pay for everybody. If a woman asks for equal pay for equal work, bosses have a tendency to reclassify jobs — that's why we seek equality for all.

Women should be in control of their own bodies. They should have the right to gain access to contraception and abortion. They should have the choice not to marry or not to have children. There must be a campaign against all organizations and people who give false information about women. Women should have sufficient protection against legal and physical violence, which they are suffering at present; most of all against rape and forced prostitution. Raising children, cooking and washing clothes should not be an individual's task — but a social one. There should be playgroups, nurseries, canteens and launderettes in every corner of the country where the women work. Remaining housework should be divided between men and women — each of them have to do their share. Women should have the right to go wherever they please, do whatever they like and meet whoever they wish. Women should fight against the 'object' identity — whether in arranged marriages, advertisements, beauty contests, in the streets or through fashions. Women must turn down all discrimination and anti-women's laws. Women should have an identity of their own — not only in relation to men. All technical courses should be opened to women. Women should run campaigns everywhere in order to free themselves. Progressive men will give us their support.

Background

Women in Mauritius have never taken their oppression sitting down. The struggle is perpetual. From the times of the Dutch settlement in the 17th Century, women have tried to voice their demands. Anna de Bengal, a woman slave, with two men slaves destroyed the entire barracks of the Dutch East India Company in 1695, and was put to death after being tortured. It is interesting to note that even the torture meted out to her and to the two men slaves was different.

Women were brought as slaves from Africa, Madagascar, and India during the period of French colonization. They were in continuous conflict with the slave-owners, and often with the men slaves as well, who outnumbered women slaves by five to one. The same fate was suffered by the women brought as 'coolies' or indentured labourers' from India during the 19th Century. Outnumbered by men, dominated by the sugar estate bosses, they were forced to submit to day after day of assault. But whenever possible there were expressions of revolt. A woman called Anjalay was shot dead in 1943 by the sugar plantation owners during a strike and rebellion at a place called Belle Vue Harel. Her death is still mourned in Mauritius.

And today, too, women are always finding ways of expressing their need for equality. Objective economic conditions have contributed. The new factories, although they exploit workers, especially women, nevertheless allow women to go out, join other women and contribute financially within the family. Nowadays men often prefer to marry a working girl — a complete reversal of opinion. As sugar prices vacillate, and as a severe economic crisis hits Mauritius, the fact that women earn money gives them an increasing right to a voice.

And, indeed, women are learning to express themselves collectively. Last year women participated massively in trade union action in support of the recognition of the Sugar Industry Labourers Union, and in support of the right to strike, went on a hunger strike. Army and riot police cordoned off the area Jardin de la Compagnie, where the hunger strikers were in a tent in the middle of Port Louis, so as to prevent the growing movement of solidarity. The area was declared a prohibited area, and the armed forces began attacking supporters of the strike. Street riots broke out. It was at this stage that two heroic groups of women, one group from Ste Croix, an urban area, and the other from Bambous, a rural area, arrived independently and braved the armed forces, chanting slogans about liberty. Such a women's demonstration was quite unheard of before. And, what made it even more significant, was the participation of women of all ages, and all communities — Hindu, Creole, Muslim and Chinese.

The women's movement has organized women's rallies — even outdoors — and received growing support from all women. Women have demonstrated in small groups with posters against unjust laws and against beauty contests, and have even organized groups to go and denounce pimps who try to force girls into prostitution — in public in the middle of Port Louis, in front of the Bank of Baroda. Once again, it is worth underlining that women have just never before been considered capable of such actions. But still, in all public events, women remain a mere 5 to 10% under normal conditions. The limitations in the struggle against oppression remain inextricably linked to the domination that women suffer.

Muvman Liberasyon Fam

Origins and development

The *Muvman Liberasyon Fam* came into existence after the mass students organized demonstrations to protest against the colonial system of education. The student movement had a vanguard of women students. This was also very unusual. The student revolt quickly brought about the politicizing of the students; the girls involved soon realized the importance of the feminist struggle.

The second factor leading to the birth of the MLF — and which coincided with the student revolt — was the opening of the Free Zone factories which were offering employment to thousands of women. This brought about very abrupt changes in the lives of Mauritian women. They now acquired the right to go out to work, even at night-time, and they could now contribute to the family budget. Thus, they now had the right to have a say in their respective households and could voice their opinions. The development of the capitalist system, which brought about these positive changes in the lives of the women workers, also led them to realize that they would have to fight hard to safeguard their jobs and demand equal wages at work. This meant joining the unions and organizing in collective ways to resist their employers' manoeuvres as well as to put forward their demands.

It was in the midst of these socio-economic changes that were upsetting the whole Mauritian traditional society that the MLF came into being. Before committing themselves to the formation of a new independent women's movement, the initiators of MLF had to reason out whether it was necessary to found a new feminist organization, in spite of the existence of other women's associations. This question was much debated. Before the MLF, there were two principal women's movements in Mauritius: the Women's Association and *La Ligue Feministe*. The first one was under the control of the Labour Party, which is the ruling party of the island, and the second one under that of the chief opposition party, the MMM. Thus, these two women's organizations had to limit their activities within the boundaries set by these political parties. They were needed merely to bring in women voters for the respective parties.

It was then decided that there should be an autonomous women's movement to take up a genuine feminist struggle. Although we believe that being tied to a political party would be fatal to the women's organization, we hold that the women's liberation movement carries with it very important political tasks aimed at radical changes in society as a whole. As soon as the MLF was launched, the two other women's movements were compelled to take stands on feminist issues, and they gradually built up autonomy from their respective parties.

Achievements of the MLF

Branches have been set up in several parts of the island. Monthly meetings are held in order to plan work in the different branches as well as on an island-wide basis, and to take official stands on issues concerning women.

Our first petition, demanding the abolition of sexual discrim- ination against women in the field of technical education, and addressed to the Ministry of Education was circulated; thousands of signatures were collected. After that, the government started opening technical schools to boys and girls alike.

FAM LITE (Women's Struggle) Review

This is the title of our magazine. In June 1977, MLF published its first edition of the magazine called *Fam Lite*. It contained articles on various feminist problems written by members of the MLF. The magazine provided a means whereby we could launch a debate on various feminist issues — we could also voice our official stand on feminist issues in our magazine. The work in- volved in the publication, i.e. typing, printing, cutting and collating were carried out entirely by the members of MLF. We were also responsible for its distribution and sale.

We are already on our seventh issue of *Fam Lite*; problems such as contraceptive methods, abortion, rape, prostitution, women's struggles in different parts of the world have been the subject of the previous numbers. We afterwards decided to publish *Nuvel Fam (Women's News)*, a feminist newspaper. This new publication differs from *Fam Lite* in many respects. It con- tains an MLF editorial on news — local or international — that affects women, as well as a newsletter section where any woman can write to the editorial board and confide day-to-day prob- lems and receive advice and information on various MLF meetings in different parts of the island.

Abortion Campaign: A nationwide campaign for the legalization of abortion was launched by MLF. During an MLF workshop on abortion, the women present took the decision to launch a common front of women's organizations for the legalisation of abortion. A petition demanding the legalization of abortion in Mauritius was circulated very widely, a press conference was called in order to announce publicly our stand on that question; other workshops have been organized on this theme; information was sent out to feminist groups in other countries, which have the same aims, e.g. NAC (England), MLAC (France), and ISIS (International Women's

Network).

We published a special issue of *Fam Lite* on abortion; we also printed a booklet which contained the experiences related to women who have had illegal abortions. A campaign was set up in order to co-ordinate national and international support for the case of Jocelyn K., a Mauritian woman who had been condemned by criminal courts for six months detention in a convent and one and a half years' seclusion in a reformatory because she had had an illegal abortion. Petitions were signed to ask for her liberation and immediate lifting of the charges against her.

Campaign for the withdrawal of Immigration & Deportation Acts: In April 1977 the Government of Mauritius passed a Bill called the Immigration and Deportation Acts. This law penalizes Mauritian women married to foreigners; by this law women could no longer bestow residence rights upon their husbands if they were non-Mauritian. As soon as the Bill was proposed to the Assembly, MLF reacted strongly against it. We contacted members of the Opposition Party and persuaded them to vote against the passing of such a law.We also stuck up posters and distributed leaflets all around the island in order to mobilize people on that issue. The MLF also called for the setting-up of a common front of all women's organizations to fight against this law. Thus the FKOF (*Fron Komin Organization Fam*) was created. Nevertheless, the Bill was passed. In spite of this, the FKOF intensified its campaign against this law. A petition containing thousands of signatures was sent to the Prime Minister; articles were sent regularly to the press, posters and leaflets distributed. The FKOF also organized a women's demonstration in front of the Parliament to protest against the voting of the law. Some members were delegated to meet the Prime Minister. A letter was sent to the United Nations to inform them about the fact that Mauritius had broken the terms of the Covenant of Human Rights, which it had signed some time ago. As the government took no steps concerning that law, FKOF decided to take the government to the UN Human Rights Committee on the grounds that it had bypassed the Covenant of Human Rights. The case is being deliberated.

Help to the unions: We work in close collaboration with different unions, the Union of House Employees, Union of Free Zone Workers, and the Labourers' Union (SILU), a union which has

Fron Komen Transpor (A common front for bus passengers): our work this year.

Fron Komen Transpor (A common front for bus passengers). We actively participated in a common front composed of political parties, the transport workers union, *Movement Chretien pour le Socialisme*, *Ledikasyon Pu Travayer*, and other social organizations. The short-term objectives of this organization were to boycott an increase in bus fares and, in the long term, to demand the nationalization of the public transport system, which is owned by big private companies. MLF has been a leader in the campaign of posters, leaflets and public demonstrations and meetings. After a huge national demonstration in the capital, Port Louis, in which thousands of people took part — members of the different political and social organizations — the government chose to arrest only 14 of them. On the day the case was to be heard in court, the Front organized a queue of other demonstrators to sign up their names at a police station in order to show solidarity to the other people who were arrested. The members of the MLF who were present at the demonstration all signed their names. When the 14 demonstrators were imprisoned, members of the MLF helped in the setting-up of MSAR (*Muvman Solidarite Anti-Repression*). We also helped to organize a night vigil in front of the prisons with the wives, children and mothers of the prisoners. We also participated in a sit-in which was organized by a group of militants in a public garden of Port Louis during a day and a night to demand the liberation of all the prisoners. The day after that, the prisoners were released.

Setting-up of an Advice Centre: In 1978–79, members of the MLF set up a weekly *permanence* in the office of an education co-operative at 36, Virgil Naz St. in Port Louis. Two of our members were responsible for it: the main problems for which women in need of help and advice called at the *permanence* were divorce, housing and family problems. We had to help such women seek legal advice and sometimes to undertake legal action.

Courses on the anatomy and physiology of women: Apart from courses organized in the different branches, two main classes have been carried out on this subject and were followed by all members of the MLF, as well as any other women who were interested. The aim of these classes was to educate ourselves on our own bodies and do away with the many taboos which, from our birth, have clouded our knowledge of our bodies' functioning; we could then organize classes for other groups of women.

Public denunciation of a pimp: One of our members met a man who expressed the wish to have sex with her. In exchange he promised her work if she brought along other girls for other men. He always drove a black Volkswagen car with the registration number F716 — this became his nickname — and he was notorious for his behaviour towards women. When our friend contacted us about the man's proposition we decided to set upon him in one of the most densely crowded areas of Port Louis, near the Baroda Bank. There we publicly denounced him, took pictures and warned women about his activities, and the next day we published an official communique in the newspaper, again warning women against him.

Camps: The MLF organizes regular camps for women only. This is a new experience in Mauritius where women are not allowed to be away from house compounds without their 'men', i.e. husbands, brothers or fathers. It needed a lot of courage and initiative on our part to organize the first camps and invite other women to join in. For many women participating in such camps, it was the first time they had ever spent a night away from home and experienced an alternative environment to their homes and families. These camps are not only meant for recreation, but also for work sessions on feminist issues, and our next camp will be organized for Free Zone working women.

Part VI:
The Struggle Against Violence

Beasts in Darkness

When walking alone
in the darkness
identifying myself with
the silent, serene mood of night

I feel
an electric current
passing through my limbs
when the car swerves past
and the lorry rushes by
roaring . . .

Oh, the dark night
frightens me not
but the sight of man
makes me shrink

Manjula C.G.

From *Manushi*, No 7, 1981

20. The War Against Rape: A Report from Karimnagar
Stree Shakti Sanghatana

This article was first presented as a paper at the Indian Women's National Conference held in Bombay in October 1980. It has been slightly edited here by Shaila Shah. *Stree Shakti Sanghatana* is a fairly broad-based women's group from Hyderabad.

Kodurpaka — Karimnagar 29 October 1978, 9 pm.

Rajavva doesn't think that the *goondas* will rape her. [*Goondas* are thugs hired by landlords to suppress peasant rebellions, etc.] She fears more for her young daughter-in-law. She tries to give cover to her and the daughter-in-law manages to escape with her baby. Rajavva's son is away but her husband is at home. The *goondas*, seven of them, tie him to the tree in front of their house and beat him. Rajavva, President of the *Mahila Sangam* [Women's Organization] and normally in full control of herself and her environment, is unnerved. She runs into the fields in front of the house and manages to cross the first one. Further along, in the second or third field, a *Sangam* meeting is taking place, if only she can reach it . . . her son is at the meeting. Someone throws a stick at her leg, she trips.

They gang-rape her. Age (she is around 50) is of no consideration. Most of the men in the neighbourhood are away. The women don't dare to come out. Kanakavva and Baravva, the two activists whom the *goondas* have actually come for, are in the office. Some children run and report the incident to others in the area. Help arrives, but by then the rapists have left. Rajavva lies unconscious, badly hurt, her clothes soiled.

They bring Rajavva home, attempts to take her to the hospital are futile — the *rickshawallas* have been threatened with violence if they assist her.

It is only the following morning that her husband is able to take her to the hospital. She carries her soiled sari, displays it, hands it in. But there is no one at the hospital to examine her. It is evening

197

by the time she is admitted, and she is then kept there for three days.

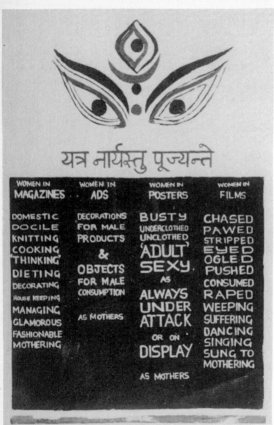

यत्र नार्यस्तु पूज्यन्ते

WOMEN IN MAGAZINES	WOMEN IN ADS	WOMEN IN POSTERS	WOMEN IN FILMS
DOMESTIC	DECORATIONS	BUSTY	CHASED
DOCILE	FOR MALE	UNDERCLOTHED	PAWED
KNITTING	PRODUCTS	UNCLOTHED	STRIPPED
COOKING	&	'ADULT'	EYED
'THINKING'	OBJECTS	SEXY	OGLED
DIETING	FOR MALE	AS	PUSHED
DECORATING	CONSUMPTION	ALWAYS	CONSUMED
HOUSE KEEPING		UNDER	RAPED
MANAGING	AS MOTHERS	ATTACK	WEEPING
GLAMOROUS		OR ON	SUFFERING
FASHIONABLE		DISPLAY	DANCING
MOTHERING			SINGING
		AS MOTHERS	SUNG TO
			MOTHERING

Rajavva's son registers a complaint at the Police Station. They jeer at him and ask 'Why don't you demonstrate what they did to her?' Joginapalli Venkatrama Rao, the landlord of the village, threatens the *rickshawalla* who took Rajavva to the hospital. He then threatens Rajavva further — he will destroy her entire family if she doesn't withdraw the case.

The legal battle, long drawn and perhaps futile, will continue. This is not the story of Rajavva alone . . .

In rural India, feudalism prevails. The landlord owns the land, and along with it, everything that grows on it. Every aspect of life here is related in some way to his power, his status. Sexual violence always has been and continues to be an integral part of this society. In the hierarchy, women occupy the lowest position and have the least power, and if the woman is a *harijan* [outcast] she is not even considered to be human. The woman is the property of the man, and all the women, children and men who till the land are in turn the property of the landlord.

One of the ways in which he asserts his rights: rape the woman and teach the peasant a lesson. The landlord, as a matter of 'right' can claim the woman, any woman. He can demand that she be brought to him — a woman on her wedding night, any man's wife, sister . . . She has no power of objection, she submits against her will. Rape is his prerogative.

Karimnagar, in the Telengana region of Andhra Pradesh state, is one of the most underdeveloped areas. The existence of very wealthy landlords and a vast impoverished peasantry characterize it. In some areas landlords own more than 500 acres of the land. The wages for agricultural labour vary from Rs. 1 to Rs. 3.50 per day [6 pence]. Women, of course, get even less. In addition to his main source of income, i.e. the land, the landlord derives income illegally from forest produce. Feudal practices such as *Vetti* [bonded labour] still persist. Peasant movements assisted and controlled by Left parties, particularly the CPI (ML) have inevitably been confronted with the state powers, and widespread and severe repression continues even today.

It is interesting to note that the first peasant organization was formed around a 'women's issue', in 1973. In Akkapalli, a widow was threatened with exile from the village because the chickens she was given by the landlord died of some disease, which the landlord accused her of causing deliberately. The *Ryotu Coolie Sangam* (RCS) fought for her, and then followed several cases of rape and murder. In 1974, the C.P.I. (ML) organized peasant struggles and uprisings in the district, but the declaration of the State of Emergency in 1975 found the various organizations in a state of disarray. In October 1978, after the Emergency was lifted, the reorganization of the struggle, the militancy of the organizations and the consequent unrest led to the declaration of these areas as 'Disturbed Areas' by the Congress Government. Ever since, police repression has been on the increase.

Peasant women have always participated in the struggles in Karimnagar dating back to the days of the Telengana armed struggle, and have been active in various ways. One instance — Lalita, a woman activist played a significant role in organizing women in the area to fight the forcible kidnap of Devamma and the murder of her husband by the landlord. The villagers, mostly women, caught the landlord, surrounded him, mounted him on a donkey and led him round the village, abused and humiliated. The police intervened and Lalita was arrested. In the neighbouring villages, solidarity protest marches were held, an increasing number of women were being politicized, and the RCS were forced to recognize the importance of the need for separate/ autonomous women's organizations, and by 1979 the first *Mahila Sangam* was formed in Kodurupaka with about 150 members. In surrounding areas too, *Mahila Sangams* came into existence.

Of course these organizations are in their initial stages, and women face difficulties in organizing themselves. Family responsibilities make it difficult for women to go underground (as the male activists can), which is sometimes necessary because of the severe repression and danger that accompanies open political activity.

There are women's organizations, but their problems are at once determined by their class and sex, their struggles are both class struggle and feminist. The fundamental problem for the peasants is that of land, and women are participating in land struggles actively. In the process of these struggles, the specific nature of their own separate struggles, i.e. the oppression they face as women, becomes asserted, and consequently the need for separate women's organizations is defined. In Karimnagar, the *Mahila Sangams* have emerged in this way, i.e. resulting from the participation of women in broader peasant movements.

Whether these *Mahila Sangams* take up issues that are feminist issues (e.g. woman- or wife-battering), function autonomously of men and take their own decisions, these questions are difficult to answer. It is premature to make any definitive analysis of their role, function and politics as yet.

But it should be noted that the demand to form independent women's organizations has come from the women themselves. *Mahila Sangams* now have their own separate offices, they meet regularly and run educationals for women, participate in cultural activities. All the time there is a growing awareness of problems, a growing awareness of strength. Now, if a woman is assaulted by her husband, she will consider reporting this to the *Mahila Sangam*, and similarly in the case of rape. Rape is such an integral part of class violence in feudal areas, that it is important to see that women are actively resisting it, questioning those 'rights' that the landlords have taken for themselves which give them freedom to abuse and violate as they wish. . . . The RCS have been participating too, by educating men to fight the taboos that are heaped on a raped woman. However, in rural areas the notion of 'virtue' is not very strong, because although the woman is considered man's property, both men and women are in turn the property of the landlord, and the political importance of questioning this has helped raise consciousness over this issue.

Other struggles that the *Mahila Sangams* have been involved in include equal pay struggles, as well as the fight for higher pay. Karimnagar has a large *beedi* factory and the women's labour force is unionized and active in wage struggles. [*Beedis* are cigarettes made of rolled up tobacco leaves, produced mainly by women's labour] Here the *Mahila Sangam* plays an important role in the fact of its existence — providing a meeting place, helping women to develop their political awareness, organizing.

The political direction of the *Mahila Sangams* and the modes of action that they will adopt will have important consequences for the women's movement. It is important to learn from historical experience however, and in this case we have seen how women's organizations affiliated to political parties (even in socialist countries) have become mere appendages of those parties. In post-revolutionary periods, women's movements have been relegated to the background, ignored, diffused. We must not allow this to happen, we have to retain our strength and our politics. It is important that women's organizations guard against such a danger, but without isolating themselves from the masses, and from other revolutionary movements.

21. Indian Women Speak Out Against Dowry
Manushi

The following article is made up of extracts from the Indian feminist magazine *Manushi*, selected and introduced by Shaila Shah.

The practice of giving dowry has been banned for decades in India. However, it continues to be practised under another guise — that of the exchange or giving of 'gifts'. Insufficient dowry has proved to have grave consequences for women, ranging from continuous mental and physical harassment and torture, to the murder of women, thereby making room for another marriage, and of course, the prospect of a fresh source of dowry.

Manushi, a magazine which has systematically campaigned for the abolition of dowry and played an important role in alerting its readership to the incidence and implications of dowry, has set it in a feminist context — as an institution that has always oppressed women.

As various individuals, families of murdered women and

women's organizations have begun to take personal and collective action against dowry, *Manushi* has recorded the protests, and has itself been a vehicle for them. For the past few years anti-dowry activities have been on the increase. Protests and actions against the incidence and fatal consequences of dowry have attracted numbers of people, and occasionally even the bourgeois media have reported these, no longer limiting reports to the usual three-lines. The development of this process of change, both in the consciousness of people, especially women, as well as in the more public sphere of action, is easily traceable in subsequent issues of *Manushi*.

What follows is a collection of various pieces of writing, some left (almost) intact and others being excerpts, all of which appeared in the pages of *Manushi* between January 1979 and December 1981. In these, individual women, as well as women's groups, speak of a range of responses to dowry, ranging from emotional to analytical pieces, from letters to theoretical articles.

I have attempted to introduce each piece or series. Obviously, the collection does not provide a whole picture, but it does offer insights into the different forms of organization that the Indian women's anti-dowry struggle has taken, and writing about it is of course, as important as any other method of protest.

The article below appeared in the first issue of *Manushi* (January 1979). It describes the first of a seemingly never ending series of similar incidents — women being killed by husbands and their families, her in-laws, for not having provided sufficient cash and goods — property that goes by the name of bride-price or dowry.

Price of a Life

An ordinary afternoon in Jangpura Extension. Suddenly the air was rent by agonizing cries. People peered out of windows — Hardeep Kaur, the 20-year-old daughter-in-law of a rich and influential neighbouring family was being beaten up, as usual. She had been married only two years, had an 11-month-old son, and was constantly being ill-treated by husband and in-laws because she had brought an insufficient dowry. After the cries stopped, everyone prepared to return to their meals, thinking it was all over for the day. A few minutes later, someone cried out at the sight of flames, and people rushed out again. The house was a melee of activity and soon the girl, wrapped in a sheet from head to foot, was bundled into a taxi and taken away.

Two private hospitals refused to admit Hardeep, so she was

finally taken to a Government hospital. At this point things begin to get more and more curious. Hardeep apparently made a statement that she had burnt herself while cooking (a cliched story) and although she was educated and fully capable of signing her name, this statement was accompanied by her thumb impression. Later, when she regained consciousness, she made another statement, properly signed, that her mother-in-law had tried to kill her by setting fire to her clothes. The police registered a case of attempted murder, but took no action, while the alleged killers went about with complete unconcern.

Then the *Mahila Dakshata Samiti* came to the locality and held a demonstration. This attracted some people, including many concerned women, though some preferred to maintain 'good relations' with the girl's in-laws, and stayed in their houses. The Samiti meeting served one purpose — the case became a political issue and was handed over to the crime branch. Detectives came around, questioning witnesses, and assured everyone that the culprits would be brought to book.

If Hardeep survived, she could perhaps be forced to alter her statement, whereas if she died, her allegation of attempted murder would be irrevocable and her killers would be in danger. So, it seems, they fought to save her life by importing medicines from the USA.

On 2 November 1978, Hardeep Kaur died of severe burns. Her murderers have not been arrested. The newspapers have not breathed a word about her death.

A woman's life has been lost — one of many such lives — and nothing has been done about it.

How long are we going to remain unconcerned spectators to such brutal ill-treatment? For how long will the dowry system continue ruining lives and be the cause of death of many young women? How many cases will be silenced by money and influence?

Urvashi Butalia

The following was an editorial in *Manushi* (No. 2), July–August 1972.

Most people are not even aware that the giving and taking of dowry is a legal offence. Since the Prohibition of Dowry Act was passed in 1961, the custom has flowered and flourished, invading castes and communities among whom it was hitherto unknown — sprouting new forms and varieties. It is percolating downwards and becoming so widespread even among the working classes that it is no longer possible to consider it a problem of the middle class alone.

With the entire bourgeois mass media oriented towards viciously promoting the religion of mindless consumerism, demands for dowry are becoming more and more 'modernized'. Marriages are made and broken for such items as cars, scooters, TVs, refrigerators and washing machines, wedding receptions in five-star hotels or an air ticket plus the promise of a job for the son-in-law in a foreign country.

In India, we have a glorious heritage of systematic violence on women in the family itself, *sati* [Hindu custom whereby women throw themselves on their husband's funeral pyre] and female infanticide being the two better-known forms. Today, we do not kill girl-babies at birth. We let them die through systematic neglect — the mortality rate among female children is 30 to 60% higher than among male children. Today, we do not wait till a woman is widowed before we burn her to death. We burn her in the lifetime of her husband so that he can get a new bride, with a fatter dowry.

'Woman burnt to death. A case of suicide has been registered. The police are enquiring into the matter.' For years, such three line news items have appeared almost every day in the newspapers and gone unnoticed. It is only lately that dowry deaths are being given detailed coverage. It is not by accident that fuller reporting of such cases has coincided with a spurt of protest demonstrations.

We, as women, have too long been silent spectators, often willing participants in the degrading drama of matrimony — when girls are advertised, displayed, bargained over, and disposed of with the pious injunction: 'Daughter, we are sending you to your husband's home. You are not to leave it till your corpse emerges from its doors.' It is significant that in all the cases of dowry murders recently reported, the girls had, on previous occasions left the in-laws' houses where they were being tortured and felt insecure. Their parents had insisted on their going back and 'adjusting' there.

Death may be slow in coming — a long process of killing the girl's spirit by harassment, taunts, torture. It may be only too quick — fiery and sudden. Dousing the woman with kerosene and setting her on fire seems to have become the most popular way of murdering a daughter-in-law, because with police connivance it is the easiest to make out as a case of suicide or accident.

And for every reported murder, hundreds go unreported, especially in rural areas where it is almost impossible to get redress unless one is rich and influential. For years, the police and the administration have hushed up these cases under the plea that people are not willing to appear as witnesses, that they are indifferent.

This myth of public apathy was exploded when the recent protests against dowry deaths in Delhi drew such immediate support from the people in the neighbourhood, passers-by and onlookers. In the demonstration at Model Town, Delhi, the organizers were not hoping to get more than 50 to 100 people for the protest. But the local people joined in spontaneously and brought with them a new vigour. By the time the protesters reached the house where the girl had died, their numbers had swelled to about 300. It was the same with the other demonstrations too.

It is obvious then, that there is a great deal of latent anger and indignation against injustice. Why then this veneer of cynicism and apathy? Why do people not come forward to give evidence against the murderers, before the police?

In most of these cases, the same people who openly joined the protest demonstrations were unwilling to give evidence before the police, the court. In one case, where the neighbours had themselves taken the initiative to get it registered as a murder case, the police threatened them into silence.

In fact, it is a matter of no small credit for those who rule this country that they have successfully trained us, the people, to accept injustice as part of our lives. The corruption and inefficiency that is cultivated by the rulers in all those forces which act as instruments of their rule — the police, the judiciary, the bureaucracy — have made the people dread these forces so much that today we fear to seek redress.

In our country, the job of subverting law by the 'guardians' of law and order has been made easier because people have lost faith in the law itself. This apathy has become the biggest asset for all those who have a vested interest in maintaining a corrupt and unjust society.

If law enforcers have been working against the law, the law itself has been a dead letter. One important reason is its consciously built-in loopholes. The Prohibition of Dowry Act declares the giving and taking of dowry illegal but allows 'gifts' at the time of marriage. No limit is set on such gifts. This has, therefore, become the most common way of demanding dowry — the girl's parents are politely asked to give whatever they 'happily wish to' (*apni khushi se*). They are of course aware that not only their daughter's *khushi* but even her life depends on these 'voluntary gifts' of theirs.

Why is it that gifts have to be given with the daughter? Hindu scriptures proclaim that the girl herself is the most precious of gifts 'presented' by her father to her husband (*Kanyadaan*). Thus the money transaction between families is bound up with the marriage transaction whereby the girl becomes a piece of transferable property. So little is a woman worth that a man has literally to be paid to take her off her father's hands. The dramatic increase

in dowry-giving in the post-independence period, reflects the declining value of women in our society. Their only worth is as reproducers who provide 'legitimate' heirs for their husband's property. It is the woman's husband who usually controls any property she inherits. So the property transaction remains between men, women only acting as vehicles for this transaction.

This will continue as long as the majority of women remain economically dependent on men and as long as this dependence is reinforced by our social values and institutions so that even those women who earn, seldom have the right to control their own income.

The problem has other dimensions too. When marriages are arranged, it is not just the boy's family who make sure that the girl's family is 'well settled and well connected' and can give their daughter a 'decent márriage'. The girl's family too, judges the boy by his job, income, inheritance prospects and social status. The worth of human beings is thus decided solely on the basis of the money and property they possess. Therefore, it is not just women who are unfree. Men too are denied their humanity when money and property are made the main criteria to judge their worth.

But this form of violation of human dignity is not even considered immoral — it is the 'normal' thing in our society based on private property. It continues to be so in countries where young people choose their own partners, so long as their choice is based on the criterion of social status or property owned.

206

The fight against dowry, therefore, has to be part of a larger fight against the system which makes human beings the slaves of money and property, which reduces human beings themselves to pieces of property. The solution is not to be found in making laws more stringent, because the essence of the existing legal system is the protection of private property.

What is needed is a widespread movement against dowry and allied social evils. A number of women's organizations have recently been galvanized around this issue. But they have been working without proper co-ordination with each other, in fact often at cross purposes with each other. This is most unfortunate as it will only dissipate the movement before it has even got off the ground. We appeal, therefore, to all the women's organizations to undertake a broad-based united action on this issue and launch an intensive, concerted campaign, instead of the isolated, sporadic protests which have so far been organized, and which can only have a short-term, limited impact.

Perhaps even more urgent is the need to begin the movement from our own homes. Are we sure that none of us who partici-pated so vociferously in these demonstrations, will take dowry from our parents or give it to our daughters in however veiled a form? That we will rather say 'No' to marriage than live a life of humiliations and comrpomises? Do we have the courage to boycott marriages where dowry is given? Even the marriage of a brother or sister of a dear friend? Will we socially ostracize such people, no matter how close they are to us? All the protest demonstrations will be only so much hot air unless we are prepared to create pressures against dowry beginning from our own homes.

A year later, assessing the direction of the anti-dowry campaign, women in Delhi wrote the following letter, an important con-tribution to the 'personal is political' aspect of feminism.

Beginning With Our Own Lives: An Open Letter to Women Activists, Women's Groups and Organizations

Though we feel very encouraged by the fact that over the past year, many more individual women, women's groups and organizations have become activized around the issue of dowry and dowry murders, we have noticed with concern a rather dis-appointing trend. Many of us who see our role as that of women 'activists' mobilizing 'other' women in protest actions against atrocities like dowry murders — we who take upon ourselves the task of changing society's attitudes — continue to live our own

lives almost untouched by the ideas with which we seek to
influence others.

We, the undersigned individuals,* feel that initiating any kind of
social, political action is meaningless unless it begins with our
own lives, that those of us who assume the role of mobilizers,
lead protest marches and speak or write against dowry, owe it to
ourselves and to all those whom we try to draw into collective
action, that we do not in any way become party to such crimes as
the giving and taking of dowry. We have no moral right to shout
slogans like '*Dahej Mat Do, Dahej Mat Lo*' [Do not give or take
dowry] if we privately continue to participate in marriages where
dowry is given or taken. If we do not dare boycott the marriage
ceremony of even our own brother or sister where lavish dowry
is given, if we do not start the campaign in our own homes, what
moral right have we to preach to others? We are not for a moment
suggesting that every woman who participates in a protest action
or starts getting involved in the campaign should be called upon to
make such a commitment. We are referring only to those who
take on themselves the task of mobilization or consciousness-
raising with other women.

It is unfortunate that the viciousness of the dowry custom
comes to be noticed only when a woman is murdered for it. We
feel that all those who give and take dowry or participate in this
ritual, are also responsible for making such murders possible. Are
they not helping perpetuate a vicious custom which reduces
women to articles of sale and barter? Why cannot a protest or
public meeting begin or end with the organizers making a commitment that they will not be a party to dowry giving or taking in
any form, that they will boycott all dowry marriages? . . .

Some of us have been practising this form of boycott for a
while. But now we publicly affirm that 1) We will not attend or
in any way participate in a marriage where dowry is either given
or taken in however veiled a form (as gifts, trousseau, money
deposited in a bank in the girl's name at the time of marriage),
even if the marriage be that of a close relative or a dear friend. We
will openly make known our reasons for boycotting such
marriages, rather than just quietly staying away from the
ceremony. We will also boycott all rituals wherein dowry continues to be given after marriage such as customary gifts to the
son-in-law's relatives at festivals and childbirth; 2) That we will
henceforth not confine protest actions to dowry murders but will
also protest when dowry is given at extravagant marriage
ceremonies; 3) That we will not attend marriages in which the
woman has no active choice — in deciding whether she wants to

* Not synonymous with Manushi Collective

get married at all or in choosing the person to whom she is to be married . . . .

Only when dowry itself is attacked in all its forms and manifestations, does the battleground shift to our own homes and personal lives. It is there that the real struggle begins.

In response to the editorial in *Manushi* No. 5, entitled 'Beginning With Our Own Lives', several women wrote to the magazine pledging commitment to their call for boycotting dowry marriages. These are yet another form of the anti-dowry struggle, important as public protests and demonstrations, a development of the personal and collective battle against dowry. Below, we reproduce excerpts from these letters.

Dear Sisters, You are absolutely correct in saying that until we boycott the marriage of even our own brother or sister, if lavish dowry is given, we have no moral right to shout slogans like 'Do not give or take dowry.' I am a student of class ten and I discussed this question with my classmate who is a supporter of *Manushi*. I feel that we must protest and boycott dowry marriages. I am making the commitment that I will not attend or in any way participate in a marriage where dowry is either given or taken in any form. And I will not attend marriages where the woman has no active choice — in deciding whether she wants to get married at all or in choosing the person to whom she is to be married.

Madhavi Sharma, Calcutta

I am the eldest in a family of three sisters and a brother. I evolved a different, a romanticist perspective on marriage, which definitely did not coincide with the ideas of my parents and grandparents. It was a period of great conflict and emotional dilemma. My mother was on the one hand, proposing an early marriage to just any one who was eligible and on the other, was instilling in me the fear that if I was too choosy, I would be left on the shelf . . .

I knew what I wanted — marriage to a man who would marry me for what I was, not for what I could bring as dowry. Also, I decided that I would spend my own savings (Rs. 500) on the marriage and the man should spend exactly the same amount. Just this and nothing more. Of course my family was sure I would not meet anyone to fit the peg and they gave me up as a bad joke.

This was way back in the early seventies when I had not been exposed to any ideology, but I had a personal abhorrence to being

bought or sold as a commodity. I did ultimately meet an old
college friend who had exactly the same views on marriage . . .

Chattisgarh

. . . Though I do not belong to a women's organization nor am I
a woman activist, I shall not be a party to such an evil in my own
life.

(Orissa)

Dear sisters, We also feel that feminism should be linked up with
personal struggles. We believe that a feminist group has to strengthen itself on the basis of our own personal experience of being
a woman and the oppression we face in our daily life. Each of us
in the group is there to fight against our own oppression as well as
to fight against oppression of women in general . . . . It is only
through the painful struggle in our personal lives that we will
emerge strong enough to fight oppression at a wider level. Male
power and male-dominated institutions oppress us all. We are all
victims of patriarchy. Let us unite as women to eradicate all
forms of male control over our bodies and our minds. We publicly
affirm that 1) when we face oppression in our personal lives we
will try to make a political issue out of it. 2) We will not attend or
in any way participate in a marriage where dowry is given or
taken in however veiled a form. 3) We will protest when dowry
is given at extravagant marriage ceremonies. 4) We will not dress
in a way which reveals our marital status.

Women from Bombay

. . . I am sure that if women overcome the temptations of wealth
and luxury, we can take our lives into our own hands and combat
those filthy hands which crush our aspirations . . . .

Sarojini Dahiya, Rohtak

Dowry is a disease which is fast spreading . . . Dowry is a disease
and so is marriage. Even women who want to remain independent
are forced to fall prey to this disease. I feel that if those of us
who do not want to get married, refuse to be pressurized into it,
this refusal too will help to eradicate dowry. But if women themselves think they are inferior to men and cannot live without being
dependent on men, then will not this dowry epidemic keep
spreading?

Sugandhi Mary, Bombay

In this section we present a few of the collective actions that
women have taken as part of their anti-dowry protests — a play,
an exhibition, public protests, including heartening directive
issued by the State Bank of India to its staff.

Women Protest, Lawyers Withdraw

As a result of a 300-strong women's demonstration on 12
September against the lawyers defending the accused in a dowry
murder case in the chief metropolitan magistrate's court, Kanpur,
the leading criminal lawyer, Sonkar Nath Dubey, withdrew from
the case, followed by the other defence lawyers. On the demand
of the demonstrating women, contained in their memorandum,
the Youth Bar Association President P. Saini, has announced that
members of the association would appear for the prosecution
without charging fees.

from *Voice of the Working Woman*

On 19 June, 1981, the State Bank of India introduced a rule
applicable to all supervising staff, officers and assistants. This new
rule prohibits employees from giving, taking, or abetting the
giving or taking of dowry, also forbidding the direct or indirect
demand for dowry. Violation of this rule can be punished by
dismissal — a significant step forward. (No. 9)

New Savitri

An exhibition on the evils of dowry.
    The *Mahila Dakshata Samiti* held an exhibition, in Hindi, on
the evils of dowry, in October 1981.
    Though small, the exhibition was visually striking, with espec-
ially strong photographs of women protesting against dowry.
Pamphlets and posters exhorted young brides not to suffer in
silence, to inform their mothers, friends, women's organizations if
they were.
    One poster demanded changes in the law — for dowry to be
made a recognizable offence; another listed the various 'rates'
for bridegrooms, and an imaginative and striking exhibit was a
mirror with a caption which read 'Are you for sale?'
    On 18 June 1980, the National Federation of Indian women
organized a demonstration in Delhi to protest against the increa-
ing incidence of atrocities against women, particularly dowry
murders, and the callous indifference of both the police and

211

government in response.

A placard read: 'In 1975, 300 women died. In 1978, 200. How many will die in 1980?'

Agitators came from surrounding areas, and the women, predominantly rural, were moved by the rally and accounts of bride-burning given by four bereaved mothers.

A petition to the Prime Minister demanded that dowry be made a recognizable offence, and that *no* gifts be given at the time of marriage. Further, they demanded that the Indian Penal Code be amended to state that driving a person to suicide be treated as murder. (No. 6)

The National Federation of Indian Women (NFIW) organized two protests against police inaction after the dowry murder of Jaswanti. Women displayed great anger and militancy, and insisted on marching to Jaswanti's husband's home. The police prevented this expression of the women's fury which might have otherwise executed summary justice for the death of Jaswanti.

Stree Sangharsh, a women's organization active in the anti-dowry campaign, staged a play, accompanied by an exhibition which explained the function of dowry and its implications. Posters traced the way in which marriage is used to transfer both capital and commodities.

The play *Om Swaha* explored the implications of marriage for a Hindu woman — denial of self-expression, a thwarted personality and a life of endless drudgery. The play ends with a song calling upon all to support the struggles of women victims of the practice of dowry. The play raised important questions about dowry as well as feminism, and they hope that it will encourage further agitation.

Stree Sangharsh have been meeting parents of dowry victims, and following up cases with lawyers and police. Yet, they felt that they also needed to resume consciousness-raising about the issue in a more concerted way, as well as developing a supportive group against the practice of dowry and its often fatal results for women. (No. 4)

And to conclude, a poem that bitterly comments on 'Marriage'.

Marriage is

12 tolas of gold
2,000 bucks for a hall
plus 200 for the Maharaj,
invitations written in red,
500 mouths to be fed
with *shrikhand* and *puri*
vessels of steel
sarees of silk . . . .
In addition, a boy, a girl,
Marriage is no trivial affair.

Nishta Desai

From *Manushi*, No 4, December 1979–January 1980

Part VII: Women and Health

Mother

Sucked into currents of married life at nineteen,
Your youth and energy were harnessed
to serve a mother-in-law's sick-bed.

Husband, pushed into background,
the family machine took over.
Speculating the promise
of the bride's fruitful womb,
they turned uneager
after the yield of three years.

They required your production unit
to function again;
as aids prescribed prayers,
gave holy water from Babas
and charms from Gurus.

Like a bucket of water
Scraped out of a low-lying well,
a son was obtained from you,
claimed from birth by each aunt, uncle
to be the product of their holy effort.

The father made hero
was congratulated, praised, feted.

The mother was given
tips on child-rearing.

Beheroze Shroff

From *Voices of Women, An Asian Anthology*, 1978

22. A Statement on Genital Mutilation
AAWORD

The Association of African Women for Research and Development (AAWORD) is a group of African women researchers dedicated to doing women's research from an African perspective. They are based in Dakar, Senegal where their first official meeting was held in December 1977.

The following statement was put out in 1980 in reaction to certain campaigns against genital mutilation that have been launched in the West. The women of AAWORD strongly criticize these campaigns for their ignorance, sensationalism and total lack of consideration of the particular context in which African women are struggling against oppression. As Marie-Angélique Savané, editor of the journal *Famille et Developpement*, expressed it in a letter to *ISIS* in February 1978 '. . . it is essentially up to African people and in particular African women to decide to mobilize and fight against certain aspects of their reality — those which seem most urgently in need of change, and to decide how that struggle should be waged' (*ISIS International Bulletin* on 'Women and Health', No. 8, Summer 1978).

In the last few years, Western public opinion has been shocked to find out that in the middle of the 20th Century thousands of women and children have been 'savagely mutilated' because of 'barbarous customs from another age'. The good conscience of Western society has once again been shaken. Something must be done to help these people, to show public disapproval of such acts.

There have been press conferences, documentary films, headlines in the newspapers, information days, open letters, action groups — all this to mobilize public opinion and put pressure on governments of the countries where genital mutliation is still practised.

This new crusade of the West has been led out of the moral and cultural prejudices of Judaeo-Christian Western society: aggressiveness, ignorance or even contempt, paternalism and activism are

the elements which have infuriated and then shocked many
people of good will. In trying to reach their own public, the
new crusaders have fallen back on sensationalism, and have become
insensitive to the dignity of the very women they want to 'save'.
They are totally unconscious of the latent racism which such a
campaign evokes in countries where ethnocentric prejudice is so
deep-rooted. And in their conviction that this is a 'just cause',
they have forgotten that these women from a different race and a
different culture are also *human beings*, and that solidarity can
only exist alongside self-affirmation and mutual respect.

This campaign has aroused three kinds of reaction in Africa:
1) the highly conservative, which stresses the right of cultural
difference and the defence of traditional values and practices
whose supposed aim is to protect and elevate women; this view
denies Westerners the right to interfere in problems related to
culture;
    2) which, while condemning genital mutilation for health
reasons, considers it premature to open the issue to public debate;
    3) which concentrates on the aggressive nature of the campaign
and considers that the fanaticism of the new crusaders only
serves to draw attention away from the fundamental problems of
the economic exploitation and oppression of developing countries, which contribute to the continuation of such practices.
    Although all these reactions rightly criticize the campaign
against genital mutilation as imperialist and paternalist, they remain
passive and defensive. As is the case with many other issues, we
refuse here to confront our cultural heritage and to criticize it
constructively. We seem to prefer to draw a veil of modesty over
certain traditional practices, whatever the consequences may be.
However, it is time that Africans realized they must take a position
on all problems which concern their society, and to take steps to
end any practice which debases human beings.
    AAWORD, whose aim is to carry out research which leads to
the liberation of African people and women in particular, *firmly
condemns* genital mutilation and all other practices — traditional
or modern — which oppress women and justify exploiting them
economically or socially, as a serious violation of the fundamental
rights of women.
    AAWORD intends to undertake research on the consequences
of genital mutilation for the physical and mental health of women.
The results of these studies could be used as the basis of an information and educational campaign, and could help to bring about
legislation on all aspects of this problem.
    However, as far as AAWORD is concerned, the fight against
genital mutilation, although necessary, should not take on such

proportions that the wood cannot be seen for the trees. Young girls and women who are mutilated in Africa are usually among those who cannot even satisfy their basic needs and who have to struggle daily for survival. This is due to the exploitation of developing countries, manifested especially through the impoverishment of the poorest social classes. In the context of the present world economic crisis, tradition, with all of its constraints, becomes more than ever a form of security for the peoples of the Third World, and especially for the 'wretched of the earth'. For these people, the modern world, which is primarily Western and bourgeois, can only represent aggression at all levels — political, economic, social and cultural. It is unable to propose viable alternatives for them.

Moreover, to fight against genital mutilation without placing it in the context of ignorance, obscurantism, exploitation, poverty, etc., without questioning the structures and social relations which perpetuate this situation, is like 'refusing to see the sun in the middle of the day'. This, however, is precisely the approach taken by many Westerners, and is highly suspect, especially since Westerners necessarily profit from the exploitation of the peoples and women of Africa, whether directly or indirectly.

Feminists from developed countries — at least those who are sincerely concerned about this situation rather than those who use it only for their personal prestige — should understand this other aspect of the problem. They must accept that it is a problem for *African women*, and that no change is possible without the conscious participation of African women. They must avoid ill-timed interference, maternalism, ethnocentrism and misuse of power. These are attitudes which can only widen the gap between the Western feminist movement and that of the Third World.

African women must stop being reserved and shake themselves out of their political lethargy. They must make themselves heard on all national and international problems, defining their priorities and their special role in the context of social and national demands.

On the question of such traditional practices as genital mutilation, African women must no longer equivocate or react only to Western interference. They must speak out in favour of the total eradication of all these practices, and they must lead information and education campaigns to this end within their own countries and on a continental level.

The Lusaka Regional Conference on the Integration of Women in Development (3–7 December 1979) ought to provide an occasion to denounce these practices and to recommend to the governments of the region to take steps to suppress them in the context of a global strategy for improving the situation of women.

At the World Mid-Decade Conference on Women at Copenhagen (July 1980), the African delegations should not let themselves be diverted by those who want to confuse 'the wood with
the trees'. The women's question is a political problem; the
African delegations have a duty to place it firmly within the
context of the demand for a new international order.

23. Report of a Workshop on Women, Health and Reproduction
Mira Savara

This is a summary of discussion which took place in a workshop
on Women, Health and Reproduction in Bombay (17–19 April,
1981). The occasion was a week-end meeting on Women and
Health, funded by the Feminist Resource Centre, Bombay. The
report, written by Mira Savara, has been slightly edited here by
Shaila Shah.

Any discussion on women's health must necessarily be related to
the status of women in society, and in particular, the role and
position of women in the family. Consequently any women's
health movement must be linked with the general movement for
women's emancipation. Of course, several other inequalities and
contradictions existing in society today have to be taken into
account if we are to provide an adequate analysis of the situation. Briefly, these are:

a) Developed — underdeveloped
Colonialism and imperialism have created and continue to maintain a dependency relationship with colonized countries. This is
forced and perpetuated in various ways and through many
institutions, supposedly for the benefit of the people of the
'dependent' colony or ex-colony. This only results in increased
dependence.

b) Urban — rural
The particular form of development encouraged within the
country is certainly directed towards industrial development.

This means that in a country like India where the majority of the population subsists on a rural, agriculture-based economy, industrial development has resulted in the unequal distribution of resources, with the rural population gaining very few benefits.

c) Rich — poor
Both in rural and urban areas, resources are distributed so that the rich benefit.

d) Male — female
Within the family it is men who have power: the women are oppressed and subordinated to the man. Women are treated as the possession of men, and women's lives have little or no value. Thus it is often that men make decisions about the condition of a woman's well-being or sickness, and decide what action is to be taken.

The above are only very briefly stated facts that we must consider in all our investigations, conclusions and analyses.

Another important issue is the actual definition of health. In the case of women, health is usually discussed in connection with our reproductive power and function, and therefore, too narrowly, e.g. mother and child care.

We think it is important to stress that women's health is concerned with all problems associated with women — mental, physical — from birth, through puberty to adulthood and beyond. The tendency to regard issues of 'health' as being synonymous with 'disease and malfunction of the body' is too narrow and must be countered. We think it is important to redefine the issue of women and health, so that we are working towards the 'total well-being of the woman', physical, emotional and psychological. In the following section, we have divided our discussion into sections which tackle various aspects of women's health, and we offer the outcome of initial discussions we have had.

Differences in Urban and Rural Situations

Urbanization has been responsible for the breaking up of some of the female networks and sources of information about healing and traditional remedies. In urban areas, along with diseases caused by the environment in which families are forced to live, there is increasing evidence of another cause that leads to women being hospitalized. This is that a number of women voluntarily attempt to gain a hospital bed in order to get out of oppressive situations in the home and in the slums. Doctors, from a totally different class background to that of the working-class woman in urban slums, treat the women by doling out tranquillizers, displaying a complete lack of understanding of the factors responsible for conditions of stress, and ill-health. Women's health groups in urban areas, therefore, need to work towards developing information and support structures for women within urban areas.

It is important not to idealize the rural situation by comparison. Many myths regarding the workings of our bodies and female sexuality are prevalent, often sustained and perpetuated by the female networks, e.g. women are rarely perceived as being ill and therefore rarely receive adequate medical attention; women are often hospitalized only at the terminal stages of illness, thus contributing to a rate of female mortality that is much higher than that of the man.

The Role of Traditional Healing/Medical Practices

We all lack adequate information about existing 'medical' practice by women in their homes, as well as knowledge on popularly held beliefs about women's health. Western science and medicine, which treats all forms of understanding other than those developed within the Western tradition as inferior to their own, has penetrated deeply and is responsible for the gradual dying out of the use of traditional knowledge and remedies, such as herbs, used by women in their homes. Thus, years of learned wisdom and practice of women is often unrecognized, or treated as backward and based on superstition even though it may have a sound basis e.g. the use of the squatting position to aid childbirth. A further contributory factor has been that indigenous traditional systems of medicine (which are now being further developed) are also male dominated — all the *ayurvedis*, *unanis* etc. are men. [*Ayurvedi* medicine is an indigenous form of healing, using herbs and oils, currently being revived in India.]

It is essential that we combat further penetration by the Western system of medicine which makes us dependent on drugs, multinationals, etc. The injection and pill culture has penetrated even the remotest village and when one rural-based group tried to bring about awareness and questioning of this, it took time and effort to prove that simple, home remedies were effective. (This group presented its accumulated knowledge of local remedies and a compilation of this knowledge was seen to be very important so that it could be shared).

We believe that a women's health movement is not a movement for the spread of modern medicine — no doubt certain practices and beliefs have to be changed once they have been studied and

understood, but there are many traditional remedies which need
to be reintroduced and their use encouraged.

Family Planning, Contraceptive Research

It is of primary importance for the women's health movement to
develop a critique and action programme on the family planning
programme in India. A large percentage of state finance is invested
in this area and we must ensure that we influence state policy
sufficiently so that this is beneficial to women. External aid is
also increasing, and has led to the increased dependency of the
receiver country on the donor. This does not encourage self-
reliance or development. Further, these programmes are directed
towards rapid birth-rate reductions, without concern for women's
health or of existing medical practice. External aid also means that
the recipient country becomes a dumping ground for often very
dangerous drugs and consequently women are used as guinea-
pigs. We felt it was necessary for us to take up concrete research
on how foreign funds are being used in India and to criticize and
publicize this use.

The Indian Council for Medical Research is the organization
responsible for contraceptive research in India. Currently, several
tests and experiments are being carried out on women: injectible
contraceptives, various pills, vaginal rings, (hormone) implants
in thighs, IUDs and nasal sprays. Most testing is related to drugs
obtained from abroad, which has an inhibiting effect on research
carried out in India itself. (Over 25 IUDs from abroad are being
tested whereas modified IUDs, based on experience here, hardly
exist at all. Research on male contraceptives is negligible.)

It was stressed that in India, where women have few rights
within an oppressive patriarchal system, women displayed a
keenness to obtain contraception, often using it in secret without
the knowledge of the men. Thus the use of *Depo-Provera* or similar
drugs has proved to be popular as it is the only contraception
which can be used without the knowledge of men and the family.
We felt that despite the popularity of these drugs, it is essential
to struggle against them because of their harmful effects. We felt
it was essential to develop forms of birth-control suited to our
indigenous social conditions, as well as to struggle against those
social conditions that determine and often damage women's
health.

We felt that hormonal contraceptives were not accepted by the
majority of women, and, given the inadequate health services and
the consequent nature of follow-up services offered to women,
that this sort of contraceptive is not geared to existing conditions

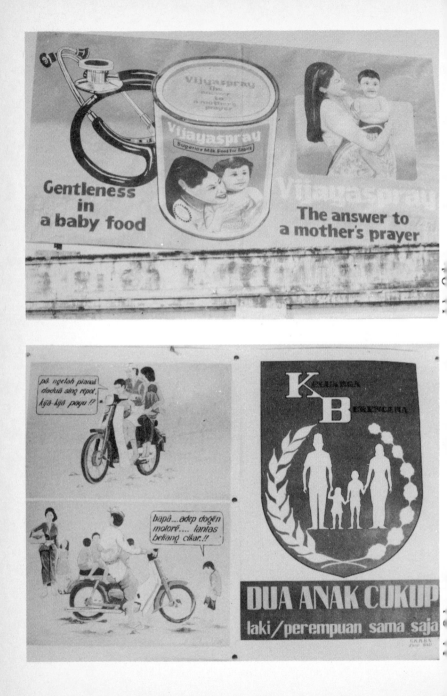

and therefore is unsuitable. We stated that we were against all
forms of testing of hormonal contraception, especially those
carried out exclusively on Third World women.

We need to develop an organization of feminists that will
investigate the contraceptives being tested on us and take action
against those harmful to our bodies.

Abortions

Of all the methods of contraception in India, abortion is the most
widely used. Between six and nine million women have abortions
each year. Although medical termination of pregnancy is legal,
only 5% of abortions performed are 'legal'. The law can be put
into practice primarily in urban areas where facilities exist, and the
law makes no provision for abortions performed in unhygienic
conditions. Abortion has not been considered to be part of the
family planning programme, and consequently abortion facilities
have not been developed.

A group is working on training nurses and *dais* to practice a
safe form of abortion — menstrual regulation — which can be done
within weeks with a simple hand-operated suction pump, without
electricity. We think it is crucial to develope safe abortion facilities
in India. [A *dai* is a midwife or nurse, often working in rural areas
outside hospitals, usually on a community care basis. She may not
be officially qualified as a nurse.]

Environmental Health and Ecology

The conditions under which women work are responsible for
serious health problems — unsophisticated cooking arrangements,
smoky rooms, long working days, all contribute damage to
women's well-being. A lot of damage is also caused by toxic
substances such as pesticides which, entering the ecology cycle,
find their way into women's bodies and effect reproduction.
Environmental health and ecology have a crucial role to play in
the women's health movement.

Mental Health

Very little available data on women and mental health exist in
India. We need to study this in both rural and urban areas in order
to develop an understanding of the nature and scope of the
problems. Certain religious festivals and practices common in
India, mostly dominated by women, involve mass trances and
fits, which could be seen as an expression of trauma and emotional
problems. Menses are generally seen as polluting but in contradiction to that view is the view that sees women as possessing strange
powers when menstruating. These contradictory conceptions can
be a source of both negative and positive feelings for women and

we need to find out much more.

Health Education

In order to contribute to awareness and understanding of how our bodies function, a few women's groups have been creating exhibitions covering areas such as the menstruation cycle, conception, pregnancy, contraceptive methods, sterilization and abortion practice. These exhibitions have proved to be highly educative and stimulating, and many women have discovered, to their surprise, problems and questions they shared with other women.

Emerging discussions also revealed existing beliefs/myths/information that women possessed on our bodies. Some of the myths encountered were: a) the fertility of the woman decides the sex of the child; b) that menstruation is 'dirty'. It was observed that certain caste practices of isolating women during their menstrual period were spreading to tribal areas. We felt that adoption of such practices which were detrimental to women should be fought; c) that sterilization is harmful for men; d) that white vaginal discharge is the cause of all weakness and sorrow.

Of course several other myths and misconceptions also exist, and, on the whole, knowledge of health matters and body functions is low, especially amongst women (in connection with our reproductive powers) and provision of knowledge and information is therefore crucial to the practice of any women's health movement or group.

Many women felt that, given the fact that it was men who defined female sexuality, it was essential that such exhibitions be open to men as well. Some groups have organized this by having different times for men and women, with good effect. However, other women felt that women should devote their scarce time and resources to raising women's consciousness and that an entirely different approach was needed in any discussion with men about sexuality. It should start from men's experience and, as such, was a task for male activists to take up.

Women Health Workers

The Community Health Volunteer scheme, set up in 1972 to make up for the inadequacy of the existing health care system, has a majority of men workers (90%) and it is mostly men who receive treatment and aid. In order to redress this, efforts are being made to ensure that one man and one woman train in each area, but an analysis of the process and training received by the workers has revealed that their knowledge is largely irrelevant to the needs of the people.

Further, the criteria stipulated by the Government on the qualifications that prospective workers need are such as to exclude the majority of women, e.g. literacy, the ability to stay away from home for three months, the need to be under 30 years old.

The Self-Help programme: this is gaining popularity amongst several groups, but some of us expressed reservations about this for two reasons: 1. this basically meant that women were responsible for the provision of 'self-help treatment', consequently this added to existing duties and work load for women; 2. in the case of serious disease, a reluctance to demand attention and treatment from the health service actually contributed to increase in the high mortality rate for women. Thus we felt that educating women about health care should not mean withdrawing from attempts to provide and improve health services.

Women health workers, especially at the lower levels, felt it important to identify and associate with their struggles. Also, for an attack on the sexist nature of medical practice in India today, we felt it would be much more valuable to involve nurses and *dais* in such struggles than to work with doctors.

Conclusion

The workshop was attended by 20 to 25 women, all of whom are interested in women and health from a feminist perspective. We hope that you will join us in our future programmes to make them richer and more meaningful. There is a way that each can contribute: by sending in material for the communications link-up; by telling us what you know about contraceptives and testing; by helping us professionally in analysing the research material that we are collecting from all over the world; by sending in all you know about herbal medicines; and by helping us to ensure that safe abortion becomes a reality to every woman so that she need no longer suffer torture and pain.

24. We Must All Speak Out
ALIMUPER

The following is a list of points publicized by Peruvian feminists
in March 1979 to celebrate an international day of action on
abortion, contraception and against forced sterilization. It is taken
from *Accion* (No. 4, March 1979), a quarterly newspaper produced
by the Peruvian socialist-feminist movement, ALIMUPER (Action
Group for the Liberation of Peruvian Women), which was formed
in 1973 when it first established women's fight for birth control.
According to a note in *ISIS*, 'When it first began seeking widespread support in 1979, the women of this group were seen as
the "crazies" of the capital city of Lima and were reviled by the
Left and Right as revolutionaries. The battle was long and hard
but it was successful in reaching women of the middle and professional classes and, from there, women of other classes. During
these first years, it published studies on women and law and
women and politics. But the most important success was that
women had taken to the streets.'

This extract from *Accion* has been translated from a special
issue which also includes articles on the role of the state and the
church in controlling women's reproduction, and a warning about
the dangers of the contraceptive drug *Depo-Provera*.

The combined problem of abortion, contraception and forced
sterilization is not unique to Peru. It's a problem faced by women
every day all over the world. Even in countries like Italy, France
and the USA, where abortion is legal, the use of the law by the
state and the medical profession, together with economic inequalities, continues to restrict these rights which should belong
to all women.

For this reason, the International Feminist Movement has
proposed the promotion of an international day of action for
abortion, contraception and against forced sterilization, under
the slogan 'A Woman's Right to Choose' and women's groups from
Colombia, Venezuela, Mexico, Brazil and Peru will be taking part.

The Catholic Church is a powerful source against abortion and contraception in Latin America.

The date chosen for this day of action is 31 March and we know that on this day feminist groups in many countries will be marching on the streets to demand their rights. We have planned a programme of solidarity which runs as follows: Statements will be put out, to be followed by a collection of signatures from supporters. There will be a meeting with organized discussion to establish relationships and make contact with other women's groups. By carrying out these tasks together we hope to continue organizing other action in the future.

ALIMUPER, together with the International Abortion Campaign for the Rights of Free Abortion and Contraception and against forced Sterilization (ICASC) invites all women to participate and unite in solidarity to publicize the following points: Everything connected with a woman's right to control her own fertility is controversial. This is because society, the system, tradition and other norms consider that others, in the form of doctors, husbands, judges, politicians, bosses, priests and the president, have the right to decide on such issues.

The result is that reproduction has become an issue for the state instead of being *our* issue. The state forces us to have or not to have children according to its interests. This is why abortion, contraception and forced sterilization are issues which must be treated as one: they all refer to the alienated state of our bodies. Life is created in our bodies, yet we don't have any rights over them. We want to claim our sexuality and have the right to a free and desired pregnancy.

Even though the law may not prohibit the sale of contraceptives, few women can afford to buy them. They have to rely on the Peruvian social services available and wait their turn. Meanwhile they have to carry on having children against their will. Neither these women nor us receive precise or responsible information about the different methods of birth-control available. Natural contraception and other methods which produce fewer side-effects aren't researched or investigated because this would only destroy business for capitalist drug companies.

We maintain that we must win the right to contraception. It must become a right for every woman and, at the same time, it should be incorporated into health programmes with sufficient information and adequate services.

We oppose the pressures of internal capitalist interests and the agents of imperialism which, without even considering the material conditions of Peruvian women, impose programmes of population control on the people and promote the use of certain dangerous methods of contraception which aren't even legal in industrialized countries.

In the face of a lack of appropriate services, abortion is widely practised as a method of contraception. This is how, directly or indirectly abortion has affected all women. Thousands die every year from badly performed abortions and many women are in prison for their involvement in abortion. Doctors practise it clandestinely and grow rich on the proceeds. And the women who can't afford doctors have to go to midwives and healers or do it with their own hands.

We believe that to allow abortion to continue as a clandestine practice would be accepting a solution that is degrading not only to women, but to the society which permits it.

We denounce the hypocrisy of those who defend the 'right to life' of a foetus, but maintain an indifferent attitude to the inhuman conditions which many women and children are suffering. The legalization of free and open abortion is the only solution to this abysmal situation.

We oppose any programme of forced sterilization, mass control over the population and indeed, any population policy in which women have no power of decision.

We believe in the need to agitate, denounce and fight against this situation in order to awaken our consciousness and gain the strength to refuse any manipulation, wherever it comes from. This is just one of the ways in which we can work towards a more egalitarian society where there will be no hierarchies or special privileges, neither in the private or public spheres, in keeping with the principles of SOCIALIST FEMINISM.

Part VIII:
Women Workers Fight Back

Temporary Girl Workers

We work for enough to live on each day,
   Without a day off, like the Labour Laws say,
But the price of noodles,twelve hours work don't pay,
   So, change our working conditions. Hey!

   Refrain
   Fellow workers, get it together,
     For prosperity in our land,
   Fellow workers, rise up together,
     To right things by our hand.

When we get our monthly paychecks,
   Our money worries merely grow,
Most of it* goes for some rice and the rent —
   Our private debts we still owe.

Lifeless, as if they were poisoned,
   Are all those fine young men
Who once promised to work hard for us —
   Oh, revive your lost bravery again.

Korean factory girls' song

From *Voices of Women, An Asian Anthology*, 1978

* 4,200 won; approximately $US12

25. Outcries of the Poor Workers: Appeal from South Korea
Asian Women's Liberation Newsletter

This article is taken from an issue of *ISIS International Bulletin* (No. 10, Winter 1978) on 'Women and Work'. It was reprinted in *ISIS* from *The Asian Women's Liberation Newsletter* which is based in Japan. The article was introduced as follows: On 6 February 1977 women workers from Dong-Il Textile Company in Inchon, South Korea held a meeting with the support of several social organizations to evaluate their long, hard struggle against the inhumane treatment by the management and the indifference of the company-controlled trade union. The following is a full text of the appeal they made public at the meeting, translated from the Japanese edition of the *National Times (Minjok Shibo)*, 25 March 1977. Dong-Il Textile is capitalized at 1.5 billion won (around US$ 15 million), and produces cotton yarn, blended yarn and cotton fabric mainly for export.

Listen to us poor workers who only seek a decent living in the face of the indifference of society and the oppression of capitalists. We appeal to those who truly wish to see freedom and equality in this society to support us in our lonely struggle to distinguish righteousness from irrationality and to recover our human rights and strengthen the voices of criticism against those who trample us down, betray, deceive and despise us as ignorant.

As there were not just one or two workers among us who were treated unfairly, we united in spite of the uncertainties, to demand our rights and to denounce the evils of society.

We, the workers of Dong-Il Textile Company in Inchon, South Korea, were deeply hurt by the cunning policy of the company to transform our union into the company's puppet union at the time of the election of the labour union delegates one year ago.

Our life in the factory is really miserable. Ours is a confined, stifling existence on the job — prohibited from talking to the workers next to us, poorly fed, not allowed to even go to toilet when necessary. The company side oppresses us by intervening in

our personal lives. After work is over, we are not free to take part
in club activities which were originally set up for us. We are end-
lessly plagued by lung tuberculosis, athlete's foot, and various
stomach diseases. Women workers have yellow, swollen faces from
inadequate sunlight. We are also tormented by temperatures of
40° (Centigrade) and by dust. We are harassed by the close
supervision and pressing demands of the company. Those who are
active in union activities are oppressed. We are struggling to free
ourselves from these miserable conditions which are too many to
enumerate.

In 1972, in spite of all the obstructions of the company, we
elected a woman chairman of our labour union and formed an
executive for a true union for workers, something unprecedented
in this country. We took pride in our union. In 1975 we again
elected a woman chairman. But in 1976 the company intervened
in the election of delegates and kept at us with threats and reprisals.
Mobilizing anti-union elements, the company itself recommended
persons it could control, used them to abort the annual congress,
and forced members during work hours to sign up to support the
anti-organization elements. On the other hand, the company
harassed active members and delegates, suspended job assign-
ments, changed sections and job positions. The company insti-
gated male headmen to give trouble to the active members. Finally
it forced the members to resign 'voluntarily'.

Prior to the congress, the company side, with the help of the
anti-organization elements, kidnapped the delegates, and forcefully
asked them to dismiss the congress. They used dirty methods to
prevent members and delegates from attending the congress. But
those delegates who wanted to get ahead in the company were
supported by the company, given alcohol, money and clothes;
the company arranged for active delegates to take care of their
families. The former took the latter to hotels overnight and
ordered them to do what the company said. They used violent,
intimidating language and action to the women union officials.
On the pretext of the congress, they excused members from work
and took them out on a picnic, thus aborting the congress. These
people are puppets who are indifferent to the pains of workers!
We were determined not to let our union fall to those puppets.
We could not retreat after six months of oppression by the
company and its schemes to suppress the labour union.

On 23 July last year (1976), the company nailed up the door of
the dormitory and closed the gate of the company so that members
of the union could not move at all, and police took away the
chairperson. All these movements were to railroad the congress
and make sure only anti-organization elements would be there. We
staged a sit-in and protested the cruelty of the company. We

continued a hunger strike for three days in the heat of mid-summer until our throats were dried up and our stomachs aching with hunger. We collapsed. Our water line was cut. We felt ourselves losing consciousness.

From outside, our parents and fellow members tried to bring in water and ice cubes. But the guardmen of the company knocked them down, kicked old parents and dragged them around, used abusive language and called them idiots. On the evening of the 25th, our parents staged a protest outside the company to protest. Then barbed wire was put up between our parents and us. Workers in blue fatigues fell and rolled on the ground and some of us continued shouting slogans unceasingly for three days.

We were completely exhausted. Police rushed into the company with a truck to disperse the struggle. We were determined to protest and not to be taken away. We took off our clothes and were half-naked. We sang the union song, our clothes in our hands. Even now we feel that song echoing in our hearts.

Though guardmen, police and other company employees beat us with police clubs, trampled us, dragged us by the hair, and pushed us into a truck, we broke windows to try to free ourselves. We crept under the truck to stop it, but we were kicked and lost consciousness. 72 of us were taken to the police station, and over 50 out of those 72 lost consciousness; 14 were taken to hospital. We were beaten and bruised all over. Two who were taken to hospital did not recover consciousness. Over 200 members rushed to the police station to demand that all the arrested be released, and over 300 people went to the headquarters of the Seoul Textile Labour Union to request them to release us.

Women on strike for the nationalization of Welawatta Weaving Mills, 1976.

Voice of Women, Sri Lanka

Ms. Lee Soon Ok, one of the two who were hospitalized at Seoul Sacred Mother (Sung Mo) Hospital, was found to be suffering from a mental disease and her very life was in danger. Sook Ok was hospitalized later, in Yoido Mental Hospital. Ms. Lee Ton Hee was released after 20 days' treatment, stating resolutely that she would continue union activities. She continued sitting on the sofa at the office of the labour union for more than two months. After the sit-in struggle, the company pressured active members to resign from the company or to write a statement that they would not participate any more; several hundred members were fired from the company.

News of our bloody struggle reached many people. At the Congress of the Central Committee on 29 July, the present chairman, Kim Yung Tae proposed and got passed a resolution of no-confidence in the former chairman of our union, Bang Soon Cho, for his poor handling of the incident at the Dong-Il Textile Company. At that time he put on a big show of concern for the cause of the workers of Dong-Il Textile Company and loudly promised to solve their problems if he were re-elected. He was elected chairman of the union.

We requested the floor of the congress to solve the present problem immediately and quickly elect delegates and announce a new congress. We asked this because chairman Bang had promised to do this when we were taken to the police station. But the new executives did not listen to our demands and only put off the solution of our problem.

We endured and waited. On 5 November the headquarters sent Lee Poong Woo, an executive of the planning board, as chairman of the co-ordinating committee. We entrusted all authority to him, believing in the good faith of the headquarters, and simply waited for the day of the election of delegates. But to our surprise, opinion at headquarters was to oppress us and to renew agreement (between labour union and the company) to allow the puppet employees membership in the union on the pretext of improving the quality of the labour union.

We immediately opposed this. Under the present situation, allowing the puppet employees into the union would be to give our union to the company. Therefore we opposed renewal of the agreement. But the headquarters used a deceptive policy of saying that they were in the process of negotiations, and that they would listen to our opinion. They ordered us not to look through the documents sent to the labour union.

We were furious when we read the official notice from Kyonggi-do dated 25 December, which proclaimed that the Governor of Kyonggi-do gave his consent to the renewal of the collective agreement between us and the company which Lee Poong Woo,

Director of the Planning Office, concluded as of 24 November at his own discretion. Inflamed with anger, we rushed to the Union Headquarters to see the chairman, only to be still more deeply disappointed.

We did our best to contain our anger and asked him for full particulars of the incident, but he replied in disgustingly violent language "What sort of women are you, who prefer the labour movement to marriage? You are simply mesmerized now. That's why you are fooling around like this.' He even started to trim his nails as if he had no interest in continuing the talk with us. Pak Ki-Yang, Director of the Seoul Chapter of Clothing Workers' Union who was in the office, pounded on the desk and shouted at us blaming us for any lack of education: 'Tell me, what on earth do you know that makes you feel qualified to make a big fuss like this?'

We are certainly uneducated. Deprived of a chance to study because of poverty, we have been despised and belittled as ignorant by society. We have been paying our union dues to the headquarters out of our hard-earned, meagre wages in an effort to gain whatever little intelligence becomes human beings. However, the very people who promised to work for us and make good use of the money looked down upon us saying that we are ignorant. We seriously wonder if the Chairman of the Textile Workers' Union is really worthy of being called a leader of a labour union, for this man while boasting of the large union membership of 150,000, looks down upon us female workers who make up more than 80% of the membership and on whom he depends for most of his livelihood. How can this be? Not only that, he even appointed company employees, the management's instruments, as directors of chapters, insisted on dividing the standing executive committee members equally between the management's yes-men and ordinary union members, resorted to a measure of co-optation to forcibly carry through elections, and made a remark that workers should be content with an increase in wages and should abstain from talking about workers' rights or human rights. We have been denied free access to the office at the Headquarters of the Textile Workers' Union that was built with our own money, and have been deceived by union leaders who are supposed to represent and fight for our rights. Whom should we trust and whom should we count on for help from now on?

We have finally made up our mind to regain our rights with our own hands, pledging to each other that we will keep fighting till the day when those at the Union Headquarters who claim to be our colleagues finish solving the problem at issue. So far they have been deliberately postponing the solution of the problem, simply to make us weary of waiting and force us to give up hope.

Now the atmosphere in the workshop is extremely rough, due
to the heavy surveillance mounted by the company and also to
the 'educational' programme whose sole purpose is to prevent
union members from meeting their representatives.

In the interests of more than 1,300 workers of Dong-Il Textile,
and also of many other fellow female workers of the Textile
Workers' Union, we are determined to expose the activities of the
treacherous union leaders and denounce the management for its
brutal measures of suppression. We are determined to do this at
all costs.

After having been betrayed by the Union Headquarters, we
issued an appeal demanding that the pains suffered by the workers
should be properly compensated. Cavilling at a passage in the
appeal — 'is it really justifiable to dispose of the rights of young
female workers who fought at the risk of their lives as lightly as
they did? Previously we only *heard about* a type of people called
labour aristocrats, but now we have had a chance to see in person
who they are' — the union leaders are unabashedly suing us for
libel. Is this what union leaders are supposed to do? The four
million workers of South Korea cannot but lament over these
shameless activities of their leaders.

How is it possible for a sensible person to say that the leaders
who have not even begun to reflect on their behaviour are *not*
labour aristocrats? Are we supposed to keep placing confidence
in these leaders, who acted in sheer violation of Paragraph 3,
Article 19 of the Labour Union Act which clearly stipulated that
a collective agreement cannot be concluded without the prior
consent of the general membership meeting or the board of
representatives, and who act in disregard of and against the interests of the ordinary members? Are we supposed to leave these
leaders to sit comfortably in their armchairs and trust them with
the proper handling of our union dues?

We have already had enough of suppression. We cannot and
ought not tolerate any more of it. We believe we should gather
all our strength and energy left, and cry out in one huge voice
of assertion that we, too, are human beings.

Lately, those in the Headquarters are trying to co-opt and
bribe our own leaders, and thereby to drive a wedge in our
movement. They reign over the executive positions as they like,
arbitrarily appointing this person as the Chief of the General
Affairs Section, and that person as the Director of a chapter. A
person who does not comply with such an appointment is
immediately accused of having called them labour aristocrats
and is threatened with expulsion from membership on the
trumped up charge of defamation.

Do you really think that we — who are determined, for the sake

Vioce of Women, Sri Lanka

of conscience and responsibility, to fight to see the day when
the problem at issue is completely dissolved, even at the cost of
receiving cold treatment which is much colder than the midnight
skies of 15–16 degrees centigrade below freezing — are a bunch
of mesmerized female workers as they claim we are?

Is it true women are better off getting married and staying
home? That we should not take part in the labour movement?

Is it true that our union will really improve in 'quality' if we
let company employees, the management's yes-men, join our
union?

All that we want is to live as human beings. Poor and uneducated as we are, we learned through our labour union activities
what democracy should be like.

Is there anything wrong with our understanding that it is an
obligation of every human being to remain true to one's
conscience and refuse to submit to injustice? And what about our
determination to keep fighting through to the end?

Let us leave these questions to your sound judgment. And
please let us enlist your heartfelt support and sympathy in our
cause.

26. Lucy, Peru: When Women Persist in their Fight . . .
Mujer y Sociedad

The following article is about the militant action of women factory workers in Peru. It has been translated from *Mujer y Sociedad* (No. 2, 15 December 1980), a feminist journal which recently started publication in Peru. The journal covers a whole range of issues from women organizing in trade unions to women's struggles in Central America and more theoretical pieces on feminist thought.

It was 11 o'clock on Friday evening. The pink house of Popular Action in the Paseo Colon did not appear to have calmed down since last July's elections. They were still prepared to prolong the dwindling hopes of a people believing passionately in justice by putting up a rather funereal flag declaring all the names of the municipal candidates.

Our thoughts were with the people. We remembered the thousands of sacked workers, weak but furious after their hunger strike, who, in the face of unfulfilled promises in this very house, now found themselves having to fight for political amnesty.

We are walking towards the doors of the Lucy S.A. factory not far away, where in the cold, dark solitude of night four women are waiting to go to sleep after a long worrying day of struggle. A white flag from Lucy Union declares in bold red letters: '*Job Security*'; '*Against the Illegal Closure of the Factory*'; and around them lie small placards for the rights of women: '*Equal Pay for Equal Work*'; '*Equality for Women*'; '*The Women of Lucy Say: We Have Had Enough*'.

We sit among them, on top of old mattresses, tired feet, and a communal cooking pot, now empty. They all tell us that the struggle in Lucy is not yet over; that there are forces still determined to continue until the achievement of self-administration, when the workers run their own factory. Virginia, Olidia, Ubaldina and Rita are four of the most important women in the struggle at Lucy. They are aged between 25 and 40. They are workers and

housewives. Rita is seriously ill. We talked to them about the
dreams and frustrations of women working in a sewing workshop
who suddenly decide to fight for their own demands as working
class women.

'The Lucy factory has been making children's clothes for 18 years.
Many of us started working on the needle machines there from a
very young age. That's all we could do — we hadn't studied at
universities. In addition, we knew that all women are taught to
sew from childhood. I used to get up at 5 o'clock in the morning
and clean my house, prepare the food, serve breakfast, get the
children ready for school and go to work.

I used to arrive at the factory at 7.30. Once inside, one of the
workers would outline our tasks for the day and there would
start an interminable day's work. We used to make at least 14
garments a day, depending on the type of orders we received.
For instance, making dresses is not the same as making coats. We
were tied to the clock, our energies imprisoned by the intensity
of piecework. Sometimes our tired eyes demanded a rest in the
workshop, but we then had to carry on working at home late
into the night. We worked for as long as it took for the overalls
or coats to be finished so we could hand them in the next
morning.

For many years it all carried on 'normally '. We looked upon
Moises Levy as a 'respected boss'. He never heard moans or com-
plaints from his quick and docile workers. Then everything changed
when we organized our union on 27 February 1979. From that
time on we no longer saw the boss as someone to be 'respected',
nor were we the docile workers. Moises Levy tried to destroy our
union, forcing two colleagues to resign. This gave us even more
courage to continue our efforts at organizing for better working
conditions, to which the boss responded by making the work even
harder and taking the simpler garments to 'clandestine workshops'.

The hostility increased with the arrival in the factory of the
boss's wife Mana Spaks de Levy in April 1979. She locked us into
the factory, put the machines so that they were facing the wall
and forbade any conversation. In January this year we presented
our first petition demanding a wage increase, better working
conditions, aprons, a better roof for our workshop and a rest
room with a table for refreshments. On 7 May, our comrade
Luiza Bustinza, defence secretary of the union, was sacked on the
grounds that she was organizing a strike. On 9 May the boss's wife
tried to take the machinery out of the factory, but this was stopped
by some of us who were standing on the doorsteps of the factory.
Since then we have been sitting in, sleeping here and taking care
of the machinery so that the boss doesn't take it away.

On 11 June the boss illegally closed down the factory and we reported it to the Ministry of Labour. On 4 August, at a General Assembly of Industrial Communities, we agreed to accept the protection of the code DL. 21584 which allows workers to administer a factory in cases of bankruptcy, abandonment or unjustified stoppage. Under these circumstances and thanks to pressure applied by feminist organizations like *Mujer en Lucha* (Women in Struggle) and other popular organizations, our case has gone from the Ministry of Labour to the Ministry of Industry. And on 25 September the Ministry of Labour granted us Mandatory Resolution No. 193, forcing the bosses to re-establish work and resume their activities in the factory.

Never before have we fought like this. For us this is still the most significant and the strongest-ever experience of struggle. When we started we really didn't know what we were getting into. We didn't know how to conduct a meeting, let alone speak in public. 'When I had to speak I used to shiver and my hands would sweat.' It was only discussions with our husbands or children, or amongst ourselves in the workshop, which taught us a way of speaking which made us feel as if we were really fighting. Nevertheless, we had to learn to speak at all costs. The demands of our struggle meant that we had to create our own propaganda from direct experience and go to other unions, so talking in public became obligatory. Not to do so would have meant silencing the struggle and losing the moral and economic support from other unions needed for the communal strike fund.

We learned to organize ourselves. We held meetings every Saturday afternoon. There we discussed our problems and organized our work for the week, the places that needed to be visited, night and day shifts and responsibilities for communal funds.

I remember that Saturday when we organized pickets in the buses and boarded them, talking to passengers and distributing propaganda. The next Saturday we realized that the comrades who had assumed responsibility for this task had not seen it through. When the time came to report on it no one said a word. Finally, and only due to the fact that the meeting's leaders requested it, someone admitted that the comrades had gone to the bus stops, but had been afraid to go inside. This started us thinking: the initial fight was a difficult one, especially for us working class women who have to face all sorts of problems, problems which male workers don't have to face. Why are we frightened? Is it because we are women starting a struggle? Is it because we are women talking about our strike? Because we are women distributing propaganda in the buses? Even our decision to sleep at the door of the factory put us in a much more difficult situation and we've shown a lot of courage. Why then should we be afraid of going into the buses? With these reflections we decided to go along to bus stops and enter the buses. At the next Saturday's meeting women informed us that they had spoken, distributed leaflets and picked up donations in the buses.

The struggle is a much harder one for women. Society has many prejudices against women. For example, on 23 September we, the women workers of Lucy y Conel, went out onto the streets to demonstrate for job security. Many men applauded us, but others shouted from their cars: 'You should go back and cook instead.' The government has never taken us seriously. So far, it has solved none of our problems. We also have problems with our husbands who try to prevent us from taking action. Look at what's been happening all this time. Our husbands have tried to stop us from coming to the factory; they have said: 'Your home and children come first.' They haven't understood our fight and they have tried to lock us in our houses to cook and look after the children. It was different when we were working since then we were bringing home a wage to the family. In those days the argument about home and children wasn't used and instead we were told 'Go to work!' This attitude of some of the husbands has sometimes weakened the struggle because some women couldn't join because of the problems they had at home. But we also have to struggle against ourselves, against all the miseducation we've received, against all our ideas of what it is to be a woman. Despite all these problems we have persisted in our fight and refused to go back. We want control of the factory and although Mr Levy still refuses, we won't stop until we have got it.

What has been happening to women in this country? For working class women, the cases of Lolas, Conel and Lucy have turned the trade union movement into an open platform, not only for the expression of demands for the right to work and higher wages for women, but also for the realization of the particular potential of women workers. We have demonstrated in the streets, held meetings outside Parliament and participated in a hunger strike. Now the women workers are causing more than one Baella Tuesta [a well-known television producer in Peru] to lose sleep. Not long ago a Sunday television programme broadcast an interview, very skilfully edited by him, pointing to the fact that the women in Conel received international support and implying that they would have been incapable of holding out without the help of national feminist organizations like Women in Struggle.

However, in a country where the economic exploitation and ideological oppression of women takes on particularly strong characteristics, the struggles being waged at Lucy y Conel have become a crucial expression against the enormous violence exercised over women's labour power. Lucy y Conel constitute the main effort on the part of women for workers' control over their factory. For those who think they understand women, it may seem as if working class women are suddenly waking up from their eternal dream of 'kitchens', but as part of the labour force they are also destroying the myth of 'tenderness and docility' of women workers.

27. The Night Shift for Women?
Voice of Women

This article is taken from the first issue of *Voice of Women* (January 1980), a feminist journal produced by women in Sri Lanka. The article contains extracts from a Sri Lankan national newspaper discussing government moves to introduce an extra shift for women workers, followed by comments from the editorial group of *Voice of Women*. Calling itself 'a Sri Lanka journal for women's emancipation', this is an excellent publication which comes out sporadically in Sinhala, Tamil and English. Using cartoons, articles, interviews, letters and poems, it covers a whole range of issues from sexism in the media to peasant women's organizations and the role of marriage and religion in the women's struggle.

The question of night work for women has become a controversial issue. At present women factory workers are on shifts of 8 hours — for example one group may work the 1st shift from 6 a.m. to 2 p.m. while the second shift works from 2 p.m. to 10 p.m. Under the International Labour Organization (ILO) Convention No. 89 which Sri Lanka has signed and incorporated in the Employment of Women, Young Persons and Children Act, women and children cannot be employed in factories after 10 p.m. Under the Shop and Office Employees Act women cannot work overtime after 6 p.m.

Writing in the *Lanka Guardian*, (1.9.79) Gamini Dissanaike raises the issue of the 3rd shift for women workers which the government if trying to introduce. He writes:

'During the recent four months strike at a leading textile mills the employers tried to introduce into the Collective Agreement a condition to employ women on the 3rd shift i.e. between 10 pm and 6 am provided, however, that such employment is not contrary to prevailing legislation or government policy. This was rejected by the workers.'

A couple of years ago, under a new ILO international programme for the improvement of the quality of working life, two experts were asked by the Geneva-based agency to study the physiological, psychological, medical, family and social implications of night work. According to the two experts Messrs James Carpentier and Pierre Cazamian the conclusions of their study are:

1) That no matter what technical or economic justification may be found for night work, they should not be allowed to outweigh the drawbacks. The study accordingly advocated the reduction of night work to the strict minimum; 2) That, to the over-tiredness [by doing night work] must be added the disturbance of the eating pattern: eating at night when one's digestive processes are sluggish, can cause various digestive disorders. The practice, unwise but commonplace among night workers, of swallowing pills to be able to sleep during the day and stay awake at night can only make matters worse; 3) The ILO further notes that the dangers inherent in night work increase with age and length of service; 4) Working at night and sleeping during the day upsets the natural rhythm. On average, nightshift workers sleep about two hours less. Not only are the hours of sleep fewer than at night, but they are often of insufficient depth, with the result that the sleeper feels groggy when he/she wakes up. They are also punctuated by awakenings due to pangs of hunger; 5) This overtiredness and the difficulties in sleeping associated with it give rise to nervous disorders. The 'night worker's neurosis' is recognized as a type of neurosis which may lead to a nervous breakdown; 6) Nevertheless, social tradition, which forces a woman into a dual role of employee

" Join the women's struggle "
" I 'll have to ask my husband "

Voice of Women, Sri Lanka

and housewife is an aggravating factor especially as women working at night will endeavour to do their housework in the morning and sleep only in the afternoon; 7) On the social side, the most obvious and irksome drawback lies in the disruption in the daily life of the family unit caused by night work, which may even seriously upset the mental balance of the workers concerned; 8) There appears to be no way of organizing the work that can counteract the harmful effects of night work at least at the present time, the study concludes.

If the Labour Department renounces Convention No. 89 repealing the other two laws, the main results of a removal of the legal obstacles could be summarized as follows:

1) Tendency to employ only young, unmarried women in industrial organizations; 2) The possibility of working three shifts in organizations which have two shifts at present; 3) The threat to both men and women, who have exceeded the age limit, of being thrown out of employment; 4) Further harassment of working women who are overburdened not only in their work places but also in their homes; 5) Opportunity for sexual exploitation of women employed in night work.

Our Views . . .

Today in the context of the social and economic changes that are rapidly taking place, it is necessary for us to continuously focus our attention on how these changes will affect women. We therefore raise certain important issues pertaining to work and especially the question of night work for women.

It is of course true that on many questions that affect women (night work, family planning, abortion, etc.) the opinions of men are canvassed — be they trade union leaders, *bhikkhus* [servant class], doctors or bishops. *Women are not asked what they think!* It is almost as if women were not supposed to have an opinion on any question — however closely it affects them. We therefore call upon women to come forward and speak up on all such issues.

While opening for discussion the issue of working women and night work for women, we would like to make the following points.

We are not against women working — on the contrary we will stand up for the *right of women to work*. It is progressive for a woman to be engaged in social production outside the home and to earn an independent income.

We oppose the exploitation, low wages and bad working conditions of all workers, be they men or women and we will be

Voice of Women Sri Lanka

specially vigilant and agitate on matters regarding the underpayment and exploitation of women.

We also feel that prolonged periods of night work are bad for both *men and women* and that all the arguments concerning the unnatural nature of this work apply to both sexes.

The night shift is done in rotation, every so many weeks, and is from 10 pm to 6 am. Many women, like nurses and doctors, already do night shifts. However to say that night work for women will 'disrupt family life' or is 'against our culture' is not a convincing argument.

What we *must* insist upon is that where women work the night shift they must get adequate rest afterwards and should not be exploited by compulsory overtime (having to do a day shift as well). We also stress that if women work the night shift, and the 2nd shift that ends at 10 pm, they be given adequate protection and transport facilities.

Our slogans are therefore equal pay for women; proper rest, canteen and toilet facilities; no compulsory overtime, proper creche facilities for working mothers, and more training facilities for women at work.

28. Adivasi Women on the Warpath
Vibhuti Patel

In Dhulia District, Maharashrtra, on May Day 1981 over 200 women participated in a working class women's convention organized by the *Shramik Stri Mukti Sanghatana* (Toiling Women's Liberation Group), formed in October 1980. The Adivasi tribal people constitute the majority of the toiling masses in this district and the *Shramik Sanghatana* have encouraged women to struggle around the specific oppressions of wife beating, dowry, rape, as well as economic exploitation and tribal oppression. The following short piece describes why they felt a convention was important and what it was like.

Shramik Sanghatana held a working class women's liberation convention at Nandurbar, Dhulia district on May Day this year.

It was an event! More than 2,000 women participated enthusiastically in this toiling women's liberation convention, on the day of heroic and militant struggle of the working class against economic exploitation and social oppression.

In Dhulia district, *Adivasis* constitute a majority of the toiling masses. It has witnessed heroic Shahada movement during last decade as a result of consistent struggles launched by *Shramik Sanghatana* (Toilers Organization). Women members of the organization have waged many struggles against rape, wife beating, alcoholism, dowry (there, the groom has to pay dowry — *hoonda* — to the bride's family). After ten years of experience women members of *Sanghatana* realize that, though *Sanghatana* fights against the economic exploitation of *Adivasis*, to fight against the specific oppression of women, an autonomous women's organization is needed, and in October 1980 Adivasi women formed *Sharramik Stree Mukti Sanghatana*. They also have their *Kalpathak* cultural group which goes to different villages with its cultural programme on women's problems of economic exploitation, sexual oppression, wife beating, and tribal oppression. This year they decided to celebrate May Day — the protest day of the working class all over the world — by holding a women's liberation convention. Since March 1981 they had been preparing for the convention. Women activists held meetings in different villages, highlighting the importance of the convention, raised finances, collected rice, *dal* and oil, prepared posters and stuck them in different villages and prepared placards, paintings and leaflets. In their invitation they wrote 'Women are divided into different strata because of economic, social and educational inequality in our society. Being 'women' they have to face sexual oppression in the family and society in this patriarchal milieu. Only toiling women are going to combat this oppression. Women perform domestic drudgery. Looking after the daily necessities of the family members is also part of the production process. All toiling women whether they are in fields or in factories, offices or kitchens, schools or hospitals are 'women workers'.

To have a real understanding of this unjust order and change it, it is necessary that we come together . . . so please be part of this convention and make it a success.'

And this sincere appeal really worked. *Adivasi* and shepherd women, mainly agricultural labourers, walked from different villages. Many women had to walk 12–33 miles in the scorching heat. There were no trucks or any other temptations by 'party bosses'. There was also no compulsion — women came voluntarily with their inner zeal and enthusiasm. When they were passing through different villages before reaching their destination they were offered food by their fellow comrades. Some women took

days to reach the place of the convention. But they didn't mind
losing five days wages, not only that, they even contributed
materially and financially to the convention. There was a lot of
excitement on the part of hosts because it was the first time such
a convention had been held in that area. In the past they had
organized workshops, *sibirs*.

On the early morning of May Day, women started pouring into
the venue of the convention. Nearly 2,000 women participated.
The convention started with songs. In the morning session two
plays were staged: one by the culture group of *Stree Mukti
Sanghatana* depicting the life of tribal women — the daily routine
of household duties, alcoholism, wife beating, and sexual abuse of
women by kulaks and their henchmen (in this area, landlords keep
their private army to 'protect' their property and to suppress any
struggle of *Adivasis*, *sahukars*) and bureaucrats — and how
organized women can combat these. The other play was staged by
women from Poona and Bombay concerning the life of city
women.

In the afternoon there was group discussion. To make discussion
more enriching and to have full participation of the women, 12
groups were formed with no 'leaders' indulging in monologues.
In spite of language barriers participants were able to build a
rapport with each other. Women from four language groups had
participated — Bhilori, Marathi, Gujerati and Hindi.

There was very interesting discussion about wearing *Mangalsutra* and *Tika* — a symbol of women's *suhag*. [*Mangalsutra* is a
necklace; *Tika* is a red dot placed in the centre of a woman's fore-
head. Both are symbols of the Hindu woman's marital status.]
Before the convention, rumour was spread by the upper class
women that women's liberation means abandoning *Mangalsutra*
and *Tika*. 'See the organizers of the convention are not wearing
Mangalsutra and *Tika*.' So the question was raised whether it is
necessary to continue wearing them to be easily accepted among
the masses. It was strongly countered by the argument that in
the past, also, Left-radical activists continued perpetuating obscur-
antist values in the name of 'getting acceptance among the masses'.
'If you are not married you won't be accepted among the masses';
'If you don't wear *Mangalsutra* or *Tika* you won't be accepted
among the masses', and so it goes on. Thus, you never challenge
reactionary stereotypes of the society. For women's meetings
Haldikumkum (a ritual in which only married Hindu women can
participate) is arranged. So we never evolve new forms, secular
non-casteist, non-communal and non-sexist, to express our feelings
of joy and fulfilment in life.

Adivasi women told how, after the formation of the women's
liberation organization, among the families of women activists,

men started sharing housework, wife beating stopped, the taking and giving of dowry also stopped. New forms of marriage were evolved where no priest is needed. Women and men in presence of their friends agreed to live together. Little money is spent for the celebration.

The women's liberation organization also held a campaign against superstition and witchcraft and for the use of [Western] medicine. They had to face strong resistance when they started telling women not to observe fasts because they have nothing to do with their husbands' or childrens' good health or long life. They find that the women's *Kalapathak* is the most effective media to spread the ideology of women's liberation.

Around 5 pm there was a big rally. Women shouted slogans and narrated their problems and struggles through songs. The evening's public meeting was a bit boring; most of the speakers gave long long speeches that most of the audience could not understand because of language problems. There *Adivasis* speak Bhilori — a mixture of Gujerati and Marathi.

After that, a meal was served — *khichri* and oil. Congratulations to the organizers for preparing a meal for more than 2,000 delegates! At night it was most entertaining, when women from different tribes performed folk dances. The songs expressed the pathos of tribal life. Some very moving songs gave account of past struggles.

The next day local organizers met the delegates from Bombay, Poona, Nagpur, Kasegaon, West Bengal and Madhya Pradesh, and discussed the problems concerning the convention and its follow-up. An informal co-ordination committee was also formed.

Not for many, many years has such a convention been seen. The enthusiasm, spontaneity, involvement and commitment of the participants in the convention was proof of its success.

Recommended Further Reading

Barrios de Chungara, Domitila, *Let Me Speak*, London, Stage 1, 1978.

Bronstein, Audrey, *The Triple Struggle — Latin American Peasant Women*, London, War On Want, 1982.

Croll, Elisabeth, *Feminism and Socialism in China*, London, Routledge and Kegan, Paul, 1978.

El Dareer, Asma, *Woman, Why Do You Weep? Circumcision and its Consequences*, London, Zed Press, 1982.

Doyle, Lesley, *The Political Economy of Health*, London, Pluto Press, 1979.

Eisen Bergman, Arlene, *Women in Vietnam*, San Francisco, Peoples Press, 1975.

ISIS, *Women in Development: A Resource Guide*, Rome, ISIS, 1983.

Jain, Devaki, *Women's Quest for Power*, Ghaziabad, India, Vikas, 1980.

Joseph, Gloria and Lewis, Jill (eds), *Common Differences: Conflicts in Black and White Perspectives*, New York, Anchor Books, 1981.

Minces, Juliette, *The House of Obedience — Women in Arab Society*, London, Zed Press, 1982.

Moraga, Cherrie and Anzaldua, Gloria (eds), *This Bridge Called My Back — Writings by Radical Women of Color*, Watertown, Massachusetts, Persephone Press, 1981.

Murphy, Yolanda and Murphy, Robert F., *Women of the Forest*, New York, Columbia University Press, 1974.

Omvedt, Gail, *We Will Smash this Prison! Indian Women in Struggle*, London, Zed Press, 1980.

Randall, Margaret, *Sandinisto's Daughters: Testimonies of Nicaraguan Women in Struggle*, London, Zed Press, 1981.

Rowbotham, Sheila, *Women, Resistance and Revolution*, London, Penguin, 1972.

El Saadawi, Nawal, *The Hidden Face of Eve — Women in the Arab World*, London, Zed Press, 1980.

Urdang, Stephanie, *Fighting Two Colonialisms — Women in Guinea Bissau*, New York, Monthly Review Press, 1979.

Young, Kate, Wollkowitz, Carol and McCullagh, Roslyn (eds), *Of Marriage and the Market — Women's Subordination in International Perspective*, London, CSE Books, 1981.

Publications

CHANGE
Parnell House
25 Wilton Road
London SW1V JJS
UK

Researches and publishes reports on the condition and status of women all over the world. CHANGE International Reports are written whenever possible by authors indigenous to the country concerned.

OUTWRITE
Oxford House
Derbyshire Street
London E2
UK

Monthly women's newspaper committed to the publication of news about 'the experiences and struggles of women everywhere, particularly those whose lives are constantly trivialised or ignored by the established media.'

Women's International Resource Exchange (WIRE) Service
2700 Broadway, Rm 7
New York NY 10025
USA

Reproduces published and unpublished accounts and analyses by and about women in the Third World.

ISIS International
Via Santa Maria dell'Anima 30
00186 Rome
Italy

Casilla 2067
Correro Central
Santiago
Chile

Resource and documentation centre in the international women's movement. Produces quarterly Isis International Journal and Supplement giving news about women's groups, conferences, events and resources around the world. Each issue of the Journal focuses on a particular theme and is produced jointly with Third World women's groups. Currently working on an extensive resource guide on audiovisuals for women.

Isis International has a sister organisation — Isis WICCE — which co-ordinates an international cross-cultural exchange programme for women. Address: P.O. Box 2471, 1211 Geneva 2, Switzerland.

WISER LINKS
173 Archway Road
London N6

Women and Third World information network and library. Produces a regular newsletter.

Women's Organizations

These are just a few of the many women's organizations, groups and publications which are growing steadily throughout the third world. Some countries, such as Bolivia and El Salvador, are not represented for reasons of safety.

BRAZIL
Centro de Defensa por los Derechos de la Mujer
(Centre for the Defence of Women's Rights)
Rua Raul Pompeia 181
30.00 Belo Horizonte

CHILE
Circulo de Estudios sobre la Mujer
(Women's Issues Study Circle)
Jose Arrieta 83-A
Santiago

Coordinadora Nacional Sindical
(National Union Coordination)
Santa Monica 2360
Santiago

COLOMBIA
Centro de Estudios de Investigacion sobre la Mujer
(Centre for Study and Research on Women)
A.A. 49105
Medellin

Mujeres en Lucha
(Women in Struggle)
A.A. 7953
Bogota

DOMINICAN REPUBLIC
CIPAF: Centro de Investigacion para la Accion Femenina
(Research Centre for Feminine Action)
Benigno Filomeno Rojas
No. 307
Santo Domingo
Dominican Republic

ECUADOR
Grupo Autonomo de Mujeres
(Autonomous Women's Group)
Soledad Martinez
Pedro Basen No 2
Quito

CEPAM
(Centre for the Promotion and Action of Women)
Los Rios 2238 y Gandara
Quito
Ecuador

ERITREA
National Union of Eritrean Women
Via Firenze 15/3
Rome
Italy

National Union of Eritrean Women in Europe
P.O. Box 7007
London WC1 U6XX

GRENADA
National Women's Organization
St George's

INDIA
Forum Against the Oppression of Women
c/o Vibhuti Patel
K—8 Nensey Colony
Express Highway
Borivili (East), Bombay 400066

INDIA

Manushi
A Journal about Women and Society
C1/202 Lajpat Nagar-1
New Delhi 110024

Saheli
Women's Resource Centre
10 Nizamuddin East
New Delhi 110013

IRAN

Iranian Women's Solidarity Group
c/o A Woman's Place
48 William IV Street
London WC2
UK

Women's Section of the Iranian
Community
465a Green Lanes
London N4

JAPAN

Asian Women's Liberation (news-
letter)
c/o Asian Women's Association
Poste Restante
Shibuya Post Office
Shibuya-ku
Tokyo 150

MAURITIUS

Muvman Liberasyon Fam
5 Rue Sainte Therese
Curepipe

MEXICO

FEM (magazine)
Av. Mexico 76, Local 1
Colonia Progreso Tizapan
Mexico 20, D.F.
Mexico

CIDHAL (documentation centre)
Apartado 579
Cuernavaca
Morelos

MOZAMBIQUE

MAGIC Women's Group
(Mozambique, Angola, Guinea
Bissau Information Centre)
34 Percy Street
London WI
UK

NAMIBIA

SWAPO Women's Solidarity
Campaign
53 Leverton Street
London NW5
UK

SWAPO Women's Council
(provisional headquarters)
P.O. Box 953
Luanda
People's Republic of Angola

NICARAGUA

AMNLAE — Asociacion de Mujeres
Nicaraguenses Luisa Amanda
Espinosa
Casa de la Mujer
Apartado Aereo 238
Managua

OMAN

Women and Revolution in Oman
(booklet)
KROAG — Committee for the
Revolution in Oman and the
Arabian Gulf
P.O. Box 86
DK 1003 Copenhagen K
Denmark

PAKISTAN

Women's Action Forum Lahore
P.O. Box 3278
Gulberg
Lahore

PALESTINE

Women for Palestine
c/o A Women's Place
48 William IV Street
London WC2
UK

Arab Women's Group
c/o Outwrite
Oxford House
Derbyshire Street
London E2

PAPUA NEW GUINEA
Women's Resource Centre
P.O. Box 520
Port Moresby
Papua New Guinea

PERU
Flora Tristan
(women's centre)
Avenida Arenales 601
Lima
Peru

Mujer y Sociedad
(magazine)
Jiron Trujillo 678
Magdalen del Mar
Lima
Peru

PHILIPPINES
Third World Movement Against the
Exploitation of Women (campaigns
against tourism and prostitution)
P.O. Box 1434
Manila 2800

PUERTO RICO
Taller de Salud (Health Workshop)
Carmita Guzman
R. 1403 Morillo
Cayey
or
Apartado 2172
Estacion Hato Rey
Puerto Rico 00919

SENEGAL
Association of African Women
for Research and Development
BP 11007 CD Annexe
Dakar

SOUTH AFRICA
African National Congress
Women's Section
P.O. Box 38
28 Penton Street
London N1
UK

Zamani Soweto Sisters Council
c/o Betty Wolport
32 Steele Road
London NW3 4RE
UK

SRI LANKA
Kantha Handa
(Voice of Women)
Kayakontha Lane
Kirula Road
Colombo 5
Sri Lanka

VENEZUELA
Liga Feminista de Maracaibo
(Feminist League of Maracaibo)
Alba Carosio
Avenida 5 de Julio cob 20
Edificio
Mirador del Lago Maracaibo
Maracaibo

ZIMBABWE
Zimbabwe Women's Bureau
152b Victoria Street
Salisbury